Complexity and Management

There is at present a great deal of interest in understanding organizations in terms of new theories of complexity, self-organization and emergence. Many of those taking up these theories do so in a way that simply presents existing views in new jargon, another management fad. The reason, this book suggests, is that they understand complexity theories solely within systems thinking.

The authors look carefully at the theoretical foundations of the ways the complexity sciences are being used to understand the sources of stability and change in organizations. As well as offering a thorough critique of the different ways in which complexity thinking is being taken up, this book, the first of a series, lays the ground for a new project. This project, which goes to the roots of Western thought, understands organizations as complex responsive processes of relating. It draws on the complexity sciences as a source domain of analogies, interpreting them through a relationship psychology that draws on the tradition of Hegel, Mead and Elias. The authors show how complexity thinking focuses attention on the emergence of genuine novelty in everyday processes of communicative action.

Timely and controversial, this book is essential reading for anyone interested in strategy, organization and management theory, and organizational change.

Ralph D. Stacey is Professor of Management and Director of the Complexity and Management Centre at University of Hertfordshire; **Douglas Griffin** and **Patricia Shaw** are Associate Directors of the Complexity and Management Centre, and consultants to organizations.

Comments on this edition include:

In a world that is discovering the power of the application of complexity theories to the day to day life of organizations, this book offers a solid rock foundation. It gives to all of us as practitioners a language on which to build our specific application of the theory to practice. It is a book that every executive concerned with the sustainability of a corporation's success can use, ranging from .com to traditional government organizations.

Alberto Bazzan, Leadership Development Leader,
World Bank Group, Washington DC, USA.

I think this book represents a remarkable synthesis and depth of reflection. What [the authors] have done in this text is to clarify all the many different strands of work that has been going on by looking at their foundations. They have really encompassed an enormous range of work, both in evolutionary thinking and in management, and explained clearly the fundamental limitations in the approaches.

Peter Allen, Head of Complex Systems Management Centre,
Cranfield School of Management, UK.

This book is the first I know of to step firmly into the new space of creative participation that has been revealed by the Sciences of Complexity, showing clearly why it is necessary to move beyond the limitations of systems thinking in order to engage with the full creative potential of life in relationship. It is a remarkable achievement that uniquely combines the philosophical depth, the psychological insight, and the practical experience that the authors have gained through direct engagement with the issues that puzzle, confuse, and frustrate people working at all levels of corporate life. It is liberating to read a text that tries to make sense of the paradoxes of creative living.

Brian Goodwin, Professor of Biology, Schumacher College, UK.

This series is a thoughtful analysis of the different models we can use to understand how and why organizations work and the implications for leaders. Of value to academics and practitioners, it will really challenge the way you think!

Vivienne Cox, Group Vice President, BP.

Complexity and Emergence in Organizations

Series Editors:
Ralph D. Stacey, Douglas Griffin and **Patricia Shaw**
Complexity and Management Centre, University of Hertfordshire

The books in this series each give expression to a particular way of speaking about complexity in organizations. Drawing on insights from the complexity sciences, psychology and sociology, this series aims to develop theories of human organization, including ethics.

Forthcoming titles in this series include:

Complex Responsive Processes in Organizations
Learning and knowledge creation
Ralph D. Stacey

Changing the Conversation in Organizations
A complexity approach to change
Patricia Shaw

The Emergence of Leadership
Linking self-organization and ethics
Douglas Griffin

Complexity and Innovation in Organizations
José Fonseca

The Paradox of Control in Organizations
Philip Streatfield

Complexity and Management

Fad or radical challenge
to systems thinking?

Ralph D. Stacey, Douglas Griffin
and Patricia Shaw

London and New York

First published 2000
by Routledge
11 New Fetter Lane, London EC4P 4EE

Simultaneously published in the USA and Canada
by Routledge
29 West 35th Street, New York, NY 10001

Routledge is an imprint of the Taylor & Francis Group

Typeset in Times and Franklin Gothic
by Keystroke, Jacaranda Lodge, Wightwick Bank, Wolverhampton.
Printed and bound in Great Britain
by St Edmundsbury Press, Bury St Edmunds, Suffolk

British Library Cataloguing in Publication Data
A catalogue record for this book is available from the British Library

Library of Congress Cataloging in Publication Data
Stacey, Ralph D.
   Complexity and management : fad or radical challenge to systems thinking? /
Ralph D. Stacey, Douglas Griffin & Patricia Shaw.
     p. cm. – (Complexity and emergence in organizations)
   Includes bibliographical references and index.
     1. Organizational effectiveness. 2. Complex organizations–Management. 3.
Interorganizational relations. 4. Organizational change. 5. System analysis.
6. Complexity (Philosophy). 7. Industrial management. I. Griffin, Douglas.
II. Shaw, Patricia. III. Title. IV. Series.

HD58.9 .S735 2000
658.4–dc21   00-062574

ISBN 0–415–24760–8 (hbk)
ISBN 0–415–24761–6 (pbk)

Contents

Series preface
Complexity and Emergence in Organizations

The aim of this series is to give expression to a particular way of speaking about complexity in organizations, one that emphasizes the self-referential, reflexive nature of humans, the essentially responsive and participative nature of human processes of relating and the radical unpredictability of their evolution. It draws on the complexity sciences, which can be brought together with psychology and sociology in many different ways to form a whole spectrum of theories of human organization.

At one end of this spectrum there is the dominant voice in organization and management theory, which speaks in the language of design, regularity and control. In this language, managers stand outside the organizational system, which is thought of as an objective, pre-given reality that can be modeled and designed, and they control it. Managers here are concerned with the functional aspects of a system as they search for causal links that promise sophisticated tools for predicting its behavior. The dominant voice talks about the individual as autonomous, self-contained, masterful and at the center of an organization. Many complexity theorists talk in a language that is immediately compatible with this dominant voice. They talk about complex adaptive systems as networks of autonomous agents that behave on the basis of regularities extracted from their environments. They talk about complex systems as objective realities that scientists can stand outside of and model. They emphasize the predictable aspects of these systems and see their modeling work as a route to increasing the ability of humans to control complex worlds.

At the other end of the spectrum there are voices from the fringes of organizational theory, complexity sciences, psychology and sociology who are defining a participative perspective. They argue that humans are themselves members of the complex networks that they form and are drawing attention to the impossibility of standing outside of them in order to objectify and model them. With this intersubjective voice people speak as subjects interacting with others in the co-evolution of a jointly constructed reality. These voices emphasize the radically unpredictable aspects of self-organizing processes and their creative potential. These are the voices of decentered agency, which talk about agents and the social world in which they live as mutually created and sustained. This way of thinking weaves together relationship psychologies and the work of complexity theorists who focus on the emergent and radically unpredictable aspects of complex systems. The result is a participative approach to understanding the complexities of organizational life.

This series is intended to give expression to the second of these voices, defining a participative perspective.

Series editors
Ralph D. Stacey, Douglas Griffin, Patricia Shaw
Complexity and Management Centre,
University of Hertfordshire

1 Introduction: getting things done in organizations

- "Getting things done, anyway"
- Ways of thinking
- Outline of the book

There is now a growing literature by management thinkers who appeal for insight to developments in the natural sciences of complexity, felt by many to be relevant because they model complex, turbulent systems. These models demonstrate the possibility of order emerging from disorder through processes of spontaneous self-organization in the absence of any blueprint. The development of these new sciences is widespread with notable centers of work at the Santa Fe Institute in the United States; centers in Brussels and Austin, Texas, headed by Prigogine; one headed by Haken in Stuttgart; and one headed by Scott Kelso in Florida. Their work has been popularized in books by Gleick (1988), Waldorp (1992) and Lewin (1993), who all talk about a "new science," even a new worldview. In taking up these "new sciences," management complexity writers mostly claim that they challenge current ways of thinking about organizations and their management.

There are differences within the natural sciences on what these "new" sciences of complexity mean. Some talk of a new dialogue with nature and the end of certainty, or they call for a science of qualities and point to the importance of a participative approach to understanding nature. Others make claims for a new ordering principle in the evolution of life. Yet others see complexity as a further step in the progress of natural science as usual. In the field of management and organization, the ideas emanating from the complexity sciences are also being taken up in very different ways. For some it justifies a return to simpler, more fundamental ways of managing that are more in touch with the deeper nature of human beings, while for others it amounts to a call for more democracy in organizations, or greater shareholder participation. Then there are those who claim that human freedom liberates people from self-organization and allows them to design or condition emergence. There are also those who see the complexity sciences as requiring managers to push their organizations into the dynamics of instability. For others, it raises question marks over strategic planning and the possibility of forecasting, so calling for a reconsideration of the nature of control in organizations. Others fear that nonlinear dynamics will be used to justify untrammeled market competition, or social and psychological "engineering."

This rather confusing situation is one reason for this book. We are interested in trying to make sense of these diverse views and in doing so develop our own perspective on the way in which notions from the complexity sciences may assist in understanding life in organizations. In doing this, we believe that it is important to look carefully at the theoretical foundations of the various ways in which the complexity sciences are being interpreted in organizational and management terms, and how these foundations compare with those of the currently dominant way of thinking about management. We also believe that it is important to understand these theoretical foundations in the context of the historical development of thinking about organizations.

Without this, it is all too easy to make loose, unjustifiable translations of concepts from the complexity sciences into organizational frameworks. Nowhere is this more easily done than when people use loose metaphors taken from the complexity sciences to make prescriptions for management action. The result is almost certain to be old prescriptions in new jargon, or careless advice. This book, therefore, is not concerned with prescriptions or universal applications of theory. It tries to move toward an understanding of human action as being in its essence a process of sense making.

One of the aims of this book, as the first volume in a series, is to examine the claims made by management complexity writers. Do they hold out the potential for a radical re-examination of how we think about organizations; that is, a re-examination that goes right to the very roots of our thinking? Or are they but the latest in the explosion of management fads we have seen over the past few decades, another superficial fashion that leaves untouched the roots of management thinking and so soon fades? We argue that a great many writers run the fad risk. This conclusion leads to the second aim of this volume; namely, to define the broad features of a project that, we think, does amount to a radical re-examination of management thinking.

This book is about movements of thought. The intention is not to provide an introduction to the complexity sciences, or why and how they have something to do with human organizations. There are now many books that do this. Instead, we assume that the reader already has some of this knowledge. Although this first volume is about the roots of organization and management thinking, and is therefore necessarily written at a theoretical level, it is animated by our conviction that there are more useful and less frustrating ways of making sense of life in organizations than those that currently dominate our thinking. Let us explain why we are convinced that more useful, less frustrating ways of making sense are necessary today.

"Getting things done, anyway"

Imagine one of those many occasions when a group of managers gather at some kind of "away day" meeting to revisit their business models, strategies and plans. They are repeatedly faced with the situation of trying to revise these frames for designing action in the light of new developments, events and opportunities. Often they have pre-reading, which analyses lists of issues, or computer graphic presentations, which do the same. Additionally, they may generate further lists of issues, which they discuss in breakout groups. As they talk they cover flip charts with bullet points. Then they come back together again and tack their flip charts to the walls. These flip charts provoke further conversation in the larger group as they mull over things that went wrong: time deadlines were not met; targets slipped; goals and aims could have been better defined; there was a lack of clarity as to strategic direction; vision and mission statements were poorly communicated; key performance indicators were ill-chosen and so on.

Some start talking about how frustrating it all is, usually because some other department did not take appropriate or timely action, or some leading figure did not give enough direction, or politics got in the way. Before the mood swings too low, however, they move rapidly to developing the action plans they need in order to correct weaknesses of the system and build on strengths. Finally they pin down accountability in terms of senior sponsors for areas of activity, or communications to be devised, or new models to be worked up. The prescriptions they return to their organization with are almost always to design more systems and install further procedures in order to stay "in control."

When invited to attend one of these sessions, the same features of the situation always strike us. What is striking is the complete lack of discussion on how they get things done in the day-by-day activity of organizing. If asked, they make a few remarks about personal connections, unexpected encounters, bending the rules and lobbying for support. However, they seem rather embarrassed about having "got things done" in this way, generally giving the impression that they do not really know how they "got things done." The situation becomes even more intriguing when we ask what they did at the last "away day" session, only to discover that they went through the same procedure and departed with a similar resolve to improve managerial processes and design better systems. In fact, when they think about it, they report that they have been doing this for years and still the planning and control systems do not work as they expected them to. Every year they find that the unexpected has happened. They also know that much the same happens in other organizations and are somewhat surprised to learn that people were writing about this phenomenon in the 1950s. The experience of being the ones "in charge" but repeatedly finding that they are not "in control" is a very familiar one to managers – one that they feel uneasy about and seem unable to discuss openly with each other.

We think that this disjuncture between what managers believe they ought to be doing and what they repeatedly find themselves actually doing is an important source of the stress that managers seem increasingly to be experiencing these days. It must, therefore, be a matter of considerable practical importance to ask a number of questions about this experience. Why do managers think that they ought to be able to design control systems and act in accordance with procedures so as to be in control of what happens to their organization? Just as important, why do they keep finding that they are not nearly as much "in control" as they believe they should be? Even more important, what then are they actually doing to "get things done, anyway"? Then, why do they repeat the same search for improved procedures and systems every year, ignoring the failure to find them in any previous year? Why do they continue, each year, not to ask how they "got things done, anyway"?

We encounter other, equally puzzling situations. For example, we frequently hear this complaint: "There is poor communication in this organization. People don't keep each other informed and this makes it really hard to do a good job." We notice a very common and immediate response to such complaints. Managers start calling for more sophisticated distributed information systems and procedures for storing and accessing that information so that they can retrieve it efficiently. They call for better briefings and fuller circulation of meeting reports. However, why has no company we know of managed to install such systems and procedures that remove the complaints? No matter how sophisticated the new information systems and procedures are, the complaints continue: "Our biggest problem is poor communication." Why do managers not discuss the fact that no matter how the information systems are developed the complaints remain the same? What if there is no alternative to a situation where information is all over the place and where meaning can only be made by many different people making sense together in many different groupings and conversations? What if this is the most effective way of developing knowledge when the future is so unpredictable?

A frequent response to the kind of situation we have just described is to set up a special meeting to discuss the problem of communication and what to do about it. Although these are perennial issues, no one quite seems to know what to do about them. Perhaps that is why it seems so important to make sure that the "right" people are invited to attend the special meeting. After some agonizing about who the "right people" are, there is further agonizing on what the "concrete outcomes" of the meeting are going to be. But just what could a "concrete outcome" be when the whole reason for the special meeting is that no one quite seems to know what to do? What if it is not possible to know who the "right" people are? Why do they have to be identified in advance, rather than leaving them to identify themselves through their interest in the issues in question? Why is it so anxiety provoking to contemplate a meeting around some issues that are not at all clear? Why is the thought that there is no agenda so horrifying? After all, in most other aspects of our lives we frequently talk to each other without an agenda. We frequently find that what others, and we ourselves, say, is unclear.

It seems to us that life in organizations is essentially paradoxical. Managers are supposed to be in charge and yet they find it difficult to stay in control. The future is recognizable when it arrives but in many important respects not predictable before it does. We sense the importance of difference but experience the pressure to conform. However, this experience of the paradoxical nature of life seems to be unacceptable. We seem to think that life should not be paradoxical, that we should be able to resolve the paradox and find the solutions to the problems it gives rise to. However, believing one thing and experiencing another must be a source of stress and anxiety. On the other hand, if we find ways of understanding the unavoidably paradoxical nature of life, we may find the liveliness of acting in the tension. We believe that this way of understanding is to be found in our ordinary everyday lives in organizations, where we do in fact cope with paradox, one way or another, finding it frustrating and exciting. What we are trying to develop in our project for this series of books is a way of understanding how people in organizations actually live with paradox in their ordinary, everyday lives in their organizations. The matters of control and difference seem to us to be centrally important paradoxes of contemporary life and we are interested in exploring how current management thought deals with these paradoxes and how alternative ways of thinking might be able to offer ways of living with them without collapsing into a search for the "right way," the solution. We need a way of understanding that places paradox at the heart of the matter.

Ways of thinking

The puzzling situations people find themselves in, the questions they ask, or fail to ask, all reflect some way of thinking. It is a way of thinking that focuses their attention on systems and procedures in the belief that this is how "things get done." It is a way of thinking that keeps turning their attention away from the details of ordinary, everyday life in organizations through which they actually "get things done." We suggest that there is nothing more important than the way managers think about the nature of their organization, particularly how it comes to be what it is. What sustains organizational continuity and what makes for creative change are central questions, and how we think about these matters is of major importance. It is this conviction that lies behind our desire to write this book, as the first in a series that is intended to explore ways of thinking about how organizations come to be what they are; that is, how they come to have the identities they have and what the role of managers is in that process. In other words, our key questions are as follows. What causes an organization to take the form it takes and what causes the pattern of its evolution into the future? Can that future be known and therefore predicted? Can that future be chosen in a rational way? Or is the future under perpetual construction and hence unpredictable to a significant extent? If so, what are the processes of perpetual construction?

In what they do and how they talk about it, managers demonstrate a particular way of thinking about questions like this. That particular way is primarily an importation of engineering notions of causality into thinking about organizations. It was engineers in the early part of the twentieth century who developed scientific management, and engineers in the middle years of that century who developed the conceptual basis of the kinds of control systems found in organizations today. This is a way of thinking that sends managers looking for the causes that will produce the outcomes they need in order to succeed. It is also a way of thinking that focuses on design. Just as engineers do, managers are supposed to design self-regulating planning, performance appraisal and quality control systems. What causes an organization to become what it becomes is then thought to be the kind of control system they have designed and the actions they have chosen. Organizational life never proceeds so smoothly that choices are always realized, so that chance events have also to be dealt with and this too is part of the management role. What causes an organization to be what it becomes is also, therefore, the way in which members deal with chance; that is, how they take risks. Risk assessment and risk management systems are another way in which the uncertain aspects of organizational life are meant to be controlled. From this perspective, then, an organization becomes what it is, and will become what it becomes, because of the systems its managers design, the actions people in organizations choose to carry out and how they deal with risk, all within a fiercely competitive struggle with other organizations in order to survive.

Do we have to continue using ideas imported by engineers to make sense of our lives as human beings in organizations? We believe not. There are alternative ways of thinking about causality, some of them suggested by the more provocative thinkers in the complexity sciences, which lead to very different answers to the questions we have been posing. These thinkers suggest that interaction itself has the intrinsic capacity to yield coherent patterns of behavior. They propose that the entities of which nature is composed interact locally with each other, in the absence of any blueprint, plan or program, and through that interaction they produce coherent patterns in themselves. There is a further suggestion too – namely, that interaction in nature takes place not primarily in order to survive but as the creative expression of identity. There is yet another provoking idea. It is only when the interaction between entities has a critical degree of diversity, emerging as conflicting constraints on each other, that there arises the internal capacity for spontaneous novelty. In other words, creativity and destruction, order and disorder, are inextricably linked in the creative process. That process is self-referential in the sense that interaction causes patterns in itself in a way that both sustains continuity in, and potentially transforms, that pattern.

If this has anything to do with organizations, it would mean that intrinsic properties of connection, interaction and relationship between people would be the cause of emergent coherence and that emergent coherence would be unpredictable. That coherent pattern might be creative or it might be destructive but it would still be a coherent pattern that emerges. People would still be understood to be choosing and acting intentionally, but this would apply to particular, local responses to others in ordinary, everyday organizational life. It would be the interaction itself that caused the emergent pattern, and plans and procedures would feature in these interactions without determining their pattern. Instead of people interacting selfishly with each other, instead of their organization interacting selfishly with others simply in order to survive, they would be understood as interacting with each other for the sake of emerging identity and difference realized in the living present. In this paradigm, an organization comes to be what it is because of the intrinsic capacity of human beings, individually and collectively, to express their identities and thereby their differences. Identity and difference emerge through self-organization; that is, relationships of a cooperative and competitive kind. What an organization becomes would be thought of as emerging from the relationships of its members rather than being determined simply by the global choices of some individuals.

Clearly this would challenge the dominant management discourse by pointing to the:

- paradoxical nature of life in organizations;
- significant constraints on predictability and individual choice;
- self-organizing relating between people in which the power, politics and conflict of ordinary, everyday life are at the center of cooperative and competitive organizational processes through which joint action is taken;
- importance of difference, spontaneity and diversity; and
- close connection between creation and destruction.

Above all, this approach would challenge systems thinking in relation to human organizations. We will be suggesting a shift away from thinking about an organization as a system and advocating a way of thinking about an organization as processes. The aim of this series of books is to develop thinking about organizations as Complex Responsive Processes of relating. The position we are defining for our project, then, is one that departs from systems thinking, the way of thinking that currently dominates management discourse. Our project is to develop an alternative to systems thinking about human organizations, not merely an extension to it. This does not mean that systems thinking has *no* place in organizations. Once problems have emerged, once activities take on repetitive features, then systems thinking is a very powerful method. Furthermore, systems thinking provides a powerful way of taking account of causal connections that are distant in time and space. This provides insight into the unintended and unexpected consequences of human action. However, systems thinking, we will argue, does not pay sufficient attention to what it is excluding and does not deal adequately with the paradoxes of organizational life. Most importantly, it cannot explain novelty in terms of its own framework. These are all matters we will take up in Chapter 4.

Outline of the book

In the chapters that follow, we return to what we think are some of the most important streams of Western thought flowing into currently dominant ways of making sense of life in organizations. The exposition is, therefore, necessarily theoretical. However, it is theory that is relevant to us in our practice in organizations. The theoretical exposition frequently triggers associations with situations we encounter in our practice and we invite you, the reader, to make your own associations with your own practice. Our intention is to point toward an alternative to systems thinking about human organizations, an alternative to be developed in subsequent volumes in this series. This volume explains why we think such an alternative is required and it briefly outlines the sources we might turn to in order to construct such an alternative. We will be arguing that the complexity sciences on their own do not supply this alternative. They are a source domain for analogies that need to be understood from particular sociological and psychological perspectives that we group together under the heading of relationship psychology.

Chapters 2 and 3 review the contrasting views of Kant, Hegel and Darwin on the nature of causality. It argues that Kant's work underlies systems thinking, the dominant perspective in current thinking about organizations and their management. We intend to found our position on the thinking of Hegel, Mead and Elias.

Chapter 4 shows how Kantian thought underlies systems thinking about organizations and sets out the problems we think that this leads to. The chapter argues that systems thinking cannot adequately explain how novelty arises in organizations or what the role of managers and leaders is in the emergence of such novelty. It is the basis of our call for a shift away from systems thinking about human organizations.

Chapters 5 and 6 review the causal frameworks underlying developments in the complexity sciences. It distinguishes between developments proceeding on the basis of Kantian thought from those that reflect the thought of Hegel, Mead and Elias. For the former the future for natural systems is an existing but hidden order, whereas for the latter the future is under perpetual construction.

Chapter 7 surveys the approaches adopted by management complexity writers. It looks at how they interpret those natural sciences in terms of human action and argues that the basis is mostly Kantian. We argue that because most of them think about complexity primarily as an extension of systems theory, they reproduce the dominant management discourse in new terms without fundamental change.

Chapter 8 explores the rationalist and cognitivist assumptions most management complexity writers make about human behavior, assumptions that also run through systems thinking. The chapter then draws on the work of a number of sociologists, social psychologists and psychologists to present an alternative to rationalist, cognitivist ways of understanding human action. We call that alternative relationship psychology and explain why we think that it provides a departure from systems thinking. This "relationship psychology" is in the tradition of Mead and Elias and provides a different way of transferring insights from the complexity sciences to human action by way of analogy. The result is a potential move from systems thinking to one that lives with paradox, particularly the paradox of the recognizable but unknowable future.

Chapter 9 briefly outlines our project – namely, the development of thinking in terms of Complex Responsive Processes as a way of understanding life in organizations. This incorporates a relationship psychology and draws on analogies from the complexity sciences, all within an understanding of causality drawn from Hegel, Mead and Elias.

This points to the approach to be developed in subsequent volumes in this series in a project that moves away from systems thinking.

Appendices provide some further information on thinking about causality, our attitude toward natural science and models, and references to how our own thought has evolved and still is evolving.

2 The age-old question of stability and change

- The claims of management complexity writers
- Moving toward a knowable future
- Human freedom and the scientific method
- The importance of Kant's contribution
- Conclusion

The purpose of this chapter and the next one is to identify a number of key concepts that will be used in subsequent chapters to make distinctions between various ways of understanding human organizations. Organization of any kind, whether in nature or in human action, can be thought of as the interplay of stability and change. This certainly becomes apparent as soon as one opens many books on human organizations and their management or participates in the conversation of practicing managers. The basic concerns are usually with how organizations function in stable, controllable ways and with how this stable, repetitive activity changes. In other words, the basic concerns are with continuity and with creativity, or innovation. One might say that any kind of organization is a dynamic interplay of stability and change, of continuity and novelty, of decay and generation, of the sameness of identity and the difference of changes in that identity. The fundamental question about organization then follows: what are the sources of both the stability and the change, of both the continuity and the novelty, of both the decay and the generation, of both the identity and the difference? This is a question that has to do with causality and it immediately links into the debate that has proceeded for thousands of years now about stability and change in general (see Appendix 1). One side in this debate emphasizes stability and the predictable nature of change. Those who emphasize change and its unpredictable nature take the other position. The question that concerns us in this and the following chapter is how we might classify the position that writers on management complexity take in this debate.

This chapter starts by briefly outlining the claims of management complexity writers. It notes the reference a number of those writers make to earlier thinkers – in particular, Kant, Hegel and Darwin. Some of their views emphasize stability and predictable change and other views emphasize unknowable futures. This chapter explores the former perspective and the next turns to those who think in terms of unknowable futures. Together, the two chapters provide a necessarily brief exploration of what these thinkers and others had to say about the stability and change in the organization of forms, including a central concept of causality in complexity theory; namely, self-organization. In doing this, these two chapters suggest a classification of notions about the causes of change and stability in organization particularly about the causal nature of self-organization. This classification will then be used in subsequent chapters as a framework for locating and comparing ways of thinking about organizational stability and change, including those based in some way on the complexity sciences.

The classification we propose is based on a distinction between five different kinds of teleological, or final cause. Since it has become so unacceptable to talk about teleology in the natural sciences we need to explain at the outset why we are doing this. A teleological cause is an answer to the "why" question. Why does a particular phenomenon become what it becomes? What is the purpose that causes the phenomenon to do what it does or become what it becomes? For thousands of years in Western thought, teleology was the all-embracing kind of cause to which other kinds were subordinate. For Aristotle, the purpose, or final state, toward which any form tended was the good, and the motivation was happiness. In the Christian era, specifically in the metaphysics of Thomas Aquinas, this became God. The purpose of everything was to reveal God's creation and the motivation was to serve the greater glory of God. It was no different in the early days of the scientific revolution. The thinkers who founded modernity and the scientific method took this teleological perspective for granted. Twentieth-century science, however, moved decisively away from this position. Now, the majority of scientists firmly confine discussions about teleology to the non-scientific or metaphysical realm (for example, Gell-Mann, 1994). Some, however, do discuss teleology as a subordinated way of understanding systems theory (for example, von Bertalanffy, 1968). For yet others, teleology becomes a nebulous background to reality. For example, Kauffman (1995) talks about "we the expected" to indicate the inevitability of human life.

The "why" question, then, is held by most to fall outside the domain of science. It is even held to be an unnecessary question by many. Anything that smacks of purpose, spiritual essence, *élan vital* or anything of that sort is immediately taken to be a sign of metaphysical or magical thinking. However, in our view, it is completely inappropriate to remove the notion of purpose from an explanation of human action. Human action is purposeful and it is important to make clear in one's explanation just how one thinks about that purpose. Furthermore, the act of banishing teleology from the natural sciences has not led to its disappearance; it has simply gone underground. It is still implicitly there in natural scientific theories, and when those theories are imported into explanations of human action it is all too easy to import the implicit teleological notions along with them. They are not then subjected to any kind of scrutiny but simply taken for granted. For example, many scientific theories assume that phenomena behave in optimizing ways. In assuming that a phenomenon is displaying some kind of optimal behavior, one is assuming the secular equivalent of some kind of perfect design, but that assumption is simply not examined.

Teleological cause, therefore, is to be the explicit foundation of our classification of causal frameworks. However, by teleology we do not mean any kind of divine purpose or inner essence. By teleology we mean two things. First, we mean the kind of movement into the future that is being assumed. A key distinction will be whether the movement toward the future is assumed to be toward:

• a known state; or
• an unknown state.

Second, we mean the reason for the movement into the future. "For the sake of what?" is a phenomenon moving? "In order to realize what?" is a phenomenon moving to the future? A key distinction will be whether it is assumed that a phenomenon moves toward the future in order to realize:

• some optimal arrangement;
• a chosen goal;
• a mature form of itself;
• continuity and transformation of its identity.

We will suggest five causal frameworks that answer these questions in different ways. These are:

• secular Natural Law Teleology
• Rationalist Teleology

- Formative Teleology
- Transformative Teleology
- Adaptionist Teleology

This chapter will be exploring the first three of these causal frameworks, which all assume movement toward a known future state, although they differ in their reasons for the movement. The remaining two causal frameworks assume movement toward an unknowable future and they will be taken up in the next chapter.

The reason for making these distinctions is this. They enable one to obtain some insight into the fundamental differences between different ways of understanding change in organizations. In particular, they assist in distinguishing between different ways in which concepts from the natural complexity sciences are being imported into explanations of how organizations change. We think that distinctions of this kind are necessary to understand the sense in which some uses of the complexity sciences in explaining human organizing simply reproduce the dominant discourse of systems theory in new jargon. We suggest that the distinctions we make offer the potential for a radical rethink of organizational change; that is, one that goes back to the roots of Western thought. Having established the distinctions in this and the following chapter, we will be using them to argue that the radical potential survives only when the complexity sciences are used as analogies that illuminate organizational change understood from the perspective of Transformative Teleology. We will be arguing that an understanding of creativity and novel change in organizations requires this perspective of Transformative Teleology.

The discussion in this and the following chapter is necessarily rather theoretical and you may impatiently wonder why you need to bother with the distinctions we make between one mode of thinking and another. It is, however, our conviction that it is extremely important to make the effort of identifying the underpinnings of complexity theories in the history of thought because without such clarity it is all too easy to use the complexity sciences in so loose a way that they simply become the latest management fad. We suggest, therefore, that you might like to read through this and the following chapter and then return to them as the necessity of the distinctions they make becomes more apparent in the arguments presented in later chapters. You might also like to connect the abstract discussion of matters such as causality, change, transformation and identity with everyday management experience. We provide an example of such experience on page 16.

The Brand Project: shifting our identity

Lawrence Rolands has recently been appointed to a new responsibility as a member of the executive team of a large multinational company. His title is Vice President – Brand, a title which did not previously exist. He is discussing with his aides the first presentation he will make to the corporation's CEO on the "Brand Project." He has to set out his initial proposals for a strategy to renew the company's brand. He insists this is not just a marketing or PR exercise, not solely a culture change initiative, not only a potential restructuring of the organization, but requires a "transformation" of the company. He and his aides are casting about for ways to structure their thinking.

"We must draw on the existing value of our brand and yet at the same time fundamentally shift our identity, create a renewed brand."

"We know we are in danger of becoming a dinosaur industry – how are we going to evolve? There are many threats and opportunities in today's environment that must galvanize us."

"We are experimenting with ways of reformulating our mission statement, to refocus the organization on a renewed sense of purpose, but the question is what kind of leadership do we need?"

"There are negative memories still of our last attempt at a transformation 'program' which was cascaded through the organization some years ago – many believed it sucked attention away from the job in hand, hit our results and generated little more than hot air. Yet obviously we must find ways of involving a broad population of stakeholders in this endeavor. We don't want another program yet we do need some kind of plan that will deliver tangible results."

"Of course we are restructuring ourselves, divesting ourselves of certain activities, forming new partnerships and alliances, entering the e-commerce world, we are in the midst of change as we speak."

"We need to re-invent ourselves, tell a new story and communicate it energetically."

There is a restless tension in the conversation. People are excited to be involved in this project – clearly it is big and complex and important, but there is also unease. The Brand project is like a code name whose use covers the uncertainty people feel about what it really implies. It's difficult to grasp the nature of this task, to think and speak clearly about it, so first one then another person seems to be convincing. The sense of urgency means that any discussion of the way people are thinking is deemed too analytical and increases the discomfort. The possible presentation simply grows like topsy, layering frameworks and models each of which is answering differently the disquieting questions about the sources of stability and change in organizational life. A tantalizing obscurity shrouds the discussion despite the intensity of contributions.

The claims of management complexity writers

Almost everyone who talks and writes about the complexity sciences in relation to human organizations claims that they may represent a fundamentally new way of thinking about the management of organizations.

The limits of mechanistic thinking about human organizations

The argument of the management complexity writers (see Chapter 7) is that currently dominant ways of thinking about organizations have their origins in Newtonian mechanics in which the universe was understood to function in a mechanistic, clockwork manner. They identify Newtonian mechanics with universal laws of a linear type, such as those of gravity and motion, that were held to drive the behavior of all phenomena in a deterministic, regular fashion to states of equilibrium; that is, patterns of change in which no novelty occurs. The reduction of any phenomenon to its parts, and the identification of the universal laws governing those parts, was thought to be the route to specifying completely the nature of, and thus predicting and controlling, the whole phenomenon. Here the whole is simply the sum of the parts, and identification of what causes the stable behavior of the parts is all that is required. This kind of part–whole thinking, so influential and successful in applied science and engineering, is directly applied to organizations in management science, according to the complexity writers. It has led to the emphasis many managers still place on predicting the future, choosing strategies, motivating individuals, measuring activities and controlling them in detailed ways.

The claim made by management complexity writers is that the new sciences of complexity undermine this reductionist, mechanistic thinking and present a more holistic perspective in which the whole is more than the sum of the parts, with both the whole and the parts following iterative, nonlinear laws. The claim is that it is of limited use to think of organizations as machines, as the old scientific perspective suggested. Rather, it is more useful to think of them as living systems interacting with each other in a nonlinear fashion, forming larger ecosystems, such as industries and economies, characterized by irregular patterns of behavior that cannot be reduced in any simple way to the parts of which any of them are composed. This new science, with its emphasis on nonlinear, holistic ways of understanding phenomena, is held to demonstrate limitations to predictability, thereby challenging the possibility of simple forms of control by humans over both nature and organizations. The new sciences are also held to point to the relationship between creativity and states far from equilibrium, often characterized by difference, conflict and crisis.

The management complexity writers recognize that there have been previous claims by systems thinkers that organizations are not purely mechanical, but rather take organic forms which are more than the sum of their parts and which display both stability and change. However, the management complexity writers, to varying degrees, argue that the complexity sciences take an important further step in identifying the paradoxically stable and unstable nature of complex systems and the limits to prediction and thus control. The key concept underpinning this claim is that of self-organization/emergence. Very briefly, self-organization is a process in which local interaction between parts of an organization produces emergent patterns of behavior of a coherent kind in the whole, all in the absence of any overall blueprint or plan for that whole. Local interaction produces a global pattern that need not be designed. It is this kind of claim that is often backed up with references to Heraclitus (see Appendix 1), Kant and sometimes Hegel.

If the claims of the management complexity writers have any validity, then they have significant implications, either directly or by analogy, for the everyday life of managers. Most managers continue to believe that their role is essentially one of designing an organization and controlling its activities. The capacity to design and control depends significantly on the possibility of making reasonable enough predictions of the internal and external consequences of one design rather than another and of one action rather than another. Question predictability and you question all of these management beliefs. Furthermore, most managers believe that it is the role of organizational leaders to choose strategic directions and persuade others to follow them. This too is questioned by the claims of management complexity writers about the limits to predictability. Most equate success with states of equilibrium, consensus and conformity. Again, this assumption is called into question by the complexity sciences. Most managers still believe that there will be no coherent patterns in the development of an organization in the absence of a blueprint or plan. The complexity sciences suggest otherwise.

It matters in a very practical way, therefore, whether the claims of management complexity writers are valid or not, for if they are, then many management and leadership activities must be based on illusory ideas about what these activities actually achieve and thus constitute a serious misdirection of attention and energy. Consequently, it becomes very important to explore carefully the basis of the claim by management complexity writers, which is essentially one to do with the nature of causality because the possibility of prediction, and thus control, depends upon managers' ability to identify causal links. Self-organization is itself an alternative concept of causality and it is important, therefore, to identify just what kind of causality it is.

We argue that it is not possible to make reasoned judgments about the validity of the various ways in which the complexity sciences are being used in relation to organizations and their management without examining what assumptions are being made about how and why organizations come to be what they are. What causes organizations to take the form they take, what causes them to display stable patterns, and also to change, is thus the central question and this makes it necessary to understand just what theories of causality underlie the complexity sciences. The distinctive causal concept in those sciences is that of self-organization. We will be arguing that self-organization as cause can be understood in one of two fundamentally different ways, the first being formative and the second being transformative. It is important to be as clear as possible about which of these alternatives writers are using because, as later chapters will illustrate, it is easy to take concepts from complexity thinking in the natural sciences, apply them indiscriminately, either directly or by analogy, and present quite unjustifiable management prescriptions. These unjustifiable prescriptions amount to little more than a new management fad and this will inevitably undermine what we believe to be the potential that complexity thinking provides for seriously rethinking the nature of management.

A basis in philosophy

A number of those writing about complexity in the natural sciences and about complexity in relation to human organizations refer back to Kant's contribution to the development of Western thought. In doing so, they are linking their own thinking about the central concept of complexity theory, namely self-organization/emergence, to the explanations put forward by Kant. We believe, therefore, that it is important to go back to this Kantian framework in order to elucidate current ways of talking about self-organization and emergence in complexity theory. First, consider some examples of how writers refer to Kant.

Mechanisms and organisms – organized or self-organizing?

Goodwin (1994) points to Kant's distinction between a mechanism and an organism. A mechanism is defined as a functional unity in which the parts of the mechanism exist for one another in the performance of a function. For example, a clock consists of a number of parts, such as cogs, dials and hands, and these are assembled into a clock, which has the function of recording the passing of time. The parts are only parts of the clock in so far as they are required for the functioning of the whole, the clock. They receive their function as parts from the functioning of the whole. A finished notion of the whole is required, therefore, before the parts can have any function and the parts must be designed and assembled to play their particular role, without which there cannot be the whole clock. Before the clock functions the parts must be designed, and before they can be designed the notion of the clock must be formulated.

An organism, however, is both a functional and a structural unity in that the parts not only exist for each other but by means of each other. The parts of a living organism are not first designed and then assembled into the unity of the organism. Rather, they arise as the result of interactions within the developing organism. For example, a plant has roots, stems, leaves and flowers that relate to each other to form the plant. The parts emerge, as parts, not by prior design but as a result of internal interactions within the plant itself in a self-generating, self-organizing dynamic in a particular environmental context. The parts do not come before the whole but emerge in the interaction of spontaneously generated differences that give rise to the parts within a unity, in a dynamic of stable repetition (Webster and Goodwin, 1996). Here, organisms develop from simple initial forms, such as a fertilized egg, into a mature adult form, all as part of an inner coherence expressed in the dynamic unity of the parts. An organism thus expresses a nature with no purpose other than its own form. Kant described this as "purposive"; that is, displaying a unified form in itself. An organism is not goal-oriented in the sense of having a movement toward an external result, but, rather, moves to a mature form which is unique in a particular context.

Kauffman (1995) also points to Kant when he says that the parts of an organism exist because of, and in order to sustain, the whole as an emergent property of holism. Marion (1999), writing about human organizations, quotes the references of both Kauffman and Goodwin to Kant when he says that organisms are self-producing and therefore self-organizing wholes, where the whole is maintained by the parts and the whole orders the parts such that it is maintained. He argues that Kant understood complexity theory 200 years ahead of his time.

Moving toward a knowable future

Today's writers on complexity appeal to Kant because he introduced a theory of wholes and parts, with notions close to self-organization and emergence, as a radical new way of thinking about causality. In fact, what Kant did was to introduce, for the first time, a systems theory and it reached a position in subsequent philosophy that was to serve as the foundation of systems thinking around the middle of the twentieth century. Such systems thinking came to have an enormous impact on thinking about both nature and human organizations. We will come to the influence on thinking about organizations in Chapter 4. Given the significance of Kant's thought and the way modern writers refer to him and are influenced by his arguments, it is important to examine just what it was that he was doing.

In his thought, Kant synthesized the central intellectual challenges of the Age of Enlightenment, which saw the collapse of the absolutist structures of the Middle Ages and formed the basis of the French Revolution. Kant rejected what he saw as the excesses of dogmatic rationalism and retained a notion of God and the immortality of the soul. On the other hand, he also rejected the excesses of dogmatic empiricism and included elements of Locke's individualism in his ethics. Above all Kant faced the conflict between human freedom and the emerging natural scientific method developed by Galileo, Bacon, Newton, Leibniz, and others, during the seventeenth century. Kant saw all of these challenges as presenting "antinomies," or mutually contradicting statements that defied human understanding. In three "critiques" of the scope of human reason, action and judgment, Kant created a new paradigm of nature and organization that resolves these contradictions. It is in his third work, the *Critique of Judgment*, that Kant develops the subtle link to understanding the first two *Critiques* as a system of thought (Pluhar, 1987). Kant rejects the argument proving the existence of God on the basis of the teleological order in nature which had been a key element of the dogmatic rationalism of the metaphysics of the Middle Ages and suggests an additional way of thinking of teleology in nature as a "regulative idea" guiding our understanding of nature.

Human freedom and the scientific method

The natural scientific method is one by which humans come to know the reality of both stability and change through careful observation, formulating hypotheses and then testing them empirically. For example, the movement of the planets was observed, hypotheses were formed about their movement and then tested by measuring the actual movement of those planets. The hypotheses suggested causal links between the action of a body and some aspect of its nature. For example, in the case of the planets, it was hypothesized that the gravitational attraction of a planet depended upon the mass of that planet. If the mass of one body increased then the gravitational attraction it exerted on others would increase in proportion. This kind of hypothesis immediately focuses attention on cause and effect links having an "if-then" structure applied to one part of the whole. The method involves isolating linear causal links, those of an efficient, or sufficient, kind (see Appendix 1). In other words the scientific method involved a reductionist approach in that attention was focused on the parts of a phenomenon. Those parts were postulated to behave predictably according to efficient causality, while the interaction between them was accorded no significance. The interaction simply followed from the nature of each part. The testing step in the method required humans to stand outside the phenomenon of interest and observe and measure its behavior in order to test the previously postulated causal links. The claim was that nature was entirely determined by necessary laws of this "if-then" kind.

To emphasize the point, the natural scientific method represented a theory of causality in which efficient cause predominated and it was this that accounted for stability and change, both of an entirely predictable kind, so that organization, or form, is equated with continuity and repetition without the possibility of novelty. Note how the past, the present and the future are all repetitions of the same pattern. This is a particular view of time in which time itself becomes unimportant. In fact, time disappeared and the laws were thought to operate in both time directions, forwards and backwards. Nature moved in a timeless way and time itself was a human illusion.

But to what end, for what purpose, was nature moving in this way? Prior to Kant's time, the purpose of nature, the teleological cause, was thought to be that of revealing God's creation. Nature was thought to be fulfilling God's purpose. Teleology here had nothing to do with movement; it was a static concept. So, by following the laws of gravitation celestial bodies orbited around each other in order to reveal the perfection of God's creation, the celestial harmony of the spheres. Teleological or final causality here is the natural law governing God's creation. As the twentieth century became more secular, natural science banished notions of teleology but the mechanistic, deterministic operation of efficient causality was retained. Natural science became exclusively concerned with what was happening. How and why it was happening were questions deemed to fall outside the legitimate sphere of the natural sciences. The "why" question itself, however, has not disappeared and we would argue that the natural sciences have continued to develop within a kind of natural law teleology that is simply not reflected upon. A form of natural law teleology survives, we argue, in notions of perfection and progress – such as optimization, a key aspect of modernism – that still have a powerful impact on how people think about organizations.

Kant recognized in his time that in the natural sciences efficient causality was being isolated and subordinated to what we are calling Natural Law Teleology to provide a deterministic, stable and predictable view of nature's behavior in which time is an illusion, change is regular and there is no freedom of movement. Organization was form that continued without the possibility of novelty.

For Kant this led to a seemingly insurmountable antinomy, or contradiction. He formulates this as thesis and antithesis:

> The first maxim of judgment is this thesis: All production of material nature and their forms must be judged to be possible in terms of merely mechanical laws. The second maxim is this antithesis: Some products of material nature cannot be judged to be possible in terms of merely mechanical laws. (Judging them requires a quite different causal law – viz., that of final causes.)
>
> (Kant, [1790] 1987: § 70)

Kant solved this antinomy in the same manner that he solved those in his other *Critiques*. He argued for a "both . . . and" position, establishing a position between dogmatic rationalism and dogmatic empiricism. On the one hand he argues against the so-called ontological proof of the existence of God as the basis of teleology in nature, and on the other he rejects Hume's argument that there is no basis for distinguishing final causes from efficient causes. Kant resolves the antinomy by arguing that understanding nature as moving toward a purpose or final cause is not an objective explanation but rather a regulative idea or principle; that is, it explains "for us." It is on this basis that Kant establishes a functional perspective on nature as systems.

It is important to note that in solving this antinomy of teleology in nature Kant is building a further argument for his resolution of the antinomy of human freedom, which he had dealt with earlier in his *Critique of Practical Reason*. For Kant, the view of teleology as a regulative idea, which he developed in the *Critique of Judgment*, could never apply to humans. Humans are part of nature, but in having souls, he argued, they are free. Humans exercise a causality that is based on freedom while nature follows a causality in which there is none. While Kant recognized the power of the scientific claim with regard to nature, he saw it as short-sighted because efficient causality driven by Natural Law Teleology left no room for human freedom, morality or ethics. Kant distinguishes between teleology as a regulative idea, by which we understand nature, and Rationalist Teleology, which is the basis of human freedom and ethics. Because humans have a soul, for Kant, human action had to be understood in terms of autonomously chosen goals and autonomously chosen actions to realize them. The predominant form of causality here is teleological – namely, that of autonomously chosen ends made possible because of the human soul. The principal concern then becomes how autonomously chosen goals and actions mesh together in a coherent way that makes it possible for humans to live together. This is a question of ethics. Kant understood ethical choice in terms of universals. In other words, ethical choices were those that could be followed by all people. Here, then, there is a particular view of ethics as pre-existing God-given universal principles of some kind. According to this view, change is the result of autonomous human choice and stability is preserved by the imperative, based in religion, which is provided by pre-existing universal codes of ethics. Human organization is continuity subject to autonomously chosen changes that reflect ethical universals.

In Kant's time this religion-based view of freedom was shifting to include the Enlightenment understanding of freedom as accessible to all humans through their intellectual endeavors. This Rationalist philosophy (for example, Locke's *Second Treatise on Civil Government*) was one in which autonomous individuals developed their own purposes; that is, chose their own goals and the actions to achieve them. It is in this Rationalist form that the Kantian view of human action continued to affect Western thinking. Here the predominant form of causality is autonomously chosen goals, but, with the religious link lost, the constraint provided by ethical universals was weakened. We will refer to this notion as Rationalist Teleology. Note how this notion postulates thought, in the form of a goal choice, before action, as the means of realizing the choice. In other words, this approach puts theory before practice and takes a view of ethics as pre-existing universal principles of human civilization.

The importance of Kant's contribution

Kant distinguished, as was pointed out in the references made to Goodwin (1994) and Kauffman (1995), between mechanisms and organisms. Mechanisms were subject to linear cause and effect links; that is, efficient causality subordinated to Natural Law Teleology. Organisms were to be understood in a systemic way. In systemic terms, causality was predominantly formative in that it was in the self-organizing interaction of the parts that those parts and the whole emerged. It was as if the system, the whole, was moving toward a subordinate final state that was already given; namely, a mature form of itself. In other words, it was unfolding an already enfolded form. For the first time in Western thought the notion of an all-embracing teleology to which other forms of causality were subordinated (see Appendix 1 on Aristotle) gave way to a notion in which the teleology was subordinated to another kind of causality, in this case of a formative kind. The key points we are making about the three causal frameworks so far discussed are summarized in Figure 2.1.

Because of the radical nature of what Kant was proposing it is important to notice what is happening here.

First he was proposing a teleology that is functional. This is not an efficient "if-then" notion in which one can take the parts separately and understand the nature of each part as adding together to give the whole. Kant is saying that the parts are functional and that the relationship between them functions to form the whole, which is a final, mature form. Although the final form is given, however, the parts can relate to each other in different ways to produce the end state. So there are variations

	Secular Natural Law Teleology	Rationalist Teleology	Formative Teleology
Movement toward a future that is:	a repetition of the past	a goal chosen by reasoning autonomous humans	a mature form implied at the start of movement or in the movement. Implies a final state that can be known. in advance
Movement for the sake of/in order to:	reveal or discover hidden order, realize or sustain an optimal state	realize chosen goals	reveal, realize or sustain a mature or final form of identity, of self. This is actualization of form or self that is already there in some sense
The process of movement or construction; that is, the cause is:	universal, timeless laws or rules of an "if-then" kind, that is, efficient cause	rational process of human reason, within ethical universals, reflected as human values. Cause is human motivation	process of unfolding a whole already enfolded in the nature, principles or rules of interaction. A macro process of iteration, that is, formative cause.
Kind of self-organization	none	none	repetitive unfolding of macro pattern already enfolded in micro interaction.
Nature and origin of variation/change:	corrective, "getting it right," aligning, fitting	designed change through rational exercise of human choice to get it right in terms of universals	shift from one given form to another due to context. Stages of development
Origin of freedom and nature of constraints:	freedom understood as conforming to natural laws	human freedom finds concrete expression on the basis of ethical universals	no intrinsic freedom, constrained by given forms

Figure 2.1 *Causal frameworks*

possible in the path toward the end state but only within pre-given limits. From this viewpoint, the source of stability is the functioning of the parts to give an enfolded final form and the source of rather limited change is the variety of ways in which the parts can relate in order to produce the final state.

Second, Kant was proposing a teleology in which there is an end state, or final form, that is enfolded in the sense that the whole exists in some sense before the parts. The purpose is to reach this enfolded end state, to repeat the past so as to move to a mature form. The parts function to form the whole, the final form. Take an acorn. It cannot grow into just any plant, only into an oak tree. So, the form exists right at the beginning in some way and is unfolded as the acorn develops into a tree. The process is one of reproduction, or repetition, of a dynamically stable form without any fundamental transformation that could lead to a form that has never existed before. We refer to this as Formative Teleology. It is subordinated in the sense that the identity of the organism, its final form or mature state, is pre-determined and the system moves toward it. The final form is already "contained" in the formative self-organizing process of interaction itself. The parts are only functional or causal parts inasmuch as they form the whole and the whole must therefore in a sense be given before one can decide what is a part and what is not. The final form is thus, in principle at least, knowable in advance. In this sense, Formative Teleology is subordinate to the formative causality of self-organization; subordinate in the sense that it is "contained" in the formative process.

Thinking in this way has an implication that is of great importance to the question of stability and change. The formative self-organizing process produces both stability and change but the pattern of change is in some sense pre-determined so that there can be no significant change at the level of the form, or the whole. This kind of explanation cannot encompass true novelty, the production of a form that is entirely new and thus unknowable.

Kant recognized the problem of subordinating teleology to formative cause in this way but argued that it provided a more powerful method to underpin the natural scientific method. However, he strongly argued that this combination of formative causality and subordinated Formative Teleology could never be applied to humankind because humans have souls and are therefore autonomous. Any application of formative causality and subordinated Formative Teleology would be profoundly devoid of ethics, or amoral. Instead, humans had to be understood in completely different terms, as acting toward autonomously chosen goals, Rationalist Teleology. Since the choice a human will make cannot be known in advance there is an element of the unknown in human futures. For Kant, a human choice is made according to "maxims"; that is, regulative categorical imperatives which assure that choices reflect universal ethical principles. The content of any given choice is, however, unknown in advance.

Kant, then, formulated a philosophy that enabled the further articulation of both the developing scientific method and the Rationalist reformulation of human freedom as autonomous individual choice. As we go forward in subsequent chapters to explore explanations of human organization we will be trying to distinguish one from another in terms of key distinctions made in the above discussion of Kant's thought. The key distinctions are:

- Nature as mechanism. The theory of causality here is that of overarching *Natural Law Teleology* in which perfection, timeless stability, is revealed through the operation of efficient causality. As a consequence, the mechanism moves in a stable manner over time and change is a predetermined and entirely predictable movement. Time is irrelevant here and interaction between parts plays no essential role in the explanation. There is, therefore, no notion of self-organization, and organization is continuity of a perfect, optimal kind.
- Nature as organism. The theory of causality here is one of functional, formative processes, formative cause, producing movement to an already given final state contained, as it were, within that process and so subordinated to it as *Formative Teleology*. Stable movement is produced by self-organizing interaction of parts that unfold to a pre-given, final form. Change is confined to regular movement from one form, say infant, to another, say child, leading to the final state, mature adult. There may be variations in the way that parts relate, producing small variations in mature form, but those are variations that do not alter the identity of that final form. Organization is continuity of form with small variations, all enfolded so that genuine novelty is not possible.
- Human autonomous action. The theory of causality here is *Rationalist Teleology* of autonomously chosen goals reflecting universal ethical principles. Notions of self-organization are absent and both stability and change are human choices. Organizations are designs chosen by humans and humans can design the truly novel.

Conclusion

In this chapter we have examined Kant's understanding of the paradox of nature as both mechanism and organism. It is important to note that this is from the perspective of the objective observer who identifies and isolates causality in nature and then tests hypotheses based on these identifications. This approach is also reflected in thinking about human organizations, as we will indicate in Chapter 4. Note also, the "both/and" nature of this way of thinking. There is both determinism and freedom, but separately located in nature and in human beings. There is both stability and change, but the end point of change is given in nature and not given in relation to human action. It is important to notice this because Kant's "both/and" resolution of conflicting arguments is still widely employed in thinking about organizations. For example, conditions in which it is appropriate to apply mechanistic approaches to management are identified and then different conditions are set out in which an organic approach should be adopted. This preserves a place for both the mechanistic and the organic by confining them to separate areas of action. In this way, contradictions are resolved, conflict is ignored and paradox plays no important part.

Having looked at causal frameworks that assume a knowable future, the next chapter turns to those that assume unknowable futures.

3 Moving toward an unknowable future

- The perpetual construction of the future
- Chance and adaptation
- Alternatives to some of Darwin's views
- Darwin and the neo-Darwinian synthesis
- Five ways of understanding stability and change
- Conclusion

The previous chapter looked at causal frameworks that explain movement into the future that is predictable, at least in the natural world. This chapter turns to two strands of thought that provide causal explanations of movement into an unknowable future.

Kant's argument, reviewed in the previous chapter, was not without its opponents. Hegel, another thinker sometimes quoted by management theorists, contested the dualism of nature and humanity and proposed a unified theory that encompassed both. The essential notion in understanding how Hegel dealt with paradox is the dialectical movement of thought. In challenging Kant's paradigm of a "both . . . and" resolution to antinomies, or mutually contradicting statements, Hegel creates another radically different paradigm of understanding organization and nature.

The perpetual construction of the future

It is important at the outset to be clear that Hegel's thinking has found its way into organizational theory after being filtered through many interpretations and simplifications. Many Marxist thinkers, for example, expressed the Hegelian notion of dialectic in the Kantian language of thesis and antithesis and for them the movement was the interaction of these polar opposites to yield a new synthesis. However, the new synthesis still contained both thesis and antithesis, which continued to interact to yield yet another synthesis. For example, Pascale (1990) takes this up in his perspective on organizations and talks about the rearrangement of thesis and antithesis in the form of a new synthesis, which can then only be further rearranged. In this view, forms unfold in a continuing evolutionary movement in which each form brings forth its opposite, and it is the interaction between these opposites that produces the movement. In this view, an unfolding dialectic, or a self-organizing process, produces emergent new states. However, in a sense, these new states are still pre-given or "contained" in the formative, self-organizing process. That which emerges is not truly novel but, rather, a rearrangement of what was already there. This is movement from a known current state to a knowable future state and teleology is already contained in the formative process in some sense. This makes some form of prediction possible.

We argue that this interpretation of Hegel misses the truly radical nature of his thought. To see what we mean, consider different ways in which one might think about the relationship between parts and whole. One way is to think of the whole as being made up of its parts where the parts are added, integrated, or fitted together to give the whole. This is Kant's mechanism and Natural Law Teleology, described above (see pp. 20–21). Alternatively, one might think of the parts as being determined by the whole, defined by it and so subservient to it. Taking the whole as prior to the parts requires that the whole should already exist. This is Kant's organism where the parts interact to produce a whole that is a repetition, perhaps with minor variation, of what went before, that is, Formative Teleology. This approach privileges the whole because the whole is thought of as if it were a part, a super part, which controls and dominates the other lesser parts. This notion of an already existing, dominant whole as a generalized abstraction or a transcendental whole creates a problem. If the parts are dominated and already determined by the whole, they cannot be constitutive of the whole in the sense of emerging from the interaction of the parts. The role of the parts is restricted to assembling into the whole.

An alternative notion of the whole is that of a whole that is never complete; that is, a whole that is under perpetual construction. Bortoft (1985) moves toward this idea with his notion of an "absent whole." He argues that it is not possible to point to a whole in the same way as it is possible to point to a part. For example, take a family. It is possible to point to the mother, the father and each of two children. However, one cannot then point to the family in this way because this would simply be numbering the whole (the family) amongst its parts (the members) so that it would be separate from its parts in the same way they are separate from each other. We would be thinking that the whole, the family, was a thing or simply a collection of individuals that already exists. However, a family is ongoing patterns of relationship between its members, arising between them in continual iteration of their interactions displaying both continuity and change. The family cannot exist separately from its members as a program governing their interactions because the family is the interactions, arising only in those interactions. The family is never there, it is never complete, because it is in a continual process of iteration in which it is perpetually constructing itself. In this way, the family is unlike the individual members who do exist separately from each other as well as together as a family, although, of course, each member of the family is also never there, never complete, because the identity of each member is also perpetually under construction. The members are constitutive of the particular family pattern emerging in their interaction, just as that pattern is constitutive of them. They form and are formed by the family at the same time. Neither the members nor the family are somehow there before they interact because what they are arises in the interaction.

It follows that while one can be aware of parts (family members) one cannot be aware of the whole (the family) in the same way. In other words, the whole is absent to awareness and in this sense it is a no-thing (the family being absent to awareness is a no-member). But this does not mean that the whole (the family) is nothing, that it does not exist. Instead, the whole (the family) is truly emergent in that it is not the result of a prior design or the revealing of an already existing, hidden whole. The absent whole is in the parts and emerges from the parts. At the same time, however, a part is only a true part, as opposed to some accidental, superficial thing, if it is essential to the emergence of the whole of which it is a part. What Bortoft is talking about here is self-reference, a phenomenon creating itself, in that the parts are being formed by the whole while they are forming it at the same time. Bortoft refers to Goethe in grounding his thought. We want to draw attention to the similarity but build on Hegel's thought in reference to his idea in which parts form the whole while being formed by the whole in paradoxical, for Hegel dialectical, movement. Kant's static resolution of paradox in a "both . . . and" paradigm is replaced by a paradigm of living experience as the paradox of movement.

In his *Phenomenology of the Spirit*, Hegel (1807) understands thought solely from within the process of thinking, drawing attention to the continuously evolving identity and change. In this movement of identity, there is both the possibility of sameness, or continuity, and the potential for spontaneous transformation at the same time. This movement is the dialectic and it is paradoxical in that it is both the repetition and the transformation of identity at the same time. The above example of a family illustrates this in that a family is formed by its members as it forms them at the same time. Family and individual identities emerge together and in so doing those identities display both continuity and potential transformation. Hegel argued that humans also experience the encounter with nature as an iteration of identity and difference.

What Hegel is getting at is really quite difficult to understand, but we think it is very important to do so in order to be able to distinguish between ways of thinking about complexity sciences and their application to organizations. For this reason we want to continue the discussion by looking at what Mead (1934) had to say about the kind of process we are talking about.

The known–unknown

In talking about communication between organisms as a social act, Mead distinguished between a gesture made by one organism and the response to that gesture by another. For example, one dog might snarl at another and that other might respond either with a counter-snarl or by lying down. Mead argued that the meaning of the communication did not lie in the gesture alone but in the whole social act. In the one case snarl and counter-snarl mean conflict, while in the other case snarl and lying down mean submission.

In conversation, we too follow the same circular movement in which one discovers the meaning of what one is saying in the response of others to it. We find ourselves recognizing the meaning of what we are saying as we speak into the response of others and, as we do this, the meaning of what we are saying may well be transforming. Note also that this is a process in which the movement is not from here (your word) to there (the other's understanding of it) but a circular movement that transforms where you have moved from (your word) and where you are moving to. To see this, you only have to think of puzzling quarrels that arise in seemingly unproblematic remarks. For example, a husband says quietly to his wife, "I was thinking of going to the football match," and she shrieks, "You are so selfish. You don't love me or the children." He guiltily explains, "But I haven't been out for three weeks," and she replies "I have been stuck here with the children for days." From there on the exchange might develop into a contrite reconciliation or a full-blown row. Notice how the movement of the communication transforms what the husband may have thought of as a tentative enquiry into something quite different – an act of extreme selfishness. As these two continue they cannot know how their interaction will develop. When he makes his comment he cannot know what it will lead to this time around, and nor can she; but, at the same time, both recognize the pattern as they engage in it. It has all happened before but each time it happens the pattern takes an unpredictable form. Note too how each statement takes meaning from the subsequent response and even changes in meaning in the light of even later responses.

This example is pointing to two important features of the paradoxical, dialectic process we think Hegel and Mead were referring to. The first is the known–unknown quality of the interaction in which there is the transformative possibility of the genuinely new as well as the possibility of simple repetition of the past. In the example given above, this couple has had similar interchanges about football in the past. As soon as it starts, they recognize it. It is known. However, at the same time what the next response and the one after that will be is unknown. Sometimes he yells back and sometimes he feels guilty. Sometimes she does not object and sometimes she does. There is always a transformative possibility. Instead of quarrelling, they might negotiate a compromise or leave each other to discover a new depth of love for each other in some unexpected way. In the unknown emerging of meaning, pattern in that meaning nevertheless comes to be recognized. Knowing is such an act of recognition. Communication here is a movement from and toward an as yet unrecognized position that comes to be recognized (known) in the act of communication itself. That recognition may sustain or shift the communicants' identities. All communication carries the possibility of change.

Time as the key to Hegel's notion of paradox

The second point to note relates to time. If one thinks in terms of Natural Law Teleology, time plays no essential part in what happens. If one thinks in terms of Formative Teleology, then the pattern that emerges now is the unfolding of what was already there in the past. Historical time is essential to this process of unfolding. The movement of time is from a given past to the present, which is a point without any temporal structure. It is simply now. The future will be a repetition of the past. This amounts to saying that the meaning is in the past and the movement of time is from the past to the present. If one thinks in terms of Rationalist Teleology then what happens now is an action chosen now to fulfill some selected goal for the future. Action is about filling the gap between what is desired for the future and what now exists. The movement of time is from the future to the living present. The meaning is located in the future, in the gesture made now as it points to the future. In both Formative and Rationalist Teleology there is no paradox in relation to time for in both cases meaning arises in the present, with one difference: in the former case meaning arises as movement from the past and in the latter it arises as movement from the future, both in a linear way. In both, the here-and-now is collapsed to a point and it has no structure itself; it refers either back to the past or forward to the future. But what of the experience of the here-and-now itself, in its own terms? When you think about it, a now that has no time structure would have little interest for human experience. And yet we do have the experience of being in the present.

In the thinking of Hegel (see O'Donohue, 1993), and also in the way Mead (1934, 1936, 1938) takes it up, there is paradox reflected in a different time structure of action. The here-and-now is not simply a point in time but also has temporal structure. One might think of a macro-temporal structure from past to present to future, and a micro-temporal structure of the present, which has a micro-past, micro-present and micro-future, a kind of fractal process. That micro-temporal structure is the gesture and the response the gesture calls forth, taken together. The here-and-now, then, has a circular temporal structure because the gesture takes its meaning from the response (micro-future) which only has meaning in relation to the gesture (the micro-past), and the response in turn acts back to potentially change the gesture (micro-past). The experience of meaning is occurring in a micro-present and it accounts for the fact that we can experience presentness. What is happening here is truly paradoxical for the future is changing the past just as the past is changing the future. In terms of meaning the future changes the past and the past changes the future, and meaning lies not at a single point in the present but in this circular process of the present in which there is the potential for transformation as well as repetition.

Notice the way in which Hegel's radical notion of time focuses attention. The two Kantian approaches focus attention on the macro sweep of time from the past to the present and into the future, with the here-and-now simply a point in that sweep. We cannot make sense of experience of a point and so we focus our attention on the past or on the future. Hegel's approach focuses attention on the micro-temporal structure of the here-and-now itself. It opens up the here-and-now point and invites us to make sense of the experience of this as the living present. This is very much about the detailed nature of interactions, micro interactions, that may be the same but may also be potential transformations. However, this is not a dismissal of the great sweep of time, or history. Within the overarching Transformative Teleology there is the transformative causation of micro interaction in which each moment is influenced by previous moments. Each moment is a repetition of the past but with the potential for transformation.

Hegel's thought is suggesting, we think, that the source of change lies in the detail of interactive movement in the living present, movement of a circular kind that is reflected in the macro-sweep of time, past and future. In complexity terms this is a fractal process. The result is a very different notion of self-organization from that of Kant. In Formative Teleology self-organization is a process of unfolding an enfolded form. In Rationalist Teleology there is no self-organization, only choice and design. In what we will call the Transformative Teleology of Hegel there is self-organization that has the potential for transformation as well as continuity at the same time. In this process identity is being created. It is in acting that meaning is formed and the acting entities realize themselves in forming this meaning. In iteration, the continuity of identity is always open to change. Self-organization is then a process of interaction characterized in an essential way by paradox and the emergence of the truly unknowable. What is being so organized is identity. It is a process that produces novelty, the creatively new that has never before existed. In Kant's notion, however, self-organization is a process of interaction producing emergent coherence already enfolded in that self-organizing process. This form of self-organization, by definition, is not a process that can produce genuine novelty.

We are arguing, then, that Hegel was presenting a Transformative Teleology that was taken up by Mead. We also agree with Mead in not following Hegel in his further development of a theory of absolute spirit. This was an expression of his time and it is generally considered to have failed. We would thus also not agree with any such Hegelian interpretations of absolute spirit to support the idea of a kind of all-encompassing transcendental whole.

The Transformative Teleology that we understand Mead to be taking from Hegel's phenomenology is not subordinate to the formative causal process of self-organization but is an overarching causality in which the "purpose" is the continuity and transformation of identity, and thus difference. The key points we are making about Transformative Teleology are summarized in Figure 3.1

Movement toward a future that is:	under perpetual construction by the movement itself. No mature or final state, only perpetual iteration of identity and difference, continuity and transformation, the known and the unknown, at the same time. The future is unknowable but yet recognizable, the known–unknown
Movement for the and sake of/in order to:	express continuity and transformation of individual and collective identity and difference at the same time. This is the creation of the novel, variations that have never been there before
The process of movement or construction; that is, the cause is:	processes of micro interactions in the living present forming and being formed by themselves. The iterative process sustains continuity with potential transformation at the same time. Variation arises in micro diversity of interaction as transformative cause. Meaning arises in the present, as does choice and intention
Kind of self-organization implied is:	diverse micro interaction of paradoxical kind that sustains identity and potentially transforms it
Nature and origin of variation/change:	gradual or abrupt changes in identity, or no change, depending on the spontaneity and diversity of variations of micro interactions
Origin of freedom and nature of constraints:	both freedom and constraint arise in spontaneity and diversity of micro interactions; conflicting constraints

Figure 3.1 *Transformative Teleology*

Review of causal frameworks so far discussed

So far, we have distinguished between four types of teleological cause and we will be using these to make distinctions between various ways of understanding organizations, including various approaches to self-organization/emergence as ways of thinking about organizations. These four kinds of teleology are:

1 Natural Law Teleology and efficient cause in which movement is perfectly regular and predictable and the parts add up to a whole. This teleology survives in modern times as an unreflected assumption about the nature of reality and as an assumption of the existence of optimal states. Everything that is possible is already given and there is no change under the sun.

2 Rationalist Teleology in which movement is toward a goal autonomously chosen by humans as an expression of universal ethical principles. Freedom means that the final form is unknown. Unpredictable, truly novel change is thus possible and stability is sustained by ethical universals. In other words, identity, or organization, evolves in essentially unknowable ways. Here the unknowable whole is achieved through choice, or design of the parts.

3 Formative Teleology in which movement is to a final form, a pre-given state already contained within the formative process that produces it. This means that change takes the form of continuity of identity, with only context-dependent variations in its manifestation. In this framework there is no explanation of true novelty. Self-organization here is repetition, with variations in manifestations of identity but no transformation in that identity. In other words, identity is developing in knowable ways.

4 Transformative Teleology in which movement is toward an unknown form; that is, to a form that is in the process of being formed, to a form that is itself evolving. Truly novel change is possible and self-organization is a paradoxical process of repetition and potential transformation. It is emergence of identity in a transformative, self-organizing process and the paradoxical experience of identity in transformation. Here teleology is not contained in the process since the teleological is itself being formed. In other words, identity, or organization, is evolving in unknowable ways, being created as it goes along. Here, the parts form and are formed by a whole that is under perpetual construction.

We want to stress again that for Kant, Rationalist Teleology would apply to human action while Formative Teleology would not. For Hegel, Transformative Teleology applied to both human action and nature. He was developing a theory of evolution as an explanation of both stability and change in human and natural phenomena.

Another major thinker who dealt with evolution and its questions of stability, change and form (organization/identity) was, of course, Darwin. To conclude our discussion of key concepts of causality it is necessary briefly to review what Darwin had to say.

Chance and adaptation

Darwin's evolutionary theory

Darwin was influenced by his reading of Malthus, who held that permanent change in any species was impossible because of the pressure of increasing population on limited space and food resources in a struggle for survival. Darwin, however, turned the Malthus argument on its head and argued that it was precisely this struggle for survival that was the motive force for change. In the struggle to survive, organisms developed biological variations that were more or less adapted to their environment, which included other organisms. The more-adapted organisms survived and their numbers increased, while the less-adapted perished. In this manner, adapted changes were retained in the population and at some point the cumulative adaptations resulted in completely new species, new forms that had not existed before. In this way, populations of species evolved into the unknown. Unlike Kant's formative process, Darwin's yielded completely new forms that were in no sense already there. For Darwin, it was the formative process of adaptation of whole organisms that accounted for change of a truly novel kind. However, he did not see this as a process in which just anything could happen or as a process in which chance or accident was central. The need to adapt exercised a constraint.

Some of the central themes in *The Origin of Species* (1859) and *The Descent of Man* (1871) run along the following lines. The body parts of an organism have particular functions, namely those of enabling the organism to survive in a struggle for survival in a particular ecological niche (the environment) that the organism finds itself in. A species consists of a number of organisms with much the same body parts, that is, mode of survival. Species change through variations at the level of the individual organism, some of which enhance its chances of survival, and thus reproductive success, in a changed environment. Other variations do not do so and so disappear from the species. In other words, some of the small individual changes turn out to be more adapted to a changed environment than others do. The more adapted changes, arising by chance (that is, unknown cause), spread through the species so that it gradually changes toward more adapted forms. If groups of the species are separated from each other by, for example, geographic barriers, then those groups are likely to change in different ways. They diverge, with each becoming more and more adapted to their separate local environments through the competitive sifting of more from less adapted changes, that is, through the process of natural selection. Eventually, the difference becomes so great that one could say that the divergent groups constitute new species.

Novelty, therefore, arises through a gradual process of chance changes (unknown causes) sifted by natural selection, the struggle for survival, so that the most-adapted forms survived to constitute a new species. Darwin, however, could not explain how these individual chance changes were passed from one generation to the next so as to spread through the population. An answer to this question was provided by Mendel who explained the genetic basis of inheritance. The combination of Mendel and Darwin became the neo-Darwinian synthesis, which will be discussed later (see pp. 44–47).

We call the process of change just described Adaptionist Teleology because the movement of form is toward the most-adapted state. This is not strictly speaking Formative Teleology because the most-adapted state is not pre-given in that the formative cause of natural selection operating on small chance variations in individual organisms could produce any number of adapted forms that have never existed before. However, it is not Transformative Teleology because the variations are not arising in micro interactions between organisms or the entities of which they are composed. The formative cause is an externally operating one. There is also an element of the pre-given in the shape of the environment to be adapted to. This makes it easy to downplay the unknown aspect of future form. There is no sense in this formulation of the paradox, of the stable–unstable, the known–unknown.

Darwin's argument, then, was that novelty arises through a gradual process of divergence in small chance variations naturally selected for their adaptive functions, and it is hard to say just when the novelty occurs. What Darwin was proposing was a formative process of variation, selection and retention, a kind of self-organization at the level of whole organisms in which truly new species emerged. This was a systemic approach in that interactions between organisms and the physical environment they inhabited produced emergent change in forms of organism. It was self-organization in the sense that the new forms did not reflect any kind of previously existing global design. There is a very important difference between Darwin's theory of evolution and Kant's thought on organisms in nature. For Kant, change in organisms was a movement through various forms to a pre-given final or mature form. He never considered the question of entirely new forms. This is precisely what Darwin did. His question was truly radical at that time: how did new species originate? In posing this question he shifted the focus of the natural sciences. It was this gradualist, chance variation at the individual level, operated on by natural selection as the struggle for survival, which was to form a crucial part of the neo-Darwinian synthesis. However, even in Darwin's time there were dissenting voices.

Alternatives to some of Darwin's views

Thomas Huxley (1863) argued that novelty emerged in a sudden discontinuous fashion. For him, novelty arose before natural selection exerted its influence. He suggested that natural selection operated to refine the newly emergent species. However, he could not explain how this occurred, just as Darwin could not explain how chance variations in an individual organism were passed on to the next generation. Around the beginning of the twentieth century, when Mendel's explanation of the genetic basis of inheritance began to attract increasing attention, William Bateson argued that mutations typically arose as small changes in genes in their recessive state where they were shielded from natural selection until they spread through the population and suddenly became dominant. Natural selection and adaptation to an environment were thus seen to be far less important in the origin of new species than Darwin thought.

Fisher (1930), Haldane (1932) and Wright (1940) developed this idea in rather different ways, and later views of this kind were expressed in the idea of genetic drift. It was argued that random variation might lead to less-fit species surviving as more-fit ones were eliminated. Some species might survive contrary to selection, or for reasons that had nothing to do with selection, such as a disaster that wiped out the more-fit species. Later, in the 1970s and 1980s, Eldridge and Gould (1972) took up this kind of argument and suggested that new species arise in discontinuous jumps in a way not due to natural selection. They called this "punctuated equilibrium."

Another line of disagreement has to do with whether natural selection operated at the level of the individual or the group. Gould and Eldridge emphasized group selection, as did Lewontin (1974). The former pointed to the particular role of regulating genes that control other genes in a move that gives more emphasis to interaction between genes rather than a simple focus on chance variation in individual genes.

So, the primacy of natural selection and gradual change has been disputed from Darwin's time to this day. These different views do not fall into our category of Adaptionist Teleology, but point toward Transformative Teleology because they look for the reason for change in some kind of micro interaction not subjected to selection and the abrupt appearance of new species not necessarily due to adaptation. However, these dissenting voices have never come to occupy the dominant position, as the neo-Darwinian synthesis did. However, before we turn to that perspective, we want to mention another interpretation of Darwin's thought – that of Mead.

Mead's interpretation of Darwin

Mead maintained that Darwin did in biology what Hegel had done in philosophy. He argued that according to Darwin's theory of evolutionary change, humans live in, and are a part of, a natural environment in which all forms have evolved and are evolving. In seeking an explanation of this evolutionary process Darwin's main concern was with how species originated. In other words, his central question had to do with change in its most radical sense, namely the emergence of forms that were not previously there, which were unknown beforehand. What was revolutionary about his answer was the assertion of a concept of time in which the future emerges as the unknown, as different from the past. In asserting this he differed from the natural scientific method and from Kant's notions of causality in nature. In Kant's formulation, nature moved to known forms and so nothing completely new was ever produced. For Darwin, as for Hegel, the opposite was true. However, for all three, Kant, Hegel and Darwin, humans were capable of producing genuine novelty.

Darwin understood evolution as causality in nature that is unknown to humans in a radical sense, and it is this emphasis on the unknown that aligns Darwin with Hegel. In Darwin's words:

> I have called this principle, by which each slight variation, if useful, is preserved, by the term Natural Selection, in order to mark its relation to man's power of selection. We have seen that man by selection can certainly produce great results and can adapt organic beings to his own uses, through the accumulation of slight but useful variations, given to him by the hand of nature. But Natural Selection . . . is a power incessantly ready for action, and is immeasurably superior to man's feeble efforts . . .
>
> (Darwin, 1859: 115)

For Darwin, nature is known to humans and it acts to produce what is unknown to humans so that what is unknown evolves from the very known context out of which and into which humans live. Nature acts in producing species that cannot be known before they emerge. The point at which variations in a species emerge as genuinely new is fuzzy and unclear. It cannot be known beforehand.

Darwin argued that humans have to deal with this kind of unknown. Humans are able to judge the outcomes of their actions, but they act in a context that is itself acting and is immeasurably superior. This paradox is at the core of Darwinian evolutionary theory. If humans ignore either aspect of the paradox they will perish in nature. If they persist in repeating the same selection then they will be surprised by natural selection and intended results will no longer be achieved. If simple trust is put in natural selection it will rapidly become fully unknown, leaving humans to starve or become the prey of other forces.

In Mead's interpretation, then, Darwin's arguments had some similarities to those of Hegel and to that extent Darwin too was putting forward explanations of a Transformative Teleological kind. On this reading, Darwin's theory of evolution is movement toward the unknown according to a formative process of variation and adaptive selection and retention at the level of the organism. As we have already said, Darwin was not clear on how the variation leading to transformation of form took place. For Mead, the source of the variation lay in the gesture and response structure of interaction between organisms. Variation with its potential for transformation arose in the micro detail of interactions between organisms. In this Hegelian perspective on the structure of time, a gesture of one organism calls forth a response in another and in so doing the gesture is changed in unpredictable ways. Mead argued that it is this process that accounts for the simultaneous emergence of human minds and human society. We will return to this notion later in this book, and later volumes in this series will explore it in more detail.

However, Darwin's thought continued to exert its most powerful influence on thought in the form of the neo-Darwinian synthesis in which there is a rather different view of the source of variation and, thus, of causality.

Darwin and the neo-Darwinian synthesis

According to the neo-Darwinian perspective, variations take place in the process of reproduction. One cause of variation is the errors arising as genetic material is copied (random mutation); the other cause is the somewhat random mixing of genetic material in sexual reproduction. New varieties of organism, therefore, appear by chance, and accident lies at the heart of the process. The explanation of variation, and thus of the whole evolutionary process, shifts from the level of the organism to the level of the gene. The explanation is reduced to the level of the individual gene and interaction between genes is unimportant. At the most important level of the explanation of evolution, the notion that interaction plays an important part thus disappears. Natural selection – that is, competition for survival – then sifts out for further reproduction those variations that adapt most effectively in the competitive environment constituted by other species of organisms. Less-adaptive variations perish, for it is only the winners which survive. Even in relation to natural selection, interaction becomes less important in this explanation and the idea that forms are evolving to the unknown slips into the background.

To see how this happens, consider the explanation given of the adaptive process of natural selection in neo-Darwinian theory (Dawkins, 1976). Two notions are widely used to explain this process, the first being that of the fitness landscape and the second being that of an evolutionary stable strategy.

Fitness landscapes

The notion of a "fitness landscape" (Wright, 1931) is an image of evolution moving across a landscape consisting of peaks and valleys. A peak represents a fit (that is, an adaptive) collection of genes (species). The higher the peak the more fit the collection of genes. A valley represents an evolutionary disaster (that is, very low levels of fitness, or maladaptations). The lower the valley the less the probability of survival. Evolution is then understood as a hill-climbing process. Another way of putting this is that evolution is a search process where the aim is to move out of valleys and up to the top of the highest peak, which represents optimal adaptation. The search process is one of trial and error in which chance variations in individual genes in a particular collection (a species) result in a move on the landscape, which may be upwards or downwards. Natural selection weeds out the downward moves and keeps evolution moving toward unknown peaks, with periodic disasters or tumbles into unknown valleys along the way. The use of this metaphor immediately creates the impression of a collection of genes moving on their own (without interacting with others) and of an optimally fit form that already exists, in a sense – the purpose of the evolutionary process being to find it. This resonates more with Formative Teleology than it does with Transformative Teleology. In Chapter 5 we will review the rather different way in which Kauffman (1995) uses this concept.

Evolutionary stable strategies

The second notion (Maynard Smith, 1976) is that of evolutionary stable states or strategies (ESS). This idea was imported into evolutionary biology from game theory in economics and its concept of Nash equilibria. Game theory is a mathematical model of interaction between agents in which the outcome of this interaction, the benefit or pay-off, for one agent depends upon the actions of that agent and the actions of the others. The starting assumption is that each agent is trying to maximize its own individual benefit in competition with others. Each player must choose a strategy before knowing anything about the others' current choices. Only after making a choice and seeing what the others have chosen can the agent know whether it was a good choice or not. As they "play," they keep changing their strategies until they reach a state in which no player can increase expected benefit by unilaterally changing strategy. This is a Nash equilibrium. In the application to evolutionary biology as ESS, the pay-off, or benefit, is defined in terms of fitness (survival) and ESS occurs when agent strategies are collectively stable. To understand what this means, consider a population of agents, all of whom are following the same survival strategy when a single mutant enters with a new strategy. If the mutant strategy can get a higher pay-off than that of the typical strategy of the population, then the mutant will "invade" the population. Each interaction between the mutant and a "native" will result in a win and the number of these mutant strategies will spread. ESS occurs where no mutant can invade the population, and this means that it is only ESS that is collectively stable. This collectively stable strategy represents a peak on a fitness landscape, a homeostatic state. Again, this approach suggests an already existing form that is discovered by some kind of adaptive search process. Notice how the emphasis is on reaching stable states, or homeostasis, in which the idea of the unknown sinks into the background.

From this perspective, then, chance (or accident) is a major cause of the emergence of any new species and there is no linear link specifying in advance that *if* a particular mutation occurs, *then* the organism will survive. In principle, any variation could emerge, the only constraints being the laws of physics and chemistry. Efficient causality is, therefore, absent. Instead, causality is of the formative kind. However, it is not the kind of formative causality to be found in Kant, or in one reading of Darwin, because the internal dynamic of the organism as a whole plays no part in the evolutionary process. Instead, the new form is "caused" by the sifting operation of competitive selection on chance variations at the level of the genes. The formative cause of the evolution of species is first of all accident – that is, chance variations in genes – and then competitive selection, which operates as a search mechanism to find a stable strategy or fitness peak. The surviving form, that to which the whole process is moving, is adaptive fitness and the search for this is at the heart of the process. Any notion of a system only comes into the process of competitive selection, which has no effect on the gene variations themselves. They arise individually by chance in a way unconnected with anything else. This evolution produces emergent outcomes in the sense that there is no blueprint or program for the pattern of evolving species, but it does so by blindly cobbling together chance changes, retaining only those that compete most successfully.

Even what appears to be altruistic behavior is explained in terms of survival advantage: cooperation occurs between relatives because this enhances chances of reproduction and so the survival of the family genes; cooperation occurs between non-relatives because this is a winning strategy. What of teleological causality? Neo-Darwinists refer to selfish genes that program organisms to reproduce in order that they, the genes, might survive, so that the teleological cause of evolution becomes the blind urge to survive, that is, to move to a peak of adaptive fitness or an evolutionary stable strategy. We refer to this as Adaptionist Teleology, which implies a largely non-systemic kind of formative causality in which competitive selection, adaptation, sifts out chance variations in individual genes. As with Kant's view of organisms this is a subordinated teleology in that it is contained within the formative process and it implies a given fitness waiting to be discovered, as it were.

Life-time development

Once a new form (species) emerges, its developmental sequence is not dependent upon chance at all. The selected genes constitute a program that specifies in detail how the lifetime development of a member of the species will unfold. All physiological features, including the most important neuronal connections in the brain, are supposedly specified in detail by this genetic program. This is a reductionist view in which specific genes, even specific markers on the genes, determine the structure and behavior of the organism. Causality here is entirely of the efficient kind. There is no formative causality because the internal dynamic of the organism does not affect its development or behavior and there is no competitive sifting. In the extreme version of this theory, the dynamic of an organism's interaction with other organisms in a context also does not affect its development or behavior. When applied to humans, this discounts the impact of social processes and diminishes the importance of learning. The process operates in this way in order to control the development of the organism in the interests of the survival of the genes (Adaptionist Teleology). This kind of thinking underlies the human genome program, socio-biology and evolutionary psychology, and in extreme interpretations there is no human choice or freedom. For time frames that matter to humans, therefore, neo-Darwinian theory posits complete predictability and, therefore, human ability to control and dominate nature, including human nature.

To summarize, from the neo-Darwinian perspective, new forms are caused by the formative operation of competition on chance variations in genes, driven by the urge to survive as reflected in adaptation to the environment. This is a formative process with a subordinated Adaptionist Teleology in the absence of any efficient cause. Once a novel form has emerged, its lifetime development is caused by the genetic program – that is, efficient rather than formative cause – and this operates in order to control that development again in the interest of gene survival through adaptation – that is, Adaptionist Teleology. The key points we make about this causal framework are summarized in Figure 3.2.

Movement toward a future that is:	a stable state adapted to an environment that may change in unknowable ways
Movement for the sake of/in order to:	survive as an individual entity
The process of movement or construction, that is, the cause is:	a process of random variation in individual entities, sifted out for survival by natural selection. This is formative cause. Meaning lies in the future selected adapted state
Kind of self-organization implied is:	competitive struggle
Nature and origin of variation/change:	gradual change due to small chance variations at the individual level
Origin of freedom and nature of constraints:	freedom arising by chance, constrained by competition

Figure 3.2 *Adaptionist Teleology*

Review of Darwin's contribution

We have been arguing that Darwin posed a radical question when he asked: what is the origin of species? His question, perhaps even more than any answers he suggested, had a major impact on the development of both the natural and the social sciences. The dominant impact in both cases came through the neo-Darwinian interpretations of Darwinian thought. In our view, this interpretation is in effect a Kantian one in that the movement of evolution is toward a form that is in some sense pre-given. The pre-given nature of the explanation is reflected in the notion of a fitness peak, or stable evolutionary strategy, which the evolutionary process "searches out." This is a kind of Formative Teleology, but one with a Natural Law flavor in that the fitness peak reflects the notion of an optimal state. Evolution here is progressive, moving up peaks toward some kind of ultimate optimum or perfection. The effect is to provide an explanation primarily of stability, the notion of homeostasis, with change to the genuinely new attracting little attention. An alternative way of interpreting Darwin is provided by Mead (1936), who took the Hegelian perspective, what we are calling Transformative Teleology. This focuses attention much more on change and less on stability. This transformative perspective had no impact on the natural sciences, but it did have an impact on the social sciences, reflected in the work of Mead (1934), Vygotsky (1962), Bhaktin (1986) and Elias (1989), which never became part of the dominant discourse. These alternative ways of understanding stability and change hark back more than 3,000 years to the debate based on the work of Parmenides and Heraclitus (see Appendix 1), and we will argue in Chapters 5 and 6 that they resurface in the development of the complexity sciences.

Five ways of understanding stability and change

The framework we intend to use to distinguish between ways of understanding stability and change in the complexity sciences and in human organizations will be based on the five different notions of teleology distinguished in this and the previous chapters:

- Natural Law Teleology, in which the concepts of self-organization and emergence do not feature at all and there is no change, other than movement to the perfect.
- Rationalist Teleology, which also has no particular implications for self-organization and change is the consequence of human choice.
- Formative Teleology, which implies a form of self-organization that reproduces forms without any significant transformation.
- Transformative Teleology, which implies a form of self-organization as paradoxical, characterized by both continuity and potentially radical transformation.
- Adaptionist Teleology, which implies a chance-based competitive search for optimality with a weak form of self-organization confined to the selection process. Change is movement to a stable state of adaptation to the environment.

We have made a distinction between five different causal frameworks. One of Kant's main contributions was to suggest that different causal frameworks applied to nature (Natural Law and Formative Teleology) and to human action (Rationalist Teleology). This split means that two different causal frameworks must be applied when it comes to explaining human action within, or upon, nature. We will argue in the next chapter that this Kantian split is manifested in split explanations of human organizations. In this split, organizations are understood to be like natural phenomena in that one causal framework (secular Natural Law Teleology in the case of scientific management and Formative Teleology in the case of systems theories) applies to "the organization" and another (Rationalist Teleology) applies to the individual choices of "the managers." The same procedure is evident when organizational theorists use some kind of neo-Darwinian theory (Adaptionist Teleology) to explain the evolution of populations of organizations, within which "the managers" make choices according to another causal framework (usually Rationalist Teleology). Chapters 4 through 6 will explain how complexity theorists, in both the natural sciences and the field of organizations, combine a causal framework approaching Transformative Teleology with either Adaptionist or Rationalist Teleology. They do this either by splitting micro and macro levels, applying Transformative Teleology to the former and Adaptionist to the latter, or they split "the organization" from individual human choices, applying Transformative Teleology to the former and Rationalist Teleology to the latter.

In the spirit of Hegel, we are interested in exploring an explanation of human organizations that does not make these splits. In our view, Hegel presented what we are calling Transformative Teleology as a causal framework applying to both nature and human action and applying at both micro and macro levels of description. This is a view of causality in which there are no splits and, therefore, no combinations with other causal frameworks.

So, we argue that it is not logical to combine Transformative Teleology with Adaptionist Teleology because this locates the process in which new forms arise in one causal framework (Transformative Teleology), while competitive constraints on those forms arise outside this process as adaptation to an environment (Adaptionist Teleology). However, from the perspective of Transformative Teleology, the competitive constraints on emerging forms arise within the micro interactions themselves and shape the form from within, not as a subsequent imposition from outside. The micro interactions themselves are simultaneously cooperative and competitive. In Transformative Teleology, it is micro interaction, in the form of conflicting constraints (see Chapter 5), that is the process perpetually constructing the future and constraining itself. The "competitive selection" occurs in the living present in the course of construction itself. The process is not producing something that is taken away and subjected to another causality. It is a process perpetually constructing itself. In Adaptionist Teleology the process of construction is that of the sifting action of competitive selection, which is external to the individual phenomena in which variation is occurring. In Transformative Teleology the process of forming variations is itself a process of cooperation and competitive selection.

A similar point applies to any combination of Transformative and Rationalist Teleology. In a comprehensive view of Transformative Teleology, human intentions, choices and plans are themselves interactions between people. They are the micro interactions within which new forms arise. It is contrary to the meaning of Transformative Teleology to imagine "the manager" standing outside the process and making choices about it within the framework of Rationalist Teleology.

To summarize, then, we will be arguing that any combination of the five causal frameworks immediately implies the kind of split upon which the dominant management discourse is built, particularly as it is influenced by systems thinking. This move increases the risk that notions from the complexity sciences will simply re-present the current discourse in a new vocabulary. We will be arguing for the development of a perspective from Transformative Teleology on its own. We see it as encompassing other types of causality, not subordinated to, or in combination with, any other in a "both/and" resolution of paradox. This means a clear move away from the way systems thinking is currently being used to understand human organizations.

A comparison of the five frameworks for thinking about causality is given in Figure 3.3

Conclusion

The purpose of the previous chapter and this one has been to distinguish between a number of different ways of talking about the causes of both stability and change in the organization of phenomena in nature and in human action. The reason for doing this is to provide a basis for comparing different ways of understanding the evolution of human organizations. We are interested in exploring the implications of Transformative Teleology as the basis for understanding change in

Figure 3.3 Comparison of frameworks for thinking about causality

	Secular Natural Law Teleology	Rationalist Teleology	Formative Teleology	Transformative Teleology	Adaptionist Teleology
Movement toward a future that is:	a repetition of the past	a goal chosen by reasoning autonomous humans	a mature form implied at the start of movement or in the movement. Implies a final state that can be known in advance	under perpetual construction by the movement itself. No mature or final state, only perpetual iteration of identity and difference, continuity and transformation, the known and the unknown, at the same time. The future is unknowable but yet recognizable: the known–unknown.	a stable state adapted to an environment that may change in unknowable ways
Movement for the sake of/in order to:	reveal or discover hidden order, realize or sustain an optimal state	realize chosen goals	reveal, realize or sustain a mature or final form of identity, of self. This is actualization of form or self that is already there in some sense	expressing continuity and transformation of individual and collective identity and difference at the same time. This is the creation of the novel, variations that have never been there before	survive as an individual entity

	Secular Natural Law Teleology	Rationalist Teleology	Formative Teleology	Transformative Teleology	Adaptionist Teleology
The process of movement or construction, that is, the cause is:	universal, timeless laws or rules of an "if-then" kind, that is, efficient cause	rational process of human reason, within ethical universals, that is, human values. Cause is human motivation	process of unfolding a whole already enfolded in the nature, principles or rules of interaction. A macro process of iteration, that is, formative cause	processes of micro interactions in the living present forming and being formed by themselves. The iterative process sustains continuity with potential transformation at the same time. Variation arises in micro diversity of interaction, transformative cause	a process of random variation in individual entities, sifted out for survival by natural selection. This is formative cause
Meaning:	has no time dimension	lies in the future goal	lies in the past enfolded form and/or unfolded future	arises in the present, as does choice and intention	lies in future selected adapted state
Kind of self-organization implied is:	none	none	repetitive unfolding of macro pattern already enfolded in micro interaction	diverse micro interaction of a paradoxical kind that sustains identity and potentially transforms it	competitive struggle

continued

	Secular Natural Law Teleology	Rationalist Teleology	Formative Teleology	Transformative Teleology	Adaptionist Teleology
Nature and origin of variation/change:	corrective, getting it right, fitting, aligning	designed change through rational exercise of human freedom to get it right in terms of universals	shift from one given form to another due to sensitivity to context. Stages of development	gradual or abrupt changes in identity or no change, depending on the spontaneity and diversity of micro interactions	gradual change due to small chance variations at the individual level
Origin of freedom and nature of constraints:	freedom understood as conforming to natural laws	human freedom finds concrete expression on the basis of reason and ethical universals	no intrinsic freedom, constrained by given forms	both freedom and constraint arise in spontaneity and diversity of micro interactions; conflicting constraints	freedom arising by chance, constrained by competition

organizations and, in particular, the way in which the complexity sciences might point to such understanding. We are interested in identifying how an explanation built on Transformative Teleology differs from others, particularly those that also draw on the complexity sciences. We will be arguing that when the complexity sciences are understood from the perspective of Transformative Teleology they offer explanations of organizational change that are potentially novel. However, when perspectives from the complexity sciences are imported into explanations of organizational change within Formative and Adaptionist Teleologies, they tend, in our view, to re-present currently dominant explanations in a different terminology. We believe that this approach runs the risk of becoming another management fad soon to go the way of others. We hold that a view based on Transformative Teleology avoids this.

To develop this argument, we turn, in the next chapter to a review of notions of causality underlying currently dominant explanations of organizational change.

4 Limits of systems thinking:
focusing on knowable futures

- Dealing with human participation and freedom
- Scientific management: ignoring interaction
- Systems thinking: splitting choice and interaction
- Conclusion

In this chapter we are going to argue that today's dominant discourse on the management of human organizations is built on two strands of thinking developed during the course of the twentieth century. The first is scientific management, and the reaction it provoked, and the second is systems thinking. What these two strands have in common is their overall approach to understanding the phenomenon of organization in human action. They both seek to apply the method of natural science to human action in ways that reflect Kant's split between causality in nature and causality in human action, discussed in Chapter 2. Let us explain what we mean by this.

The natural scientist takes the position of the external, objective observer of some selected phenomenon in nature. From this perspective, one way is to regard the selected phenomenon as a mechanism and understand it by analyzing it into its parts and then identifying the necessary laws governing their behavior. The necessary laws have the "if-then" structure of efficient cause. Although teleology is usually banished as a causal principle in the natural sciences, we hold that it remains as an implicit causal factor (secular Natural Law Teleology) because the necessary laws are understood to be producing movement toward optimal patterns of behavior. Alternatively, the natural scientist may understand the selected phenomenon in systemic terms, that is, in terms of the interaction of the parts, much as Kant did when he talked about nature as organism. The necessary laws then relate to interactions between parts rather than simply to the behavior of a part. And what causes the form of the whole is then the interaction itself, that is, formative cause with subordinated teleology (Formative Teleology), in which the movement of a system is toward a final or mature form of itself, a form already enfolded in the system (see Chapter 2).

Scientific principles of both the mechanistic and the systemic kind are then applied, for example by engineers, in order to operate on the natural environment for the benefit of at least some humans. This application is understood as a human choice governed by Rationalist Teleology, that is, choice determined by human reason exercised as an expression of ethical principles.

Natural science, in its theorizing and its application, therefore preserves the split Kant argued for between the causality applied to nature (Natural Law or Formative Teleology) and that applied to human action (Rationalist Teleology).

Mainstream approaches to understanding the phenomenon of human organizations take much the same approach. The organizational researcher also typically stands outside the phenomenon of human organization, like the natural scientist, and seeks either to identify necessary laws driving the organization as mechanism, or the rules of interaction between the parts of the organization understood as a system that forms behavior. In doing so, the organizational researcher applies the same notions of causality to the phenomenon of human organization as the natural scientist does to a phenomenon in nature: Natural Law Teleology when it is thought of as mechanism and Formative Teleology when it is thought of as system. Having understood the phenomenon of "human organization" in the same way as the natural scientist understands phenomena in nature, the organizational researcher then moves to the equivalent of applied science. The researcher points to the chosen goals of the organization and designs a system of rules and procedures to achieve them, or identifies systemic interactions that might undermine their achievement. This is Rationalist Teleology just as in applied natural science. This whole approach is then presented as a prescription for managers who should design and apply (Rationalist Teleology) the rules and systems that constitute an organization's functioning as optimizing mechanism (secular Natural Law Teleology) or system for achieving given patterns of behavior (Formative Teleology).

Mainstream approaches to using the understanding of human organizations, therefore, preserve a split between Rationalist and

Formative Teleology just as in natural science, but they apply both to human action in a move that Kant argued vigorously against. The way in which both of these teleologies are applied is as follows. Rationalist Teleology applies to the choosing manager (theorist, researcher, decision-maker), from whom the organization itself is split off as a "thing" to be understood. The organization, that which is to be explained and operated on, is then regarded as an objective phenomenon outside the choosing manager (theorist, researcher, decision-maker), equivalent to a natural phenomenon, to which Natural Law or Formative Teleology can be applied. There are two major problems with this move, problems that many think have bedeviled management thinking for decades. First, managers and researchers are humans participating in the very phenomenon their approach splits them off from: they cannot be objective observers in the manner of the natural scientist, but they proceed as if they can. Second, and closely related to the first, the split locates human freedom entirely in the manager (theorist, researcher, decision-maker) and reduces other members of the organization to inhuman parts without freedom, just as Kant warned.

Dealing with human participation and freedom

There have, of course, been moves by systems thinkers to devise explanations that deal with these problems of participation and freedom, which we will discuss later in this chapter. However, in our view, those moves have met with little success within management science or systems thinking. The reason for this lack of success, we argue, lies in the very notion that organizations can be thought of exclusively either as mechanisms or as systems. This is because as soon as one thinks of "the organization" as a "mechanism" or as a "system," this thought itself immediately reifies and objectifies human action and subjects it to necessary laws or systemic rules. This immediately locates human freedom and participation, that which we are trying to explain, outside the mechanism or the system we are using to explain it. This is clearly understood by many systems thinkers and they have developed methodologies to widen participation in systems identification and design in organizations. Basically, the approach is to extend the boundary of the system to include more people in democratic processes, so empowering them. In doing this, however, they always locate some kind of choosing agency outside the system, a point we explain later in this chapter. The split, therefore, continues. The split between manager and organization is essential to thinking about an organization as mechanism or as system. Any attempt to remove the split while continuing to think in terms of mechanism or system must fail because the split cannot be resolved while it is retained and it must be retained if the organization is to be thought of as a mechanism or a system. The result is that both management science and systems thinking provide powerful ways of thinking about, and designing means of securing, organizational stability and continuity and, in the case of systems thinking, unfolding potential change already enfolded in the system. However, they both encounter difficulties when it comes to explaining, within their own frameworks, the role of ordinary human freedom and the closely related possibility of transformative change. The nature of ordinary, everyday freedom and participation, not necessarily of a democratic or empowered kind, is not adequately incorporated. Furthermore, organizational change of a fundamental kind, and how that change comes about, also cannot be adequately understood from either mechanistic or systems perspectives. Another perspective is required. We suggest one of complexity understood as Transformative Teleology.

Why does this rather abstract point matter to practical managers? We started this book by pointing to a common frustration experienced by managers. The systems they design hardly ever work as expected and yet managers "get things done anyway." However, instead of paying attention to how they "get things done anyway," they put even more effort into identifying systemic obstacles and designing better systems. Since these can never capture the novelty so often experienced, frustration levels rise even further. The experience is of continual, irregular change, but the ways of thinking employed to understand that experience are essentially about stability and regular change. Why are managers doing this? Because, we argue, they are caught in ways of thinking that do not pay adequate attention to their own participation in what is happening. Instead, they pay attention to the "systems" that attempt to control ordinary, everyday human freedom in order to preserve stability or secure regular, globally intended change.

We all know, however, that rules, procedures and systems on their own are not what make an organization function. One of the most reliable ways of bringing an organization to its knees is for its members to do precisely what the rules and systems stipulate and nothing more. In other words, systems in organizations can only function if the members of the organization weave their day-to-day interactions with each other through and around the rules of the systems they have designed. Systems work, to the extent that they do, because of the informal, freely chosen, ordinary, day-to-day cooperative interactions of an organization's members, and this cannot be controlled. It seems that this is how they "get things done anyway." If this is so, then such activity cannot be understood from either mechanistic or systemic perspectives because the underlying theories of causality upon which those perspective are built exclude the very human freedom upon which the kind of day-to-day cooperative interaction we are referring to depends. That ordinary, everyday freedom is not necessarily democracy or empowerment, but the ordinary choices people make as they weave their daily activities through and around systems guiding and constraining their work.

The very practical problem with thinking about organizations in either mechanistic or systemic ways is that no sooner has the mechanism or the system been identified or designed than real organizational life moves on. This suggests that change of any fundamental kind, including change in systems, arises outside the system and any explanations of such change in systemic or mechanistic terms can only be given with hindsight. Organizational mechanisms and systems are simply formalizations of changes after they have occurred and so systems design can never keep up, by definition. Perhaps that is why managers keep finding that their systems do not work as expected. Again, the reason for this gap between what happens and what is expected is due to the underlying theory of causality upon which both mechanistic and systems thinking is built, a theory that excludes ordinary human freedom and the essentially linked quality of the unknown, both features of fundamental change.

We are not arguing that management science or systems thinking have no use at all or that managers should abandon rules and systems. On the contrary, we are pointing to the need to pay careful attention to how people go on with each other in their day-to-day organizational lives as they use the rules and systems they have designed, despite the drawbacks of those systems; namely, that they cannot cope with all eventualities and they cannot keep up with the pace of change. We are also not saying that systems thinkers, for example, have not identified the problems we point to. They have, as we will indicate in the section after the next one in this chapter. We are arguing, however, that their attempts to deal with the problems do not really succeed because they try to deal with the problems on the basis of systems thinking itself. The problems arise because of the theory of causality underlying systems thinking. No attempt to deal with the problems can succeed while this theory of causality remains the exclusive focus. Ultimately, Formative Teleology cannot be applied to human action and Rationalist Teleology is too limited a way of understanding human action. Hence our interest in exploring a shift to Transformative Teleology.

The tools of "systems" managers, then, fail to function as expected in a turbulent world precisely because they focus so much on stability and in the process inevitably ignore ordinary, everyday human freedom. We believe that this everyday frustration of ordinary practical managers requires a careful examination of flaws in the dominant thinking about organizations, right at the very roots of that thinking in its theory of causality, and a search for an alternative way of thinking.

This chapter seeks to explain why we take the position set out above. Consider the first strand underlying today's dominant discourse on organizations and their management, namely scientific management.

Scientific management: ignoring interaction

Frederick Taylor (1911) in the United States and Henri Fayol ([1916] 1948) in Europe, the founding figures of scientific management, were both engineers. Taylor's central concern was with the efficient performance of the physical activities required to achieve an organization's purpose. His method was that of meticulously observing the processes required to produce anything, splitting them into the smallest possible parts, identifying the skills required and measuring how long each part took to perform and what quantities were produced. His prescription was to provide standardized descriptions of every activity, to specify the skills required, to define the boundaries around each activity and to fit the person to the job requirement. Individual performance was to be measured against the defined standards and rewarded through financial incentive schemes. He maintained that management was an objective science that could be defined by laws, rules and principles: if a task was clearly defined, and if those performing it were properly motivated, then that task would be efficiently performed. Fayol's approach to management was much the same. He split an organization into a number of distinct activities (for example, technical, commercial, accounting and management), and he defined management as the activity of forecasting, planning, organizing, coordinating and controlling through setting rules that others were to follow.

What concepts of causality are structuring this way of thinking about organizations? Management science equates the manager with the scientist and the organization with the phenomenon that the scientist is concerned with. The particular approach that the manager is then supposed to take toward the organization is that of the scientist, the objective observer, who regards the natural phenomenon as a mechanism. The whole mechanism is thought to be the sum of its parts and the behavior of each part is thought to be governed by timeless laws. An organization is, thus, thought to be governed by efficient causality and the manager's main concern is with these "if-then" causal rules. There is a quite explicit assumption that there is some set of rules that are optimal; that is, that produce the most efficient global outcome of the actions of the parts, or members, of the organization. This is what we are referring to as the secular form of Natural Law Teleology and in scientific management the underlying teleology is never examined.

There is an important difference between the scientist concerned with nature and the analogous manager concerned with an organization. The scientist discovers the laws of nature while the manager, in the theory of management science, chooses the rules driving the behavior of the organization's members. In this way, Rationalist Teleology is brought into play but it is one that differs in important ways from Kant's notion. First, this Rational Teleology applies only to the manager. It is he who exercises the freedom of autonomous choice in the act of choosing the goals and designing the rules that the members of the organization are to follow in order to achieve the goals. Those members are not understood as human beings with autonomous choice of their own but as rule-following entities making up the whole organization. Closely linked to this point about freedom is that of acting into the unknown. Kant argued that the choices humans make are unknown. In its use in scientific management, Rationalist Teleology is stripped of the quality of the unknown, and also of the ethical limits within which action should take place, to provide a reduced Rationalist Teleology. In fact scientific management does what Kant argued against. It applies the scientific method in its most mechanistic form to human action, whereas Kant argued that it was inapplicable in any form simply because human freedom applies to all humans. Second, Kant's coupling of autonomous human action with universal ethical principles is absent in the Rationalist Teleology of management science, which regarded human action as reflex-like responses to stimuli in accordance with the behaviorist psychology of its time.

The ethical aspect of Rationalist Teleology appears to some extent in the Human Relations reaction to scientific management. By the 1930s, the view that Taylor and Fayol took of human behavior was being actively contested by, for example, Elton Mayo (1949), a social psychologist. He conducted experiments to identify what it was that motivated workers and what effect motivational factors had on their work. He pointed to how they always formed themselves into groups that soon developed customs, duties, routines and rituals and argued that managers would only succeed if these groups accepted their authority and leadership. He concluded that it was a major role of the manager to organize teamwork and so sustain cooperation. Mayo did not abandon a scientific approach but, rather, sought to apply the scientific method to the study of motivation in groups.

From the 1940s to the 1960s, behavioral scientists (for example, Likert, 1961) continued this work and concluded that effective groups were those in which the values and goals of the group coincided with those of the individual members and where those individuals were loyal to the group and its leader. Efficiency was seen to depend upon individuals abiding by group values and goals, having high levels of trust and confidence in each other in a supportive and harmonious atmosphere. In extending freedom to all members of an organization and paying attention to motivational factors, the Human Relations school took up a fuller notion of Rationalist Teleology but still thought of this as encompassing an organizational whole driven by efficient causality with an implicit Natural Law Teleology in that the movement of the whole organization was toward an optimal state of harmony.

Taking scientific management and Human Relations together, we have a theory in which stability is preserved by rules, including motivational rules, that govern the behavior of members of an organization (a mixture of Rationalist Teleology and Natural Law Teleology). Change is brought about by managers when they choose to change the rules, which they should do in a way that respects and motivates others (Rationalist Teleology) so that the designed set of rules will produce optimal outcomes (secular Natural law Teleology). Because they are governed by efficient cause, organizations can function like machines to achieve given purposes deliberately chosen by their managers. Within the terms of this framework, change of a fundamental, radical kind cannot be explained. Such change is simply the result of rational choices made by managers and just how such choices emerge is not part of what this theory seeks to explain. The result is a powerful way of thinking and managing when the goals and the tasks are clear, there is not much uncertainty and people are reasonably docile, but inadequate in other conditions. Truly novel change and coping with conditions of great uncertainty were simply not part of what scientific management and its Human Relations consort set out to explain or accomplish.

The principles discussed above were developed a long time ago, and they have been subjected to heavy criticism over the years, but they still quite clearly form the basis of much management thinking.

Systems thinking: splitting choice and interaction

During the 1930s and 1940s, a number of scholars were working in related areas, very much in conversation with each other, culminating in the publication of some important papers around 1950. The related areas covered systems of control, the development of computer language, and the development of a new science of mind in reaction to behaviorism, namely cognitivism (McCulloch and Pitts, 1943; Gardner, 1985). These ways of thinking amounted to a new paradigm in which the whole came to be thought of as a system and the parts as subsystems within it. A system in turn was thought to be part of a larger supra system. The parts were now not simply additive in that they affected each other. The focus of attention shifted from understanding the parts, or entities, of which the whole was composed, to the interaction of subsystems to form a system and of systems to form a supra system.

The new systems theories developed along three pathways over much the same period of time: general systems theory (von Bertalanffy, 1968; Boulding, 1956), cybernetics (Wiener, 1948; Ashby, 1945, 1952, 1956; Beer, 1979, 1981) and systems dynamics (Tustin, 1953; Philips, 1950; Forrester, 1958, 1961, 1969). All three of these strands began to attract a great deal of attention in many disciplines from around 1950, as did the new cognitivist psychology and, of course, computers. Engineers, bringing with them their notion of control, took the lead in developing the theories of cybernetic systems and systems dynamics, while biologists, concerned with biological control mechanisms, developed general systems theory. This systems movement, particularly in the form of cybernetics, has come to form the foundation of today's dominant management discourse, so importing the engineer's notion of control into understanding human activity.

Some brief remarks are made on each of these strands of development in systems thinking before looking at the theories of causality underlying them.

The central concept in general systems theory (von Bertalanffy, 1968) is that of homeostasis, which means that systems have a strong tendency to move toward a state of order and stability, or adapted equilibrium. They can only do this if they have permeable boundaries that are open to interactions with other systems. Such systems display the property of equifinality, which means that they can reach homeostasis from a number of different starting points along a number of different paths. It follows that history and context are unimportant. All that matters is a system's current state in terms of boundaries and how systems are relating to each other across these boundaries. Disorder is corrected at all levels by boundary and role definitions and change takes place through change in boundaries. It is easy to see how these notions lead, in organizational theories, to an emphasis on clarity of roles and task definition and the equation of management with a controlling role at the boundary (Miller and Rice, 1967). This notion of boundary is fundamental to systems thinking, a point we develop below.

Cybernetic systems are self-regulating, goal-directed systems adapting to their environment, a simple example being the central heating system in a building. Here, the resident of a room sets a target temperature and a regulator at the boundary of the heating system detects a gap between that target and the actual temperature. This gap triggers the heating system to switch on or off, so maintaining the chosen target through a process of negative feedback operation. All planning and budgeting systems in organizations are cybernetic in that quantified targets are set for performance at some point in the future, the time path toward the target is forecast, and then actual outcomes are measured and compared with forecasts, with the variance fed back to determine what adjustments are required to bring performance back to target. All quality management systems take the same form, as do all incentive schemes, performance appraisal and reward systems. The same point applies to change management and culture change programs. Total Quality Management and Business Process Re-engineering projects are also fundamentally cybernetic in nature. The thinking and talking of both managers and organizational researchers, therefore, tend to be dominated by cybernetic notions. It is easy to see the consistency of this way of thinking with that of scientific management, despite the shift to a "systemic" perspective.

The third development of systems theory was also developed largely by engineers who turned their attention to economics (Goodwin, 1951; Philips, 1950; Tustin, 1953) and industrial management problems (Forrester, 1958). In systems dynamics, mathematical models of a system are constructed, consisting of recursive, nonlinear equations that specify how the system changes states over time. One important difference from the other two systems theories is the recognition of amplifying, or positive, feedback as well as negative feedback. Another is the introduction of nonlinear responses into a chain of circular causality that could lead to unexpected and unintended outcomes, which means that it can no longer be assumed that the system will move to equilibrium. The system is then no longer self-regulating but it is self-influencing: it may be self-sustaining or self-destructive. Systems dynamics originally had little impact on management thinking, but more recently it has attracted much interest as a central concept in the notion of the learning organization (Senge, 1990). Here, instead of thinking of a system moving toward an equilibrium state, it is thought of as following a small number of typical patterns or archetypes. Effective management requires the recognition of these archetypes and the identification of leverage points at which action can be taken to change them and so stay in control of an organization, in effect controlling its dynamics.

The underlying theory of causality

The development of system–environment thinking amounted to the rediscovery of formative causality (see Chapter 2). Systems theories hold that the internal dynamics of a system, the form of the system, play a major role in determining its behavior. This formative causal link, however, is thought of in linear terms in that the form, or internal dynamic, causes the behavior but that behavior does not cause the form, or internal dynamic. The internal dynamic is a given. In the theories of cybernetics and general systems there is also linear causality of an efficient kind. For both, if there is a change in the environment, then the system will adapt. It is a gap between environment and internal state that triggers a change back to an equilibrium state in a straightforward linear manner. History here is unimportant since change toward equilibrium is triggered only by the current gap between environmental conditions and internal state. In the systems dynamics strand, as well as formative causality, there is also efficient causality but this time it takes a circular nonlinear form. The behavior produced by a system in one period of time feeds back through the system to determine behavior in the next time period. In systems dynamics, history does, therefore, play a part. However, with this one difference we can say that, in all three strands of systems thinking, the notion of efficient cause is expressed as a feedback process and linked to a formative causality. While predictability and movement toward equilibrium are not at all problematic in part–whole thinking, they become so when a shift is made to system–environment thinking, particularly in the systems dynamics strand.

Comparison with part–whole thinking

Consider how this systems thinking compares with the earlier framework of scientific management. The manager continues to be equated with the natural scientist, the objective observer, and just as the scientist is concerned with a natural phenomenon so the manager is concerned with an organization. Now, however, the organization is understood not as parts adding to a whole but as a system in which the interactions between its parts are of primary importance. The manager understands the organization to be a self-regulating or a self-influencing system and it is the formative process of self-regulation or self-influence (formative cause) that is organizing the pattern of behavior that can be observed. In the case of general systems and cybernetics, that pattern is movement toward a chosen goal, an optimally efficient state, and the pattern of behavior is held close to this goal/state when the system is operating effectively. In the case of systems dynamics, the form toward which the system moves is a typical pattern or archetype enfolded in the system, which the manager can alter by operating at leverage points. In all of these systems theories, therefore, the final form of the system's behavior (teleology), that toward which it tends, is a state already enfolded, as it were, in the rules (efficient cause) governing the way the parts interact (formative cause). The teleology is therefore subordinated to the formative process. The goal may have been set outside the system but its own internal formative process determines its movement toward the goal. This is the same causal framework as Formative Teleology. It is unclear how many of these systems theorists were familiar with Kant's *Critique of Judgment*. It is certain that von Bertalanffy was not and that some recent theorists such as Kauffman are. But there is a close resemblance between Kant's notion of organism and his related theory of formative cause, although here it is applied to human beings regarded as systems.

In the terms we are using in this book, therefore, the move from part–whole to systems thinking about organizations amounts to a new theory of causality, a move from a theory of secular Natural Law Teleology to one of Formative Teleology. An implicit secular Natural

Law Teleology also continues in the belief in cybernetics and general systems theories that the system moves toward an optimally efficient state.

In management science, the manager is the objective observer who designs rules of individual behavior to do with task performance and motivation. In cybernetics and general systems perspectives, however, the manager is the objective observer who designs the whole system, including the rules of interaction between members that drive it. In systems dynamics the manager is the objective observer who detects system archetypes and operates at leverage points to alter them. In early systems thinking, the freedom was located in the manager to choose the system or to choose changes in it. The Rationalist Teleology of management science continued as before and the first wave of systems thinking about organization paid as little attention as management science did to ethics, ordinary human freedom and the unknown nature of the final state toward which human action tends. However, some more recent developments of systems thinking in the 1980s and 1990s actively took up the issues of participation and ethics, but they did so in a way that did nothing to alter the underlying theory of causality. The systems movement continues to build on a theory of Rationalist Teleology applied to the understanding and design of organizations as systems that are governed by Formative Teleology, as the following section explains. The focus of the systems movement is on problem-solving and action to improve a system so that it moves toward an optimal state (Phelan, 1999).

As soon as one thinks of a human organization as a system that can be identified or designed one immediately encounters the problem that the identifier or the designer is also part of the system. If one then continues to think of an organization as a system it seems quite natural to seek to remedy this by widening the boundary of the system to include the identifier or designer within the system. To see the difficulties this leads to, consider first how second-order cybernetics (Bateson, 1973; von Foerster, 1984; von Glasersfeld, 1991) sought to accomplish this inclusion and then how the later development of soft systems (Checkland, 1981; Checkland and Schles, 1990) and critical systems thinking (Churchman, 1968, 1970; Flood, 1990, 1999) dealt with the problem.

Learning and the inclusion of the observer in the system

Bateson (1973, 1987) starts with the classic example of the cybernetic system, that of central heating mentioned above. The resident of a room sets the desired temperature at the system's regulator located at the boundary between the system and its environment, which is the temperature in the room. The system then regulates itself through the feedback of information about the gap, or error, between desired and actual room temperatures. The system cannot change its own setting and so it cannot learn or evolve. It simply repeats its error-activated behavior.

Bateson then introduces the resident into the system. Now the system consists of the resident and the central heating system. The environment is still, of course, the temperature in the room. However, the boundary of the system has now been extended to include the skin of the resident, who changes the temperature setting. When the skin of the resident registers an uncomfortably low temperature for a while, he turns the regulator setting up and the boiler is turned on. Later the resident may feel too warm and turn the setting down. In this way, the brain of the resident is seen to be a cybernetic device in much the same way as the heating system and together they constitute the expanded system.

The structure of this larger system has changed in an important way because now the number of states it can move through is much larger. The change in the total system is not due to responses to one specific error as it was before, but to a range of errors that do not fit the resident's requirements. From the perspective of the logically lower system, the heating system, the addition of the resident amounts to the inclusion of the observer who can control it and this has implications for learning:

- The resident/heating system displays what Bateson calls Learning Level 1 in that the resident changes the lower level system by changing the setting, so increasing the number of alternatives open to the whole system. This learning is error-activated in that it is triggered by a gap between the resident's habitual comfort levels and his current experience. Later, Argyris and Schön (1978) used this idea to talk about single loop learning, which occurs when people alter their behavior without changing their mental models; that is, habits. Through the work of Senge (1990) this idea has come to occupy a central position in the idea of the learning organization.
- If the resident were to change his habits of altering the setting, then the system would display Learning Level 2 because there is once more a

widening of the range of alternatives open to the system. This level of learning is of a higher logical category in that it expands the range of Level 1 alternatives. Once again it is error-activated in that the resident will change his habits because the old ones do not meet some new or higher required standard. Argyris and Schön (1978) called this double loop learning, and it too features as a central concept in the learning organization as a change in mental models (Senge, 1990).

● The system could potentially display Learning Level 3, which expands the range of Level 2 alternatives. Bateson thought that humans very rarely achieved this level of learning and the examples he gave of it were religious conversion and personal change through psychotherapy.

Human beings are regarded, in this development of systems thinking, as living cybernetic systems that can understand and control lower level cybernetic systems, which include themselves. Note what is happening here.

First there is a self-regulating system that works automatically to remove an error, a gap, where the action is triggered by the detection of the error. This applies to the central heating system, but the notion of error-triggered action is then used to form a theory of human learning, which becomes a cybernetic, error-detecting process.

This happens when the perspective is widened to take in the human observer, designer or controller of the system. It is the human who sets goals for the system. In other words, the human specifies what an error would be and he does this according to some mental framework in his mind, a mental model. The system now includes the person who makes a choice and he can detect an error, a gap, between what he experiences and what he wants as determined by his habits, or mental model. He can respond to this error and set a new goal for the system without in any way changing his habits, his mental model, his understanding of his world. In other words his mental model, which remains the same, is now part of the higher order system and this higher order system can learn. This learning is itself a cybernetic process in that experience of an error triggers a change in the goal set for the lower order system. Mental models, then, are higher order cybernetic devices that change the goals for the lower order cybernetic system. This is Learning Level 1, or single loop learning, made possible by including the objective observer's fixed mental model in a widened system. Note that the process of changing mental models remains outside the definition of the Learning Level 1 system.

However, the system can now be widened to include this observer's observing of himself performing the single loop learning. He may find that as he changes the temperature setting according to his habit, or mental model, this does not yield the satisfaction he is seeking. This error could trigger him into changing his habits, his mental model. The process for changing the mental model is now part of an even higher order system and the mental model can also change as a result of the choice of the human. When it does so Learning Level 2, or double loop learning, is achieved. The system is now widened to include the process of changing mental models and this too is thought of as a cybernetic system. However, the process that triggers the process of changing the mental model, something to do with satisfaction and dissatisfaction, or preference, is still outside the definition of the Learning Level 2 system.

However, the system can now be widened even further to include this observer observing himself changing his preferences that trigger the choice to change his mental model. He becomes aware of himself learning in a double loop way and this is presumably made possible by a mental model of the process of changing his mental model. This process of changing preferences is now included in an even wider system. However, once again, there is now the problem of defining the process by which he becomes aware of the need to change his preferences. Bateson found he could not identify what this would be and fell back on mysticism or deep personal change that nobody finds easy to explain.

The problem with this kind of explanation, then, is that it rapidly runs into an infinite regress and has to be abandoned to some kind of mysticism. The source of the problem, in our view, lies at the very roots of systems thinking in the theory of causality it is built upon, and cannot be addressed simply by widening the boundaries of the system to include the observer. Let us explain what we mean.

The problem with boundaries

In systems thinking, certainly as it is applied to organizations, there is always an observer, that is, someone who delineates a system of interacting parts and identifies or designs rules of interaction for those parts. The act of observing or designing a system is, therefore, immediately an act of applying the causal theory of Formative Teleology. This is because the act points to, or sets up, interactions in which the patterns of behavior they will produce are already there in the identified or designed rules of interaction. The system, in systems thinking, can only do what it is designed to do. A central heating system can only regulate room temperatures and a budgetary control system can only regulate financial flows. In other words, the pattern of behavior produced by the system is formatively caused by the system's process and the pattern of behavior so caused is the one already there in the process.

To avoid an immediate assumption of Formative Teleology, one would have to design a system where the rules of interaction evolved of their own accord. The system would have to take on a life of its own. Systems thinkers are not concerned with models of this kind, although some of those working in the natural complexity sciences do explore the behavior of such models. If the model of a system takes on a life of its own, however, it will most likely deviate rapidly from the phenomenon it is trying to model. It is difficult to see how this could assist in controlling the phenomenon, the central concern of systems thinkers. We will return to this point in Chapters 5 and 6, but here it suffices to notice that systems thinking does not encompass models of this kind and is therefore built on the foundations of Formative Teleology.

In open or cybernetic systems the behavior tends to an equilibrium state and in the systems dynamics of the learning organization the pattern of behavior tends to one or more archetypes (Senge, 1990). To labor the point, then, that which a choice is being made about is a system driven by Formative Teleology, according to systems theories. The system moves to some optimal (secular Natural Law Teleology) or archetypal state that is already embedded in it (Formative Teleology). However, the choice itself, the choice about the system and its rules, is made by an observer outside the system. It is Rationalist Teleology that applies to the observer; that is, the observer has the freedom to choose goals for the system, even the freedom to design it, hopefully within ethical principles. Systems thinking, therefore, right at its roots proceeds by making a Kantian split, but, unlike Kant, applies Formative Teleology to a system of human beings. Freedom is confined to the observer.

This is the problem second order cybernetics must deal with and it does so by incorporating the observer in the system as in the Bateson example above, when the resident of the room is seen as part of the system. However, this does not solve the problem because now the resident is subject to Formative Teleology. Bateson says that the resident makes choices about the room temperature according to habits, that is, according to patterns that are already there in the now expanded system in the form of mental models or sets of rules in the brain/mind of the resident. In order to change his habits, the room resident has to choose to change his mental model, but the process by which he does so is not part of the system as it has just been delineated. All that is part of the system is the resident's current mental model. Some process outside of the system so delineated is required to change it, a process of choice characterized by Rationalist Teleology outside the system.

Bateson, therefore, expands the boundary of the system to include this process of a change in mental models. However, nothing has yet been said about how an individual changes his mental model. As this individual is incorporated into the expanded boundary of the system he "arrives," as it were, with a learning model of how to change his mental model. Argyris (1990, 1993) suggests that there are two learning models: one where people compete with each other as to whose mental model is to apply and another where they engage in dialogue. If the expanded system consists of people trying to change their mental models according to the first learning model they will not succeed, but if they arrive with the second they might. In other words, the pattern of change in learning models is already there as soon as they are incorporated in the system – Formative Teleology again. The choice about how to change learning models is located outside the expanded system in metalearning models – Rationalist Teleology again. The system could be expanded to include not only learning models, but also models of learning how to learn. But then the question arises as to how people choose to learn how to learn and we are right back to a distinction between Formative Teleology applying within the system and Rationalist Teleology applying outside it.

Our argument, then, is that systems thinking contains a fundamental difficulty right at its roots. This is to regard human interaction as a system. This assumption leads to thinking about that interaction as something about which another human standing outside it makes choices according to Rationalist Teleology. Every move to incorporate the observer into the system simply repeats the split, applying Formative Teleology ever more widely and thus inevitably removing human freedom more and more thoroughly from consideration. Instead human freedom, as Rationalist Teleology, is located at higher and higher levels of abstraction in infinite regress. Each move to expand the system not only locates free choice somewhere outside the system, it also locates the source of any novelty or fundamental change outside it too. Systems theory cannot explain novelty within its own framework but always has to displace it to some unexplained location outside the system. The reason for this lies in the theory of causality being used and in the notion that there can be an external observer of human interaction, matters we will take up below. It is because we think that the split between Formative and Rationalist Teleology is fundamentally inappropriate for understanding human action that we want to explore how explanations based on Transformative Teleology might yield more useful insights.

Consider now how soft systems and critical systems thinking deals with the problem of the system and the human being.

Participation

The criticism leveled at early systems theories was that they implied that organizations were physical entities like organisms with clear boundaries, structures and functions. Allied to this was the criticism that systems theories presented individuals as deterministic, thinking machines and ignored the emotion, conflict, politics and cultural aspects of organizational life. The response of systems thinkers to these criticisms, we think, has typically taken the form of redefining the boundaries of the system.

First, the definition of the system is widened to include politics and culture. Instead of just thinking in terms of the immediate, probably technical, aspects of a problem in systemic terms, the connection with other relevant subsystems is included (Trist and Bamforth, 1951). For example, Checkland (1981) and Checkland and Schles (1990) advocate an interpretive approach to systems thinking in which account is taken, presumably by the designer of the system, of the social rules and practices of participants in the system. These are constitutive of meaning, which lies behind them. They define a model, a learning cycle with a number of steps, that constitutes the Soft Systems Methodology (SSM). This is a methodology for systems designers to follow when facing soft, ill-structured problems that include social practices, politics and culture. Intertwined with this designed intervention is an investigation of the process of designing the intervention itself and the culture and politics this process involves.

Early on in the SSM learning cycle is the requirement for systemic thinking about the world and the building of systems models of that world. So, in order to cope with the ill-structured problems created by "soft" issues such as culture, the system boundary must be widened to include such matters and incorporated in models. The model is then taken to the real world problem area and change proposals are thought through. This approach recognizes that problems are not isolated or confined to a delineated technical system but are part of even wider cultural and political systems. However, the recognition takes the form of expanding the systems definition and takes account of culture and politics as systems themselves, systems that intertwine with and impact on the problem that is the focus of attention. The goal here is to surface divergent models that individuals have of the system of concern to them. The purpose of surfacing these divergent models is to generate a shared understanding and consensus so that action can be taken to improve the system (Phelan,1999). The approach is one of facilitating a participative approach to learning about a system as part of problem-solving.

However, the participating researchers or managers still stand outside the system, now including cultural and political subsystems that include them, and they observe it. The political and cultural subsystems including participating managers and researchers are now also subjected to a causality of Formative Teleology. In the previous section the criticism that humans are removed from the system is dealt with by including higher logical levels, a vertical extension of the definition of the system, and here it is dealt with by widening the horizontal definition of the system to include more factors and people of relevance. This move does not remove the need for an external observer or alter the fundamental theory of causality. The problems with freedom and novelty remain.

Systems of meaning and ethics

Various systems thinkers (Ackoff, 1981, 1994; Checkland, 1981; Checkland and Schles, 1990; Churchman, 1968, 1970) address the criticisms of systems thinking by arguing that human systems are better understood as systems of meaning (ideas, concepts, values) and learning.

Ackoff, for example, holds that obstructions to change lie in the minds of the members of an organization, their mental models. Ackoff does not agree with surfacing these mental models and changing them because, for him, it is not practically feasible to do so. Instead, members of an organization should participatively formulate an idealized design of the future they desire and create ways of achieving it. They should seek to close the gap between their present and this desired future. Ackoff has developed a method of interactive planning to do this, one that focuses on the participative development of scenarios for desired futures. The very first step in the rather detailed process he proposes is systems analysis, the formulation of a detailed picture of the organization as it is today in terms of process, structure, culture and relationship with the environment.

Churchman, the originator of critical systems thinking, displays his adherence to mainstream systems theory when he sets out the conditions required for a system to be purposeful. Purposeful systems are characterized by a decision-maker who can produce change in performance measures, a designer whose design influences the decision-maker, a design aimed at maximizing value and a built-in guarantee that the purpose can be achieved. He stresses the importance of critical reflection on system design and operation and the importance of moral practice. For him, the first step in systems thinking is to draw a boundary around the system, and this is essentially a choice that opens up ethical questions. But drawing a boundary always includes some and excludes others, dominating some and liberating others, and for this reason it is an ethical choice. Here, the aim is to emancipate people from domination so that they can participate on a free and equal basis in the process of system design. The way in which particular views are privileged over others is identified (Flood, 1990) and exposed so that people are liberated from dominant worldviews (Phelan, 1999).

So, the idea of human systems as systems of meaning is closely linked to an emphasis on participation as equality, and an idealized, democratic freedom. However, when participation is approached from the perspective of systems thinking it becomes an activity that is to be analyzed and organized, another system. For example, Beer (1994), in later developments of his work, presents what he calls "team syntegrity." This is a method of forming work processes in which each member of a team can make maximum use of his or her capacity, as well as benefit from the synergies of group dynamics. This model lays down, in some detail, how people are to proceed to work effectively in a team. Checkland and Churchman also stress participation, debate and trans-discipline and trans-function team working.

Review

The response to the criticism that systems thinking does not take account of obvious features of human action to do with participation, culture and politics takes a number of forms. The first is vertical expansion of system definition to include higher and higher cognitive levels, including more and more aspects of human cognition and sense-making within a framework of Formative Teleology. As we go up each level there is always a higher order cybernetic system that controls and changes the one below understood as Rationalist Teleology. The second response is a horizontal widening of the boundary to include cultural and political systems in the definition of the relevant system. This brings more and more aspects of human action within a framework based on Formative Teleology. What these moves do, then, is deepen or widen the area covered by the system: the response is to redefine the boundary. At each stage of boundary widening there is a bigger and bigger area covered by Formative Teleology and, standing outside it, a process of design and choice to which Rationalist Teleology applies. Here Rationalist Teleology is understood as a participative, democratic process aimed at surfacing hidden obstructions and securing consensus.

However, there has to be a limit to deepening and widening the boundaries because the former runs into infinite regress and the latter into a degree of complexity that cannot be dealt with (Flood, 1990). The major criticism of this move from our perspective is that in the extension of Formative Teleology to ever wider areas, the issue of how fundamental change occurs is progressively pushed outside the selected area of action. Formative Teleology, by its very nature, cannot explain novelty. So at each stage in deepening and widening the boundary of the system, the source of novel change is located outside the system in the heads of the designers. In other words the explanation lies in Rationalist Teleology. The implicit assumption is that human intellect and reason leads to choices of novel change. But how is the choice to be made? The answer is always more systems thinking. This is a strange conclusion. It is implicitly being assumed that people can create the truly new through a process of reasoning, systems thinking, that excludes the possibility of the truly new from its very framework. How is anyone to use a reasoning tool to choose something new when that tool excludes the very notion of anything new?

The response to the criticism that systems are designed by technocrats who exclude people is to focus on democracy and participation in the process of design. What this move does is substitute a group, be it a democratic or some other kind, for the individual designer of the system. The understanding of a system or the design of a system is now a task for a team in dialogue with each other. The method of their thinking and talking to each other is still supposed, however, to be systemic. If there are problems with the notion of a "system" then simply adding more people to the endeavor will achieve very little.

For us, the problem with systems thinking of any form is this. When you think in terms of Formative Teleology, important interlinked matters are excluded at the very roots of the explanation and adding them in later cannot cure this. These interlinked matters are human freedom, the unknown and ethics. These exclusions have practical consequences of great importance. When you think in terms of a system in which freedom of action of its members, their ways of coping with the unknown and ethical implications are merely incidental matters, then you miss the importance of the myriad ordinary everyday choices people are making in order to cope when the system does not work as expected. This goes back to "getting things done anyway." Another very practical matter is that systems thinking offers little assistance in understanding how true novelty arises.

When we talk about freedom here, we are not concerned with a noble call for democracy or a sad reflection on how people mess perfect systems up. What we are getting at is the unsoundness, in terms of understanding, of temporarily suspending the micro details of human free interaction of an ordinary everyday kind in order to be able to conceptualize some kind of macro system that can be generalized and more easily understood because we can then approach it as we approach natural phenomena in science. This move encourages us to miss the essential feature of human action, namely its cooperative nature in the living present. It is in this way that we get things done and change them too. Furthermore, the soft systems and critical systems responses to criticism of systems thinking assume that diversity and difference must be eliminated before action is possible. They do not incorporate the essential roles that difference and diversity play in the creative process, a matter we will take up in Chapters 5 and 6. These problems with systems thinking call, we believe, for a way of understanding within Transformative Teleology.

If you want to structure problems and your concern is with continuity then systems thinking can be a powerful aid. It has shown itself to be so. However, if your concern is with how you get things done day by day, on the one hand, and how it all radically changes, on the other, then systems thinking is inappropriate. It is inappropriate at its roots, in its theory of causality. If your question is about novelty and about how choice and intention arise in the first place, then systems thinking cannot help. This suggests that if the complexity sciences are taken into thinking about organization within the framework of systems theory they will not add much. This is a matter we will return to in Chapter 7 but here we want to make the point by briefly looking at a recent importation of complexity ideas into systems thinking.

The danger of regarding complexity theory as another strand in systems thinking

In a recent review of systems thinking, Flood (1999) identifies complexity theory as another strand in systems thinking. The insights he draws on from the complexity sciences are the limits to predictability and the way in which self-organizing interactions at a local level can produce coherent global patterns of behavior. For him, this means that self-organizing systems produce emergent order that is unknowable to the human mind. This questions whether long-term intended action is possible and it leads him to conclude that the most we can do is manage what is local. Managing what is local means managing over a small number of interactions between people and over short time periods into the future. This is, he says, how we learn our way into a mysterious future in a process of continually revisiting what might be going on, what we are doing and achieving and the way we are doing it. He calls this getting to grips with complexity, knowing within the unknowable or managing within the unmanageable, in order to produce emergent outcomes.

For Flood, systems thinking is thinking about wholes and complex interrelationships in which ultimately everything is related to everything else. This means that systemic appreciation is an ever-expanding exercise, and according to him the way complexity theory points to the unknowable and to the importance of self-organizing interactions makes this ever-expanding exercise even more impossible. In order to overcome this, he advocates the "bounding of thought" to yield a viewpoint that is relevant and manageable. This means drawing a boundary around the issues to be considered, around the system that is to be the focus of attention – a central point of Churchman's approach. Flood agrees with this need to make boundary judgments and the ethical questions it immediately brings to the fore. He sees ethics as central to systems thinking. Having drawn the boundary, which is a mental construct that sketches out an action area, Flood then recommends deepening judgment by systemic appreciation. This appreciation requires judging issues according to four subsystem categories: process, structure, meaning, and power-knowledge. These provide four bases of possible interpretation, four images of action. He advocates deepening systemic appreciation of each of these action areas by applying the systems designs to be found in the systems literature.

In seeing complexity as simply a strand of systems theory, therefore, Flood takes it to mean that the application of systems models can now only be to a selected area of the total system. Having selected this local area he proceeds as before. What we see as the fundamental problem of the whole of systems thinking, its reliance on a split between Formative and Rationalist Teleology, is thus confined to a local area of a system rather than the whole of it. In seeking to contain complexity theory within systems thinking, any potential it has for very different insights is thus cut off. This is an example of the kind of use of complexity theory we will return to in Chapter 7, the kind of use we think leads to a fad rather than radical challenge.

A word on the contribution of systems thinking

In this chapter we have argued that both scientific management and systems thinking provide limited ways of understanding life in organizations because of the theories of causality upon which they are built. In this section we want to make it clear that this conclusion does not in any way detract from the significant contribution both of these ways of thinking have made to human understanding and practice of management in organizations. Scientific management greatly enhanced the understanding and practice of efficiency in management. Systems thinking represents a significant extension of scientific management in its focus on interaction and in so doing makes at least three important contributions:

● The emphasis on interaction leads to an improved understanding and design of regulatory procedures and so secures more reliable continuity and a higher degree of self-regulation in organizations.
● Thinking in terms of interconnections and the consequent awareness of causal links that are distant in space and time alerts managers to the unintended and unexpected consequences of their action.

- The awareness that managers are also part of the systems they identify and design leads to greater attention to matters of participation and ethics.

These contributions offer the potential for more creative management, a potential that the following story illustrates.

A thumb-nail sketch of systems consulting

A group of strategists arranged a meeting with an expert in systems thinking to discuss projects in a developing country. In the course of the meeting the systems thinker drew elements of the conversation together and pointed to a matter that the strategists were all aware of but were paying little attention to, namely the scarcity of water supply as the central problem facing the country. All of the development projects being considered at that meeting would clearly aggravate this problem because they would all lead to greater water consumption. The systems thinker quickly demonstrated this with a few simple systemic models, showing how water shortages could lead to unexpected consequences for all of the development projects, so potentially undermining them. In his hotel room that night the consultant developed more sophisticated models. He arrived at the insight that an important project, one on which all the others would have to rely for success, was a project for recycling water supplies, a process completely absent at that time. His presentation of this model on the next morning generated great enthusiasm among the strategists.

The story is a small-scale version of the currently popular scenario tool. Similar stories could be told about Business Process Re-engineering and other systemic tools. Their modeling produces powerful arguments that managers can use in participating in the political decision-making processes of an organization. In the argument we present in this volume, these political processes are central. For us, they are where one must look for the creativity in organizations. Our difference from systems thinking has to do with how we think about the kind of systems tools being used in the above example. In systems models, the past is idealized in the sense that it consists of elements selected from a very complex context to form a certain pattern. The same is true for the scenario of the future. Here, systemic modeling provides insights based on resolving the paradox of time in the living present by talking about "both" the past "and" the future. This is valid and helpful when it is a question of choosing the optimum alternative from a set that is already known. But how does a completely novel idea arise? It is this question that leads us to focus on the living present having the time structure of paradox (see Chapter 3). Furthermore, once an alternative is selected, such as the water recycling projects, it has to be carried out. The processes of "getting it done" are the complex responsive processes we want to draw attention to. We are not trying to dismiss the tools of systemic thinking, but rather trying to understand how they are tools used in much more complex processes that are much more than tools.

Conclusion

In this chapter we have traced out the move from understanding an organization within a framework of scientific management and human relations to a framework of understanding organizations from a systemic point of view. The move from one framework to another amounts to a shift in underlying theories of causality.

The management sciences/human relations perspective focuses on actions of individuals and teams (the parts), and does so within a theory of causality in which Rationalist Teleology is applied to parts governed by efficient cause. This framework leads to a focus on reasoned choices, or designs, for the parts such that they produce optimal behavior – secular Natural Law Teleology. There is a split between Rationalist Teleology to do with choice and secular Natural Law Teleology to do with that over which the choice is exercised. There is no notion of self-organization here and the movement of time is from the past to the present. The focus is on repetition, and this locates meaning in the past (see Chapter 2). The major criticism of this approach is that it ignores the importance of interaction between the parts, especially since those parts are human beings.

In meeting this criticism, the shift to systems thinking moves attention from the parts to interactions between them where those interactions are governed by a different kind of causality. There is Rationalist Teleology taken to mean systems thinking itself and it is applied to the "organization," basically assumed to be governed by Formative Teleology in which systems move toward final forms, often optimal states (implying secular Natural Law Teleology) that are already contained in the system. So, while the shift to systems thinking represents an enormous increase in the capacity to understand the complexity of real human action, it continues with a split causality, this time a split between Rationalist and

Formative Teleology. There is now a concept of self-organization, but of a kind that unfolds an enfolded pattern rather than producing any novel pattern. Time is now movement from the future as a desired state to the present so that meaning lies in the future.

Our criticisms of systems thinking focus primarily on what we see as the consequences of this split, namely the objectification of human interaction as a system and the exclusion of human freedom from the system itself into the realm of reasoned choice (Rationalist Teleology). The criticisms amount to objections to the exclusion of recognizably human behavior from the specification of a system and the relegation of explanations of that human behavior to reasoning processes that are themselves not adequately explained. The responses of systems thinkers to these criticisms amount to redrawing the boundary of the system so that it includes that which the critics have objected to as excluded. These boundary movements, however, simply relocate the essentially human behavior to another level outside the redrawn boundary, once again to be explained in terms of Rationalist Teleology. The boundary is either extended in a horizontal direction to incorporate observed features of culture and political activity or it is extended in a vertical direction to include people as participants in identifying and designing the system that is supposed to govern their action. Or, when complexity theory is recognized, it too prompts a redrawing of the boundary, this time narrowing it to encompass only the local, known interactions, once again relegating the unknown to a position outside the boundary where it and its impact are not open to explanation within the terms of systems thinking itself. These acts of redrawing boundaries are described as judgments, but how those judgments come to be made is not explained.

For us, organization is a process of joint action in which patterns in that action are both repeated to preserve continuity and stability and at the same time opened up to create the possibility of transformation, the truly novel. The systems approach of redefining boundaries in response to criticism does not address how people "get it done anyway" in their ordinary everyday activities. The boundary redefinition response also does not enable any increased understanding of transformation or of how people actually cope with the unknown. It does not encompass the close connection between diversity, conflict and creativity. It is our belief that the boundary redefinition response is inadequate because it leaves untouched the roots of systems thinking, namely the split between Formative and Rationalist Teleology. When complexity theory is seen as simply requiring yet another boundary judgment it too is inadequate for the reasons just given.

Our interest, therefore, is to explore whether a fundamental move, from the Kantian-type split between Rationalist and Formative Teleology to a more integrative Transformative Teleology, offers a more adequate explanation of the day-to-day process of "getting things done anyway," and of the process in which true novelty emerges, and – covering both of these questions – how members of an organization deal with the unknown they experience as free human beings. Here, time is the circular movement of meaning within the present as described in Chapter 3 and self-organization is a process that can produce novelty. We are interested in exploring whether complexity theories have any contribution to make to such a move, for it is only then that they might open up a radical challenge to the currently dominant discourse on management. Continuing within the Kantian split on causality, we believe, is likely to lead to a complexity approach to management that is simply another fad. In the next chapter we turn to an examination of the theories of causality underlying the natural complexity sciences to see whether they point to such a shift in underlying theories of causality.

5 How the complexity sciences deal with the future

- Chaos theory: unfolding an enfolded future
- Chaos theory as Formative Teleology
- Dissipative structure theory: constructing an unknowable future
- Conclusion

There is as yet no single science of complexity but, rather, a number of different strands comprising what might be called the complexity sciences. Those writing about complexity in human organizations usually draw on concepts to be found in one or more of three of these strands – namely, chaos theory, dissipative structure theory, and the theory of complex adaptive systems. The first two strands model natural phenomena at a macro level. In other words, they think of these phenomena as whole systems, populations, or ensembles of entities and then construct mathematical models of relationships applying at the level of the whole system, just as the system theories discussed in the previous chapter do. The third strand in the complexity sciences referred to above adopts a rather different approach to modeling much the same phenomena. It uses an agent-based approach. Instead of formulating rules or laws for whole populations, these models formulate rules of interaction for the individual entities making up a population or system. This chapter provides a brief review of those concepts in the theories of chaos and dissipative structures that management complexity writers most frequently refer to; the next chapter does the same for the theory of complex adaptive systems.

This chapter will explore the extent to which theories of chaos and dissipative structures employ what we are calling Formative and Transformative Teleology (see Chapter 2) in their underlying assumptions on causality. The concern will be with what insight these theories have to give on the origins of novelty. In what way might they help us understand how creative new forms come into being? In what way might they help us to understand how very complex phenomena sustain continuity and stability? The questions dealt with in the previous two chapters to do with stability, change and self-organization are thus also central to this chapter.

Chaos theory: unfolding an enfolded future

This section first reviews the central features of chaos theory, matters that are now well understood and do not give rise to much contention. The contention comes when chaos theory is used to explain some real world phenomenon and has to do mainly with whether chaos theory applies to that phenomenon or not. We will be arguing that the underlying causality in chaos theory is that which we have called Formative Teleology. As Chapter 2 explained, Formative Teleology excludes the possibility of true novelty; therefore, when a principal feature of a phenomenon is its capacity for novelty, it is not much use appealing to chaos theory for any kind of direct explanation of that phenomenon's behavior. The most chaos theory could do here would be to supply some rather loose metaphors, with considerable potential for misleading rather than illuminating. Before explaining why we reach this conclusion, however, we review the central features of chaos theory, on which there is now fairly general agreement in the scientific community.

The central features of chaos theory

Chaos theory (Gleick, 1988; Stewart, 1989) provides an explanation of the behavior of a system that can be modeled by deterministic nonlinear equations in which the output of one calculation is taken as the input of the next. In other words, the equations are used recursively, or iteratively, in exactly the same way as they are used in the systems dynamics strand of systems thinking (see Chapter 4 for comments on systems dynamics and its use in the theory of the learning organization). Chaos theory shows how particular control parameters, determined outside the system, cause its behavior to move toward a particular state space called an attractor. Such systems have the potential to move to one of a number of different attractors, depending upon the parameter values.

Strange attractors/fractals

Attractors describe global patterns of behavior displayed by a system. For example, the control parameter might be the speed of energy or information flow through the system. At low rates of energy or information flow, the system is drawn to a point attractor in which it displays one form of behavior, namely a stable equilibrium state. At higher rates of energy or information flow, the system may switch to a periodic attractor. This too is a stable equilibrium state in which behavior cycles between two values. Then, at very high rates of energy or information flow, the system is attracted to explosive growth or even random patterns of behavior. In other words, behavior becomes highly unstable and the system may disintegrate. Furthermore, at some critical level of the control parameter, between levels that lead to equilibrium attractors and those that lead to instability, behavior is drawn to a strange attractor.

In precise mathematical terms a strange attractor may be depicted as a spatial pattern abstracted from time, or in process terms as rhythmic variations over time. Strange attractors are reflected in patterns of behavior (that is, shapes in space or movements over time) which are never exactly repeated but are always similar to each other. A strange attractor has a distinctive shape, or cyclical movement, but that shape or movement is much more complicated than a single point or a regular cycle. A strange attractor displays a recognizable pattern in space or over time but that pattern is irregular. In other words, strange attractors are paradoxically regular and irregular, stable and unstable, at the same time. They are neither equilibrium nor random states but, rather, an intertwining of both at the same time: within any stable space or time sequence there is instability and within any unstable space or time sequence there is stability. Another term used to describe patterns of this kind is "fractal." It is the identification of strange attractors, or fractals, which distinguishes chaos theory from systems dynamics – indeed, from all of the systems theories discussed in the previous chapter.

The weather is usually used as an example of a system that displays patterns typical of a strange attractor. The abstract representation of the weather system's attractor has a shape rather like a butterfly, in which patterns of air pressure, temperature, and so on, swirl around one wing and then shift abruptly to the other wing, never ever exactly repeating the same movement. The heartbeat of a healthy human also follows a strange attractor reflected in temporal rhythms (Goldberger, 1997). Although heartbeats are regular when averaged over a particular period of time, movements within that average display a regular irregularity. A failing heart is characterized by a loss of complexity in which it moves to a periodic attractor.

There is not much that is contentious in what we have so far described. More contentious would be the drawing of a general conclusion that chaos theory points to a connection between health, or viability and success, on the one hand, and strange attractors or fractal processes, on the other. Even more contentious would be any link to human organizations and the use of chaos theory to challenge mainstream management thinking in which success is equated with stable equilibrium. Such links do not simply follow from chaos theory but would have to be separately established by a careful examination of the area to which chaos theory was being applied. However, as a metaphor, the notion of deterministic laws producing strange attractors, with their paradoxical properties of stability and instability, is certainly very thought provoking. Chaos theory, then, presents properties that may stimulate challenges to mainstream management thinking at a metaphorical level.

Predictability and unpredictability

Returning to matters of general agreement, strange attractors, also referred to as mathematical chaos, have important implications for predictability (Stewart, 1989).

The precise parametric conditions required to produce a strange attractor for a given mathematical model are predictable. Once revealed by iteration, the spatial shapes and time contours of the strange attractor are also predictable because a given equation, or set of equations, can produce one and only one strange attractor for given parametric conditions. It is as if the equation enfolds an implicit, or hidden, order that is revealed by iteration. For example, the strange attractor followed by the weather system has the characteristic shape already referred to and any deviation from it is soon drawn back into it. The shape of the attractor bounds the movement of the system in space and time, that is, it establishes the limits of the behavior that it is possible for the system to produce. The overall shape of weather movements can therefore be predicted. It is possible to predict the limits within which temperature will vary over a particular season in a particular geographical area, for example. Furthermore, the specific behavior displayed by the system within these limits is reasonably predictable over short ranges in space and short periods of time.

However, over long ranges in space and long periods of time the specific behavior of a system caught in a strange attractor cannot be predicted. This is due to the system's sensitivity to initial conditions, more popularly known as the butterfly effect, which means that the long-term trajectory of the system is highly sensitive to its starting point, the property known as sensitive dependence on initial conditions. The usual example is that of a butterfly flapping its wings in São Paolo. The flapping will alter air pressure by a minute amount and this small change could be escalated up by the system into a major change in specific behavior. Long-term predictability would then require the detection of every tiny change and the measurement of each to an infinite degree of precision. Since this is a human impossibility, the specific long-term pathway is unpredictable for all practical purpose. The long-term behavior of such a system, therefore, is as much determined by small chance changes as it is by the deterministic laws governing it. Deterministic laws can therefore produce indeterminate outcomes, at least as far as any possible human experience is concerned.

Chaos theory, then, produces a rather clear conclusion. Any system governed by recursively applied nonlinear laws may display behavior of the strange attractor type at certain parameter values. When it follows a strange attractor its behavior is predictable at global, macro levels of description, but only in qualitative terms. At the specific micro level, predictability is confined to short-term local occurrences, leaving the specific long-term trajectory unpredictable due to the inability of humans to measure with infinite accuracy.

Chaos theory as Formative Teleology

We come now to our interpretation of the theory of causality underlying chaos theory. Chaos theory establishes the properties of systems that can be modeled by recursively applied nonlinear equations, just as systems dynamics does (see Chapter 4). These mathematical models display movement toward and within pre-given patterns called attractors, a mathematical description of an end state toward which a system moves. The attractors are given as soon as the equations are formulated.

Furthermore, chaos theory models a system at a macro level (that is, at the level of a whole system), implicitly assuming (Allen, 1998a, 1998b) that the entities of which the system is composed are all homogeneous, or at least normally distributed about an average. The same assumption applies to interactions between entities. These assumptions of average behavior at the micro level, also made in the other systems theories discussed in Chapter 4, mean that complicated dynamics between entities are ignored and, as will be explained in the next section, this means that the model cannot simulate novelty. This is another way of stating a point already made, namely that any equation, or set of equations, in chaos theory models can only ever produce a limited, given number of attractors. The model does not have the capacity to move of its own accord from one attractor to another. It can only move if some external agent changes the parameters. In other words, chaos theory does not model internal or intrinsic creativity, a point that applies equally to the systems theories discussed in the previous chapter that underlie the dominant management discourse.

In other words, chaos models display the unfolding of patterns in a sense already enfolded in the specification of the model. As for the models in systems thinking, therefore, the underlying causality is what we have called Formative Teleology. Here, causality is of the formative kind in that the nonlinear structure of the equations, the iterative process and the sensitivity to initial conditions together formatively cause the attractors, the final state toward which, and within which, the system moves. The critique of system thinking presented in Chapter 4, therefore, applies with much the same force to any extension of systems thinking to include chaos theory

What is distinctive about chaos theory, compared to the other systems theories discussed in Chapter 4, however, is the clear identification of the limits to predictability. In doing this, chaos theory challenges the manner in which systems dynamics is used in organizational theory because, while systems dynamics points to the likelihood of nonequilibrium behavior, the way in which it is used continues to equate success with attraction to a state that is as close as possible to equilibrium. From a chaos perspective, this move toward the simplicity of equilibrium could be interpreted as a move toward failure, where health and success are strange attractors in which long-term predictability of specific trajectories is impossible. For systems dynamics thinkers, the aim is to identify leverage points for interventions that will enable them to identify where, when and how to initiate change. However, the ability to do this in a system that is sensitive to tiny changes is also called into question. That obviously has serious implications for the human ability to stay "in control."

Why does this matter? It matters because, as we have indicated in the previous chapter, currently dominant ways of thinking and talking about management are squarely based on Newtonian and system–environment notions of efficient and formative causality in which good enough long-term prediction is possible. The efficacy of the whole process of choosing aims, goals and visions (Rationalist Teleology) in order to be "in control" depends utterly on this foundation of predictability. If a system's specific long-term behavior is unpredictable, then setting specific goals for it is a questionable activity. The models of chaos theory take exactly the same form as those of systems dynamics. Whereas those using systems dynamics models of the learning organization conclude that humans can identity leverage points and stay in control, chaos theory models lead to the conclusion that long-term success is a paradoxical dynamic in which specific long-term states cannot be predicted, making it impossible for humans to stay in control. If systems dynamics and its chaos theory extension were to indicate anything at all about human action, then currently dominant ways of thinking about management would be undermined.

In the end, however, both systems dynamics and its extension to include chaos theory cannot be applied directly to human action, and nor can any of the other systems models discussed in the previous chapter. This is because human interaction is not deterministic, while the models of systems thinking, including systems dynamics and chaos theory, are. The equations in these models are fixed, while the principles of human interaction change through learning. All of these models are built on the same theory of causality, that of Formative Teleology. Building on Kant's distinctions (see Chapter 2), what we are calling Formative Teleology excludes the central feature of human action, namely human freedom and its ethical principles. Chaos theory might provide a loose metaphor for the unpredictability of autonomous human action but it can do no more. Even then, the inability to model processes of learning and creativity severely restricts even the metaphorical use of chaos theory for understanding management, and this restriction applies with just as much force to the systems theories underlying currently dominant ways of thinking about management discussed in the previous chapter.

So, chaos theory cannot apply directly to human interaction but its insights to do with strange attractors and unpredictability could present a challenge, at the level of metaphor, to systems thinking about organizations, which also can only be metaphors for the reasons given above. However, given that both chaos theory and systems thinking are built on the same theory of causality, it is likely to be difficult to take up the challenge to develop new ways of thinking about organizations, as evidenced by the discussion of Flood's attempt at the end of the previous chapter.

Consider now another strand in the complexity sciences – namely, the theory of dissipative structures, which also develops models of systemic interaction at the macro level.

Dissipative structure theory: constructing an unknowable future

The discovery of a distinctive kind of dynamic between stable and unstable states is not restricted to chaos theory. The same phenomenon is also revealed in the theory of dissipative structures (Prigogine, 1997; Prigogine and Stengers, 1984; Nicolis and Prigogine, 1989), and it too points to the potential that deterministic nonlinear systems have for producing unpredictable behavior.

Convection: an example of a dissipative structure

An example of a dissipative structure that is frequently referred to by management complexity writers is that of convection. As Nicolis and Prigogine (1989) point out, this is not a trivial example because convection is the basis of the circulation of the atmosphere and oceans that determine weather changes. It is also the basis of the transfer of heat and matter in the sun. The connection with life on earth is immediately evident. Furthermore, the frequent use of this example by writers on complexity in organizations makes it important to look carefully at it, as a basis for the critique of these writers in Chapter 7.

A laboratory experiment may be used to explore the complexity of the phenomenon of convection, but it should be remembered that any such experiment is an idealization of, or abstraction from, the reality one is trying to understand. If one is trying to understand the phenomenon of convection in nature and seeks to do so by means of an artificial abstraction in a laboratory, then one is taking essentially the same step as building a mathematical model or making a computer simulation. The experiment to do with convection involves taking a thin layer of liquid and observing its behavior as increasing heat is applied to its base. At thermodynamic equilibrium, the temperature of this liquid is uniform throughout. Consequently, it is in a state of rest at a macro level in the sense that there are no bulk movements in it. However, at the micro level, the positions and movements of the molecules are random and hence independent of each other. They fluctuate without correlations, patterns or connections and there is therefore symmetry in the sense that no point in the liquid differs from any other point. However, as heat is applied to the base of the liquid it sets up fluctuations that are amplified through the liquid. In other words, molecules at the base stop moving randomly and begin to move upward, so displacing those at the top, which then move down to the base of the liquid. The molecules display bulk movement in the form of a convection roll. Consequently, the symmetry of the liquid is broken in that one position in it is different from some others. At some points in the liquid, molecules are moving up and at other points they are moving down. In that sense correlations between them appear. There is now diversity at the micro level and motion at the macro level.

When a critical temperature point is reached, a new structure emerges in the liquid. Molecules move in a regular direction setting up hexagonal cells, some turning clockwise and others turning anticlockwise. The result is long-range coherence, where molecular movements are correlated with each other. In the laboratory experiment, the experimenter, as external objective observer, turns up the level of the heat to the critical point but does not impose the subsequent pattern from outside the liquid. Rather, the pattern, in which some convection rolls move in one direction and others move in the opposite direction, is produced by the internal dynamic. The direction of each cell's movement is unpredictable and cannot be determined by the experimenter. The direction taken by any one cell depends upon small chance differences in the conditions that existed as the cell was formed. This unpredictability is not due simply to practical difficulties. It is intrinsic. Although a change is imposed from outside this experimental system, its response is determined by its own internal dynamic. In effect, some rolls spontaneously "choose" one direction and others spontaneously "choose" another. Prigogine calls the point at which this happens a bifurcation, and the process of spontaneous "choice" is what he means by self-organization. He calls the emergent pattern a dissipative structure.

As further heat is applied to the liquid, the symmetry of the cellular pattern is broken and other patterns emerge. Eventually the liquid reaches a turbulent state of evaporation. There is movement from one state, characterized by perfect order at the macro level and perfect symmetry at the micro level, to other states of more complex order and this occurs through a destabilizing process at bifurcation points. The system is pushed away from stable equilibrium in the form of a point attractor, through bifurcations to other attractors, such as the periodic attractor of convection rolls, and on to deterministic chaos. There is unpredictability at each bifurcation point in the sense that no subsequent state is simply deducible from the previous one.

The formation of dissipative structures

This experiment is typical of many others and has led Prigogine and his colleagues to identify a dynamical pattern of change.

- A liquid, or a gas, is held *far from equilibrium* by some *environmental constraint*, such as heat.
- In this condition, small *fluctuations* (that is, variations in molecular movements in the liquid, or gas) are *amplified* to break the microscopic *symmetry* of the entities comprising it.
- At a critical level of environmental constraint the system reaches a *bifurcation* point. This is a point at which the system becomes unstable and has the possibility of developing along a number of different pathways.
- At this bifurcation the whole ensemble of entities *spontaneously self-organizes*, in effect "choosing" a pathway, one of which could produce a new pattern, such as a laser beam. In other words, long-range *correlations* form between the entities and a new coherent pattern suddenly *emerges* without any blueprint, one that cannot be explained by, or reduced to, or predicted from, the nature of the system's component entities.
- That pattern is a *dissipative structure*, that is, one that dissipates energy or information imported from the environment, so continuously renewing itself. The structure is an evolving interactive process that temporarily manifests in globally stable states taking the form of irregular patterns, and it is essentially a contradiction or paradox: symmetry and uniformity of pattern are being lost but there is still a structure; disorder is used to create new structure.

When it comes to the phenomenon in nature, rather than in the laboratory, there is an important difference. In the case of convection in nature there is no experimenter standing outside the system objectively observing it and turning up the heat parameter as there is in the laboratory experiment. Instead, the patterns of convection in the earth's atmosphere and oceans are caused by variations in the earth's temperature, which are in turn partially caused by the convection patterns. Outside of the laboratory, the system itself is changing the parameters and it is this that the experiment is trying to model. As Chapter 7 will show, this point about the role of the experimenter and what it is that the experiment is trying to model tends to get lost by many management complexity writers. They then equate the manager with the experimenter and argue that the manager's role is that of operating on the parameter to move the organizational system to a bifurcation point where a creative new choice can be made. In Chapter 7 we will explain why we think that this is an invalid move.

Formative Teleology

The above example easily leads to the conclusion that, like chaos theory, the theory of dissipative structures is built on a notion of formative cause. The form, or pattern of behavior, of the system is caused by a formative process. However, there is an important difference between chaos theory and the theory of dissipative structures. A chaos model of a system cannot explain how a system might move from one pattern of behavior, one attractor, to another. The theory of dissipative structures does just this and the reason lies in the way that the formative process differs in the theories.

In the theory of dissipative structures, a central feature of the formative process, one lacking in chaos theory, is that of fluctuations. To reiterate, fluctuations are small variations in the movement of the entities comprising a system, or in the environmental context within which the system operates. When the system is close to equilibrium, fluctuations are unimportant because they are rapidly damped away by the system's movement to equilibrium.

However, far from equilibrium, the dynamic is such that fluctuations are amplified to the point where symmetry is broken. In other words, the dynamics of instability break existing patterns so that the system approaches a bifurcation point at which behavior becomes highly unstable. At this bifurcation point, a number of different patterns of behavior, different pathways for future development, become possible and the system, in a sense, "chooses" one of these. In other words, the system displays the capacity to move from one attractor to another. While the macroscopic equations describing the system specify the different pathways, there is nothing in those equations that determines the "choice" (Prigogine, 1997). It is a spontaneous movement of the system that depends upon the micro detail of the fluctuations at that particular point in time (incorporated in the equations as a randomizing factor), and that movement may be the emergence of a new complex order. In other words, the system not only moves from one attractor to another but it does so spontaneously of its own accord, due to its own dynamic, and the feature that is central to this dynamic is that of fluctuations. This is the difference from chaos theory, a difference reflected in the capacity to self-organize and produce emergent change from one attractor to another, a capacity lacking in chaos theory models.

Prigogine lays great stress on how bifurcations break the symmetry of time, making the past different from the future. This means that the future is unpredictable and what happens to the system depends upon the micro detail of interactions in the here-and-now of the bifurcation point.

How is one to understand this in terms of the different kinds of causality that we have been distinguishing? In a sense, the causality is that of Formative Teleology in that the pathways available for selection are already given in the model or experiment. In the convection example, the hexagonal convection rolls could move in one of two different directions. However, which of these pathways is selected is not given beforehand but emerges unpredictably in the micro interactions prevailing at a particular point in time. This is not a feature of Formative Teleology in which movement is always toward an already enfolded form. Also, although the direction the system takes depends on small fluctuations, it does not do so in the sense found in the Adaptionist Teleology of neo-Darwinism (see Chapter 3) because there is no suggestion that adaptation to the environment plays any part in the system's movement. The fact that the system can unpredictably move in one of a number of different directions, depending on the detail of here-and-now interactions, points to what we have called Transformative Teleology, although it is easy to see how the theory might be taken up as Formative Teleology. This interpretation within the framework of Formative Teleology is, we think, what most management complexity writers do (see Chapter 7).

However, Prigogine himself, it seems to us, takes his thinking in the direction of Transformative Teleology. In considering what he has to say, the following point needs to be borne in mind. The kind of experimental evidence on dissipative structures described above is widely accepted in the scientific community, and indeed it was work of this kind that won the Nobel Prize for Prigogine. When he extends his ideas to the wider area of evolution in general, however, there is a great deal more contention and many scientists reject his argument.

Transformative Teleology

When Prigogine considers the wider implications of his work, we think he makes a clear move to Transformative Teleology. At the beginning of his book, *The End of Certainty* (1997), he poses what he sees as a central question: "Is the future given, or is it under perpetual construction?" In the terms we are using, this translates into "Is causality in nature (including humans) better understood as Formative Teleology, or is it better understood as Transformative Teleology?" His answer to the question is very clear: he sees the future for every level of the universe as under perpetual construction and he suggests that the process of perpetual construction, at all levels, can be understood in nonlinear, nonequilibrium terms, where instabilities, or fluctuations, break symmetries, particularly the symmetry of time. He says that nature is about the creation of unpredictable novelty where the possible is richer than the real. When he moves from focused models and laboratory experiments to think about the wider questions of evolution, a move that many scientists would question, he sees life as an unstable system with an unknowable future in which the irreversibility of time plays a constitutive role. He sees evolution as developing bifurcation points and taking paths at these points that depend on the micro details of interaction at those points. Prigogine sees evolution at all levels in terms of instabilities, with humans and their creativity as a part of it. For him, human creativity is essentially the same process as nature's creativity and this is the basis for his call for "a new dialogue with nature." These features, unknowable futures emerging in here-and-now interactions, are essentially what we have defined as the causal framework of Transformative Teleology.

Central to Prigogine's approach, at all levels, is the distinction between individual entities and populations, or ensembles, consisting of those entities. He points to how classical physics, within which he includes relativity and quantum mechanics, takes the trajectories of individual entities as the fundamental units of analysis. He then argues that individual trajectories cannot be specified for complex systems, not simply because humans are unable to measure with infinite precision, as in chaos theory, but for intrinsic reasons as follows. Poincaré identified two kinds of energy for dynamical systems, the first being the kinetic energy of a particle itself and the second being the potential energy arising in the interaction between particles. When potential energy is zero the world is static and when it is positive the world is dynamic, the reason being the existence of resonance. Resonance occurs when the frequencies of particles are coupled, so increasing the amplitude of their motion. Resonance, therefore, makes it impossible to identify individual trajectories because the individual trajectory depends not only on the individual particle (kinetic energy) but also on the resonance with frequencies of other particles (potential energy). Resonances tend to be unimportant for transient interactions but become dominant for persistent ones, and resonances drive instabilities. Resonance, an intrinsic property of matter, therefore, introduces uncertainty and breaks time symmetry, making the future unknowable.

Since individual trajectories cannot be identified for intrinsic reasons, Prigogine takes the ensemble as fundamental and argues that change in whole ensembles emerges over long periods through the amplification of slight variations in individual entities; that is, the variability of individuals in the case of organisms or microscopic collisions in the case of matter. It is this variability that is amplified to reach bifurcation points where a system spontaneously self-organizes to take completely unpredictable paths into the future. He sees whole populations, or ensembles, changing at bifurcation points where symmetry is broken by intrinsic differences between parts of a system and between the system and its environment. Self-organization is the process in which a system chooses a path at a bifurcation point as a result of individual variability, or fluctuations. Prigogine is arguing, therefore, that at the most fundamental levels of matter it is the individual variability of entities and the interactions between them that lead to change in populations or ensembles. He sees this process as extending to every level, including that of human action. Again, what he is describing are central features of what we mean by Transformative Teleology.

Demonstrating the importance of individual variability: micro diversity

A former member of Prigogine's research team, Allen (1998a, 1998b; Prigogine and Allen, 1982), distinguishes between four different ways of modeling reality using nonlinear relationships. The distinction he makes may help to clarify the above summary of Prigogine's views.

Cybernetic models

Allen first describes equilibrium (cybernetic) models. These models assume that:

- the reality being modeled moves rapidly to a stationary state;
- the discrete, or microscopic, events making up that reality occur at their average rate;
- real individual entities of any given type are all identical, or at least normally distributed around an average.

These assumptions make it possible to construct a mechanistic model of reality; that is, a set of deterministic equations describing the dynamics of the model, which produce stable, predictable outcomes. This is Formative Teleology. The conclusions drawn when one takes an equilibrium perspective are seriously defective because equilibrium models ignore the importance of time in the development of dynamic patterns of interaction and because they ignore the obviously complex dynamics of interaction at the level of microscopic events and entities found in real life.

System dynamics and chaos models

The first step in dealing with these problems is to drop the assumption of movement to a stationary state. When this is done, a second type of model is constructed, taking the form found in systems dynamics and chaos theory. Now, equilibrium is a special case but, in addition, there are much more complex patterns of behavior – different possible stationary states, different cyclic states, or mathematical chaos. Again, this is Formative Teleology and because the assumptions about average events and entities at the microscopic level are retained, the model does not reproduce the internal capacity to move from one attractor to another that is possessed by complex systems in reality. When one thinks within the systems dynamics/chaos theory framework, one therefore ignores a vital facet of evolution: that to do with how patterns of behavior change of their own accord, that is, without outside intervention.

Self-organizing models

When a further assumption is dropped the third type of model is constructed and this model exhibits self-organizing behavior in that movement from one attractor to another does take place entirely due to the internal dynamics of the model. The dropped assumption is that to do with microscopic events occurring at their average rate so that events of different probabilities that occur in reality are incorporated. Instead of moving according to a trajectory, this kind of model displays collective adaptive capacity in that it can spontaneously reorganize itself. Dropping the assumption about average events amounts to introducing fluctuations into the model (usually in the form of "noise"), and the capacity to move spontaneously from one attractor to another is then directly due to the presence of these fluctuations. In other words, a different form of order can emerge in the presence of fluctuations or noise. This is the kind of model discussed above in the example of convection and it too is Formative Teleology for the reasons given above. Shifting one's thinking from systems dynamics and chaos frameworks to a self-organizing one, therefore, increases one's understanding of how a system can shift spontaneously from one pattern of behavior to another, but the underlying theory of causality remains the same. This approach ignores the possibility that the elements of the system are internally affected by their experiences and by the collective structure of which they are parts. There can, therefore, be no transformed future.

Evolutionary complex systems

When yet another assumption, that to do with identical or normally distributed individual entities, is also dropped, then a fourth model is obtained, which Allen describes as an evolutionary complex system. This model generates entirely new attractors. Now, in addition to possessing the capacity to move from one existing attractor to another, the model can evolve in novel ways. The possibility of the evolution of novelty depends critically on the presence of microscopic diversity. When individual entities are the same – that is, when they do not have any incentive to alter their strategies for interacting with each other – the model displays stability. When individual entities are different and thus do have incentives to change their strategies of interaction with each other, the model displays rapid change of a genuinely novel kind. The "openness" of the individual entities to the possible, through some "error-making" or search process, leads to a continuing dialogue between novel individual "experiments" and (almost certainly) unanticipated collective effects. Since this kind of possibility will out-compete an equivalent system without it, the process might be described as an "evolutionary drive." The collective system conditions the response that any particular new behavior will receive, and this then leads to a characteristic restructuring of the collective system. Allen describes these models as having an evolutionary drive, and what he is talking about, we think, is a move toward Transformative Teleology.

This fourth kind of model, then, provides an analogy with what we are trying to get at in the notion of Transformative Teleology. The model takes on a life of its own, in which its future is under perpetual construction through the micro interactions of the diverse entities comprising it. The "final" form toward which it moves is not given in the model itself, nor is it being chosen from outside the model. The forms continually emerge in an unpredictable way as the system moves into the unknown. However, there is nothing mysterious or esoteric about this. What emerges does so because of the transformative cause of the process of the micro interactions, the fluctuations themselves. Prigogine and Stengers write as follows:

> "Order through fluctuations" models introduce an unstable world where small causes can have large effects, but this world is not arbitrary. On the contrary, the reasons for the amplification of small events are a legitimate matter for rational enquiry. Fluctuations do not cause the transformations of a system's activity . . . Moreover, the fact that fluctuations evade control does not mean that we cannot locate the reasons for the instability its amplification causes.
>
> (Prigogine and Stengers, 1984: 206–207)

This passage makes it clear that the origin of change does not lie in chance or accident that requires no further explanation, as is the case in Adaptionist Teleology. Rather, the source of change lies in differences between individual entities that are amplified, differences and their amplification that can be understood and explained:

> We believe that models inspired by the concept of "order through
> fluctuations" will help . . . to give more precise formulation to the
> complex interplay between individual and collective aspects of
> behavior . . . This involves a distinction between states of the system
> in which individual initiative is doomed to insignificance on the one
> hand, and on the other, bifurcation regions in which an individual,
> idea or behavior can upset the global state. Even in those regions,
> amplification obviously does not occur with just any individual, idea,
> or behavior, but only those that are "dangerous" – that is, those that
> can exploit to their advantage the nonlinear relations guaranteeing the
> stability of the preceding regime. Thus we are led to conclude *the*
> *same* nonlinearities may produce an order out of the chaos of
> elementary processes and still, under different circumstances, be
> responsible for the destruction of this same order, eventually
> producing a new coherence beyond another bifurcation.
>
> (Prigogine and Stengers, 1984: 206)

What emerges, then, is always potentially transformed identity: the
identities of the whole and of the entities constituting it at the same time.
And therefore the differences between the entities themselves, and their
collective difference from other wholes, also emerge at the same time.
Micro interactions transform global patterns and themselves in a paradox
of forming while being formed, and an explanation of what is happening
requires an understanding of these micro interactions.

A word on models

Allen explicitly recognizes the limitations of his complex evolutionary
models when he says that they give insight rather than predictions, and
Prigogine says that such models are very risky because:

> In complex systems, both the definition of entities and of the
> interaction among them can be modified by evolution. Not only each
> state of a system but also the very definition of the system as
> modelized is generally unstable, or at least metastable.
>
> (Prigogine and Stengers, 1984: 204)

However, they both continue to place importance on model building in
their work. For us, the kind of evolutionary model being suggested here
creates very serious problems when it comes to human action. The
systems thinkers, discussed in the previous chapter, develop models that
they hold can be directly applied to organizations. We argued in the
previous chapter that this is an invalid move if one is interested in

significant change because it assumes Formative Teleology, which cannot take account of the emerging novelty we experience in organizational life or of human freedom. The evolutionary models discussed above are of a very different kind, much closer to Transformative Teleology in that they do model emerging novelty. However, we believe, along with Prigogine and Allen, that this very difference makes it just as impossible to apply evolutionary models directly to human action. The reason is this. If a model takes on a life of its own, as it does in these evolutionary models, then there can be no assurance that the model will take on the same evolutionary pattern as the real life phenomenon it is modeling. Any relevance such a model has will have to rely upon the experience-based judgment of anyone who proposes to use it. Instead of having value as direct application, the value of this kind of model lies only in the insight it gives into the dynamical properties of micro interaction between diverse entities in general. These models demonstrate general possibilities. They show that, in principle, it is possible for self-organizing micro interaction between diverse entities to produce coherent emergent patterns. What these insights and possibilities mean for human interaction requires careful interpretation within sociological and psychological understandings of human behavior. The need for such careful interpretation is made evident when one considers how micro diversity is often incorporated in the models. This is often done by introducing statistical noise into the models. Diversity in human action arises in human freedom and it seems rather unlikely that human freedom can be represented by statistical noise. As Prigogine quite explicitly says, fluctuations and diversity do not just happen by chance, but require careful explanation. The model is then only pointing to what requires further explanation rather than having any direct value in application.

Conclusion

There is an important distinction between the formative causality in dissipative structure theory and that in chaos theory.

In the models used in chaos mathematics, a move to a different attractor requires an objective observer outside the system to alter a control parameter. This alteration results in a move to a new attractor, where the move itself is not dependent upon the internal dynamic in any way. More precisely, formative causality does not incorporate micro diversity. However, how such a system moves within the bounds of the strange attractor is determined by its own internal dynamic, affected by small changes. This is Formative Teleology.

Many of the mathematical models used in dissipative structure theory incorporate micro diversity and, therefore, the model system moves to another attractor without any intervention by an objective observer outside the system who changes a parameter. In all cases, of course, an external observer designs the model of the system, but what is being discussed here is a model design that simulates an internal capacity to change spontaneously without any outside intervention. In other words, diversity enters into formative causality. The property of system flexibility, the capacity to move easily from one pattern to another, turns out to be an intrinsic property of a nonlinear system when it is characterized by difference. This points to what we mean by Transformative Teleology. This may be a difficult point to hold in mind. It might be thought that the model designer is somehow setting the conditions for the changefulness of the system. However, the designer is trying to design a system that has its own internal capacity to change and this would be defeated if the change depended upon the designer setting the conditions. What the designer is doing is constructing a model with the characteristics of difference and showing that this can cause emergent change in the absence of any external interference or control. The purpose is to demonstrate the possibility of such a process in nature, where there is no external observer in control.

However, the resultant model of the system can only be used as an analogy, not a direct application. The conclusion we reached in Chapter 4 is that systems thinking about organizations, while it may be very useful for understanding and controlling behavior of a repetitive kind, cannot deal with the question of novelty. Systems and systems thinking are some of the tools of communication people in organizations use to accomplish joint action. The ongoing patterns of communication and joint action that are an organization, however, cannot appropriately be thought of as a system for the reasons we gave in Chapter 4. Here we reached the conclusion that models of systems that have a life of their own can provide analogies for novel change but cannot be directly applied to human action. Analogies always require interpretations in terms of human interactions, which cannot usefully be thought of as a system. We hold, therefore, to our conclusion that when it comes to novel change and human freedom, thinking of human action as a system is not appropriate.

This is a very challenging notion for the dominant management discourse, which has no way of thinking about inherent capacities for spontaneous change in which managers participate but over which they have little or no control.

Furthermore, currently dominant ways of talking and thinking about organizational change, based on the engineer's notion of control, make the implicit assumption that successful change occurs when people are persuaded to hold the same beliefs. Those who give a central role to conflict are rare (Pascale, 1990) and the call is usually for strongly shared cultures and harmonious teamwork. Managers seek to remove or suppress the conflicts that arise when people differ, seeing such conflict as disruptions to orderly processes of change. It is all part of a framework of thinking, drawn from Newtonian logic and systems theories which equate equilibrium and harmony with success. The work of Prigogine and his team, in focusing on a notion of transformative causality incorporating difference, challenges this perspective, suggesting that the very difference managers seek so strenuously to remove is the source of spontaneous, potentially creative change. Living beings, including humans in organizations, need to evolve in novel ways in order to survive and if the theory of dissipative structures reveals anything about life in organizations it will mean that many of the current ways of making sense of life in organizations are completely antithetical to this need. Managers may be struggling to change their organizations in ways which ensure that they stay the same.

6 Complexity and the emergence of novelty

- Complex adaptive systems: a life of their own
- Review of the management complexity writers' claim
- Conclusion: the challenge

This chapter continues the discussion of how the complexity sciences deal with the future, this time reviewing the area known as complex adaptive systems.

Complex adaptive systems: a life of their own

A complex adaptive system consists of a large number of agents, each of which behaves according to its own principles of local interaction. No individual agent, or group of agents, determines the patterns of behavior that the system as a whole displays, or how those patterns evolve, and neither does anything outside of the system. Here self-organization means agents interacting locally according to their own principles, or "intentions," in the absence of an overall blueprint for the system. These adaptive systems, just as with the chaos and dissipative structure models discussed in the previous chapter, display broad categories of dynamics that include stable equilibrium, random chaos and a distinctive dynamic between them, at the edge of chaos.

One type of simulation of a complex adaptive system assumes that each agent follows the same small number of simple local rules. For example, three simple rules are sufficient to simulate the flocking behavior of birds (Reynolds, 1987). Here, each agent is the same as every other agent and there is no variation in the way that they interact with each other.

Emergence is therefore not the consequence of non-average behavior, as was the case with dissipative structures. Instead, emergence is the consequence of local interaction between agents. Unlike dissipative structures (see Chapter 5), and because of the postulated uniformity of behavior, these simulations do not display the capacity to move spontaneously, of their own accord, from one basin of attraction to another (Allen, 1998a, 1998b). Instead, they always stay within one attractor and do not evolve. It is important to stress this point because, as Chapter 7 will show, many of those using complexity theory to write about organizations propose that if people follow simple rules in an organization then they will produce complex behavior. They may do, but it will certainly never be novel. Complex adaptive system models of this type fall into the category of Formative Teleology. The process of interacting according to simple rules forms the behavior of the system, a form that is already there, enfolded in the simple rules.

However, other simulations of complex adaptive systems do take account of differences amongst agents, or classes of agents, and different ways of interacting (for example, Ray, 1972). They do, therefore, display the capacity to move spontaneously from one attractor to another. Even more than that, such systems seem to display the capacity for evolving new attractors as the local rules of interaction between agents in the system as a whole evolve at the same time. These models therefore produce much the same evolutionary possibilities as those of Prigogine (1997) and Allen (1998a, 1998b) discussed in the previous chapter. They too are models that take on a life of their own and may, therefore, also offer insight into the nature of Transformative Teleology by way of analogy, although they too cannot be directly applied to human action.

Consider in a little more detail the nature of this group of complex adaptive system models that have the capacity to evolve. They are agent-based models that incorporate the notion of efficient causality because each agent behaves according to "if-then" rules. The agents are algorithmic entities of a cybernetic kind. However, at the level of the whole system causality is of the transformative kind. It is the nonlinear structure of the system and the replicating activity of the agents comprising that system that cause the patterns of behavior that the system produces. Causality, then, is primarily transformative in that it is the evolving local interaction that shapes the behavior of the system. When the system is characterized by micro diversity, it displays the capacity to evolve. The micro diversity here takes the form not only of non-average events but also of different types of agents. These differences in the agents emerge though the process of replication where there is error, random variation, or mixing of code. In this kind of transformative causality, outcomes are caused by chance as well as by the form of the system. The agents are co-creating the evolution of the system they comprise. In other words, the internal dynamic of agent interaction causes the emergent global pattern and simultaneously the emergent change in the mode of interaction, that is, the internal dynamic. Transformative causality takes a circular form, unlike cybernetics, systems dynamics and chaos theory where formative causality is linear in that the internal dynamic causes the emergent global pattern but does not cause itself. So, although in complex adaptive systems models of this kind the local rules of interaction are deterministic, taking the "if-then" form of efficient causality, they are not fixed. Instead, they spontaneously evolve. Here, self-organization and emergence lead to structural development, not just superficial change, and this is "spontaneous" or "autonomous," arising from the intrinsic nonlinear, interactive nature of the system.

In terms of the framework we are using in this book, what kind of teleology do complex adaptive system models of this kind imply? One could argue that they operate according to Formative Teleology because the very act of designing the model and starting it running from an initial position immediately implies the range of attractors it is possible for it to display. For example, when a model uses limited computing time to simulate limited space and food supplies as some models do, this immediately predisposes the model to search for survival strategies that conserve limited computer time. However, the feature distinguishing Formative Teleology from either Adaptionist or Transformative Teleology is not that the Formative limits the range of possibilities for the system, while the other two do not – our notion of Transformative Teleology, for example, is not one in which just anything could happen without any limitation whatsoever. The distinguishing feature of Formative Teleology is, rather, that the specific forms toward which the system moves are already given in the design of the model. It is arguable that complex adaptive system models incorporating micro diversity, like those of dissipative structures, do not do this. To the extent that such models have a life of their own, they may therefore be pointing to the nature of Transformative Teleology. On the other hand, one might argue that these models operate within Adaptionist Teleology because variety in individual agents is generated by random mutations and some principle for the selection and survival of the agents is usually stipulated.

One could, therefore, make rather different interpretations of the causal nature of complex adaptive system models incorporating micro diversity. The important point, then, has to do with interpretation, just as it did with regard to the models of dissipative structures in the previous chapter. There too, they could be taken up as models of Formative Teleology, or they could be interpreted from a perspective that we think approaches what we are calling Transformative Teleology. How do those working in the field of complex adaptive systems interpret their work? It is to this question that the rest of this chapter turns.

Adaptionist Teleology

Some interpretations of complexity theory differ very little from neo-Darwinian views on causality (see Chapter 3). Gell-Mann (1994), for example, talks about chance events that become frozen into regularities, which enable prediction thereafter. As the universe, planetary systems, planets and ecosystems evolve, they encounter bifurcation points. These are points at which evolution could proceed in a large number of different directions. For example, as language evolved, so this view goes, any one of a number of possible grammatical structures could have been selected. However, as soon as one is selected and its use spreads, it becomes frozen or locked in. A particular selected structure arises by accident but becomes frozen and, in doing so, provides a new regularity that governs development thereafter. The same point applies in economics where products can be thought of as becoming "locked in." Frozen accidents are founding events that constrain the emergence of other possibilities. Frozen accidents become rules, or laws, that govern subsequent evolution. This does not challenge neo-Darwinian causality at all but, rather, suggests a reason for the branching pattern of evolution and so accounts for the reasonably limited variety observed. It seems to us that in his interpretation of complexity theory Gell-Mann downplays the importance of self-organization and emergence. He certainly does not elevate them to new causal principles. Despite pointing to unpredictability, he emphasizes predictability. His views on complex adaptive systems fall very much within the causal framework of neo-Darwinism, that is, our category of Adaptionist Teleology.

Formative Teleology

Holland (1998) takes a similar tack, but with a rather different emphasis. He holds that emergent patterns are predictable and regular. He accepts the long-term unpredictability of complex systems but claims that this does not matter because the scientist should focus on levels of detail and time spans for which predictability is possible. He dismisses the importance of long-term unpredictability and holds that it is possible to get by through focusing on the short term. Holland holds that if the current state of a model is specified then that state, processed through the structure of the model, determines the next state, which in turn determines the state after that. He claims that the only uncertainty relates to the appropriateness of the level of detail in which the current state is specified, and to the faithfulness of the correspondence between the model and reality. In other words, uncertainty lies in the interpretation that the modeler makes of a deterministic reality. The future, for him, is fully and unambiguously determined. It is a hidden, pre-given reality. Presumably, unpredictability lies in the models of reality being used, not in the unpredictability of that reality itself. For him, complexity theory is not a fundamental challenge to the dominant scientific discourse but simply another model that is useful in the pursuit of "science as usual." He retains the centrality of efficient causality but adds to it notions of formative cause. Holland's interpretation of complexity theory is quite clearly made within the framework of Formative Teleology.

Others working with complex adaptive systems – for example, Kauffman (1993, 1995) and Goodwin (1994) – provide interpretations that certainly challenge Adaptionist Teleology. This challenge comes from the elevation of interaction between agents to the level of primary causative principle. But do they mount this challenge from the perspective of Formative Teleology or do they make a move to Transformative Teleology? To answer this question consider first some key points that Kauffman makes about causality.

Kauffman's second ordering principle

Kauffman demonstrates in his computer simulations of the evolution of life that a system consisting of a large number of entities, or agents, interacting randomly with each other, is highly likely to evolve into a connected, autocatalytic network in a relatively short period of time. In other words, as entities interact randomly with each other (chemicals in the primordial soup before life emerged, for example), some entities are highly likely to come to play a part in the construction of others, the process of catalysis. Sooner or later, the strings of catalytic interaction that emerge will bend back on themselves and form autocatalytic networks. This means that entity A plays a part in the construction of B, which plays a part in the construction of C, which plays a part in the construction of A. There is no design or blueprint for this network. It emerges and sustains itself in a self-referential manner which can be thought of as self-organizing. This happens in the absence of competitive selection. Here, then, self-organization is an inevitable cooperative, participative dynamic, which is an intrinsic property of interaction and causes the emergence of pattern. Causality here is of a formative kind that is very different to the neo-Darwinian version, because it is interaction, or relationship, that causes emergent form, rather than competition operating on chance. Kauffman is clearly not arguing within the framework of Adaptionist Teleology.

Instead of chance and adaptation, the first ordering principle, Kauffman is arguing that there is a more important second ordering principle. This second principle, the fundamental dynamic in evolution, is interactive cooperation, having the intrinsic capacity for producing novelty and coherence, rendering their emergence inevitable although what emerges is radically unpredictable. This has immediate implications for thinking about organizations. The metaphor of competitive selection as the fundamental formative cause of evolution has had a major impact on how economists, sociologists and organization theorists talk about the evolution of human systems. The assumption that competitive survival is the driver of all things organizational is deeply embedded in the talk and thought of managers today. It would be a major shift to think of competitive survival as less important than the internal, intrinsic dynamic of human relating and competitive cooperation.

The importance of connection

To continue with Kauffman's argument, he shows how the dynamics of a self-organizing network consisting of a number (N) of entities is determined by the number (K) and strength (P) of the connections between these entities.

When the number of connections is low the dynamics are characterized by stable attractors; when the number is high the attractors have properties similar to mathematical chaos, or they may be completely random. In an intermediate state, between stability and instability, the dynamic known as "the edge of chaos" occurs; namely, the paradox of stable instability. In other words, the dynamic has a fractal quality in that no matter what the detail in which the attractor is examined, it displays intertwined stability and instability. So, if one selects what looks like a stable part of a spatial or temporal pattern at the edge of chaos, it always contains chaos, or instability, and vice versa.

When the strength of connection between agents is lowered then the number of connections producing stability is higher.

At the edge of chaos, novelty emerges in a radically unpredictable way. In the light of this, Kauffman calls for a shift from the scientist's concern with prediction to a concern with explanation. Goodwin also emphasizes the radical unpredictability of emergent novelty and calls for a shift from a science concerned purely with quantities to a science of qualities, given that it is interaction that causes emergent qualitites rather than quantities.

In his work, Kauffman is developing a notion of formative causality in which numbers and strengths of connection between entities in a system cause the patterns of behavior of that system. The patterns of behavior are not, initially anyway, caused by chance and competitive selection, on the one hand, or by an agent's choice, on the other. No agent within the system is choosing the pattern of behavior across the system and neither is Kauffman, the simulator. Instead, that pattern emerges in the interaction between the agents, neither by chance nor by choice, but through the capacity to produce coherence that is intrinsic to interaction itself.

If this notion of causality were to apply to human organizations, its implications would be profound because it would mean that organizational change, strategic direction, is caused neither by chance nor by the choices of managers, but by the nature of interaction, relationship or cooperation between people in that organization. If one thinks along these lines, it immediately leads one to ask what managers are doing when they think they are choosing and planning their organization's future. The notion that managers can choose what happens to their organization as a whole is so deeply ingrained that it leads to a typical response. The response is to argue that if managers cannot choose a creative outcome because it is radically unpredictable, then at least they can choose those numbers and strengths of connections, those qualities of relationship that produce the dynamics at the edge of chaos where creative change is possible. However, this misses the whole point because no agent within the system is choosing the numbers and strengths of connections for other agents in the system, or for themselves either; even if they were, this is not enough to determine the dynamic, a point to be explained later in this chapter.

Fitness landscapes and conflicting constraints

To return to Kauffman, he illustrates his argument using the metaphor of a fitness landscape where peaks represent highly fit states for a network of agents and valleys represent unfit states, fitness being defined as survival chance for the network determined outside that network (see Chapter 3). Networks of agents are assumed to seek to survive by moving out of valleys and up peaks on the fitness landscape, that is, by hill-climbing to more adapted states – in effect "searching" for variations that are more fit. This is where Kauffman incorporates into his scheme neo-Darwinian arguments to do with chance, adaptation and the urge to survive (see Chapter 3). Networks of agents change through random mutation in the rules governing the way in which they interact with each other. These changes in the network are represented as movements across the fitness landscape of all possible fitness states as the network "seeks" peaks. The shape of this landscape, whether it has few high peaks or many low peaks, determines how easy or difficult it is for a network to find a fit state. A very rugged landscape with large numbers of low peaks makes it difficult for a network to find a reasonably good state of fitness simply following the hill-climbing rule because they are so easily trapped on a low peak. Given its importance, then, the question is: what causes landscapes to be more or less rugged?

Kauffman shows that it is the number and strength of connections between agents in the network that determines the ruggedness of the landscape across which it has to move in search of fitness. High K produces a very rugged landscape and this means that agents are imposing many conflicting constraints on each other. Consider why this is so. Connections create constraints in that one agent acts in response to the actions of the other agents it is connected to. The connection imposes the constraint of responding. If an agent is connected to two others and they each call for a different response, then the agent has to handle two conflicting constraints.

The greater the number of connections, the more the potential conflict in the constraints that agents impose on each other. The more the conflicting constraints that a network has to accommodate, the less smooth the walk across the landscape, that is, the more rugged it is. It is then extremely difficult for the network to find a reasonably good state of fitness because, as it follows the hill-climbing rule, it will easily get trapped on a low peak. In competition with others, networks with low fitness will experience waves of extinction.

At low K, however, the landscape will be rather smooth with a small number of very high peaks, that is, a small number of very good survival strategies that are very easy to find. Conflicting constraints will be minimal. However, this makes it easy for competitors to find the same survival strategy, removing the competitive advantage of the first, making it too subject to waves of destruction. In other words, landscapes that are too smooth or too rugged are bad news for chances of survival.

However, at a critical level of connection, at a critical point between low and high K, the landscape will be rugged but not too rugged and it is here that survival chances are greatest. Conflicting constraints will be neither too numerous nor too few and the network will be neither too stable nor too unstable.

Kauffman is arguing, then, that the manner in which competitive selection operates on chance variations depends upon the internal dynamic of the evolving network, that is, upon the pattern of connections, the self-organizing interaction, between the entities of which it is composed. Note how this conception moves away from the notion that the fitness landscape is a given space containing all possible evolutionary strategies for a system, which it searches for fit strategies in a manner driven by chance. The fitness landscape itself is being constructed by the properties of the system itself. The notion of fitness landscape, its ruggedness, becomes a metaphor for the internal dynamic of the system, not an externally given terrain over which it travels in search of a fit position. These internal properties of the network are the connections between its entities, and these connections create conflicting constraints. The internal dynamic is thus one of enabling cooperation and of conflicting constraints at the same time, a paradoxical dynamic of cooperation and competition. In human terms, connections between agents may be taken as analogous to relationships between people, and relationships immediately constrain those in relationship. Power is constraint; conflicting constraints, therefore, translate in human terms to power relations. In other words, the emerging strategies of a human organization may be caused by the nature of power relations between its members, by chance and by competitive selection.

This challenges the manner in which dominant ways of thinking and talking about management today downplay power relations and conflict. Kauffman's view of causality points to how power and conflict, inevitably intertwined with cooperation, are fundamental to the emergence of coherence.

Stability in change

Another important aspect relates to control. While no agent is "in control" of the system's evolution, it is nevertheless evolving in a controlled manner and the source of this control lies in the pattern of conflicting constraints. This is a very important point because it is the conflicting constraints that sustain sufficient stability in a network at the edge of chaos. At the edge of chaos, a network configures itself into closely connected clusters, separated from each other to some extent, making it difficult for perturbations to cascade through it. This happens because of canalization, which means that many agents follow the same rules so that there are many chances of the same responses and patterns of response being reproduced. Canalization is the same as redundancy or loose coupling. It is not efficient but it preserves stability in a dynamic of change. At the edge of chaos, there are tendrils of contact between clusters of agents so that some but not all perturbations cascade through the network. Another way of putting this is in terms of the power law. It is a property of the edge of chaos that many small perturbations will cascade through the network but only a few large ones will. In other words, there will be large numbers of small extinction events but only small numbers of large ones. It is this property that imparts control, or stability, to the process of change at the edge of chaos.

Furthermore, Kauffman uses the concept of self-organizing criticality (Bak and Chen, 1991) to argue that living systems evolve of their own accord to the edge of chaos. The concept of self-organizing criticality is usually illustrated with the example of a sand pile on a table. As sand is trickled onto the pile it builds up as a mound until it reaches a particular height, after which further additions of sand lead to avalanches of sand falling off the table. The sand pile sustains its shape in a dynamic self-organizing way through the avalanches. It is the internal dynamic of the sand pile that sustains the shape.

This is a very challenging way of thinking about the causes of stability in human organizations. The dominant discourse places enormous importance on efficiency, that is, the removal of redundancy. Managers usually try to design out processes in which people repeat each other's activities. For example, having two teams working on the same project is normally regarded as unacceptable because it is inefficient. However, from a complexity perspective, such redundant activity, although inefficient, is a source of stability for an organization operating in a turbulent world. This means that an overwhelming concern with efficiency, secured by downsizing and the removal of redundancy, may well be destroying the source of stability and resilience in an organization.

Fitness as co-creation

Picking up once more on Kauffman's argument, the next move is to understand fitness: what is a peak and what is a valley? This depends upon what the other networks constituting the environment are doing in response to what the single network so far considered is doing. The emergence of autocatalysis, (that is, self-organization), produces many networks that become interconnected and so have to cooperate and compete with each other in order to survive in the network of networks. They co-evolve, that is, they deform each other's fitness landscapes.

This requires taking account of the number of networks (S) and the number of connections between them (C): the lower C, the less networks deform each other's landscapes. The dynamic is now rather complicated. Stability (that is, landscapes with little deformation) occurs when S and C are low and K is high. The landscape keeps heaving about, the networks never stop co-evolving in a chaotic manner when S and C are high and K is low. At some intermediate point between high S and C and low K, on the one hand, and low S and C and high K, on the other, the dynamic of the edge of chaos arises. Once again, it is characterized by the power law. Finally, Kauffman shows how such a network of networks evolves in a spontaneously self-organizing way to the edge of chaos where it is neither too stable nor too unstable.

Note here four important points. First, the dynamic experienced by a single network is not simply determined by its own internal dynamic, its own "choice" of K, but also by the size of the larger system it is part of and the connection between it and others, and between those others. High

K produces chaos in isolation but stability in interaction. This will be very important when we come to look at how management theorists use complexity theory. Many tend to lose sight of the limitations on the "choice" open to any single system. This point also presents a significant challenge to the currently dominant management discourse, which is conducted on the taken-for-granted assumption that managers can choose strategic directions for their organization. The notions of causality described in this section point to how limited that choice might actually be when one thinks of an organization in interaction with others, together producing the emergent dynamics of that interaction. Each will be making choices, trying to influence outcomes and the dynamics in which those outcomes emerge, but what transpires will emerge from the conflicting constraints they place on each other, not the simple choice of any one of them. This calls into question the whole notion of strategic choice.

Second, there is the point about micro diversity made in relation to dissipative structure theory in the previous chapter. Kauffman's model incorporates micro diversity in that agents follow different rules of interaction, hence the conflicting constraints. Then there is the introduction of random mutation into the rules governing agent interactions. This leads to further diversity amongst interacting agents. It is this property of diversity, the fact that the interacting agents are different from each other, that imparts the capacity to move spontaneously to novel attractors.

Third, the notion of formative causality presented by Kauffman, unlike that of systems theories or neo-Darwinism, is a self-referential one. In the latter, the dynamics of the system formatively cause the patterns of behavior that emerge but the dynamics do not cause themselves. In the concepts put forward by Kauffman, the dynamics cause themselves as the system evolves of its own accord to the edge of chaos.

Fourth, it is important to understand that Kauffman uses the concept of fitness landscapes as a metaphor for the internal dynamic of a network or a network of networks. He is trying to explain the dynamics of connection between agents within a system and between systems. Since the metaphor is a spatial one being used to illuminate a dynamic temporal process it can easily be misunderstood. Some, who will be referred to in the next chapter, seem to interpret fitness landscapes as if they were external to the network that is "moving" across them. As soon as one slips into thinking about the fitness landscape as a kind of environment outside the system across which it is moving, one loses the insight that it is the dynamic of the system itself that is shaping the landscape. The internal dynamic is the landscape. When this insight is lost, people talk about landscapes of knowledge and landscapes of strategies and think about an organization, a group or a person selecting knowledge or strategies that are more fit. This is very different to the use of a fitness landscape as a metaphor for the dynamics of relationship.

Formative or Transformative Teleology?

Kauffman's challenge to Adaptionist Teleology is clear. In the latter, the only source of variety is chance variation in the most fundamental individual entities. In Kauffman's scheme such random mutation plays a minor part, the major source of variety lying in the interactions between entities. It is the number and strength of connections between entities in a network that forms the dynamic of the network, including the dynamic at the edge of chaos, where endless variety is an intrinsic possibility of the interaction itself. Furthermore, the dynamic of the whole network is not solely determined by its own internal connections but also by its connections with other networks. The dynamics of individual networks form and are formed by each other at the same time. From an Adaptionist Teleology perspective, natural selection operates on every chance variation, determining whether it survives or not. Forms gradually emerge, therefore, through, and only through, the grinding process of natural selection. In Kauffman's scheme forms emerge through the self-organizing process of interaction and are only then subjected to the pressures of natural selection. Rather than simply moving toward a stable state of adaptation to an externally given environment, as in Adaptionist Teleology, forms in Kauffman's scheme are in perpetual construction by the very movement itself. There is one aspect, however, where Kauffman's scheme coincides with Adaptionist Teleology. For both, the motivating force of evolution, the "for sake of which," the "in order to," is that of the selfish, individual urge to survive. We take this point up later in this section.

It seems clear, then, that Kauffman's explanation does not take the form of Adaptionist Teleology but, rather, exhibits the main features of what we have called Transformative Teleology. In his explanation, networks of networks are in perpetual construction moving toward an unpredictable future. The process of construction is that of forming and being formed at the same time and it produces repetitive patterns always with the potential for transformation. Variation arises in micro interactions between entities and networks, characterized by micro diversity and the paradox of conflicting constraints that both enable and constrain. His models take on a life of their own. There is, however, an aspect of his thinking that seems to reflect Formative Teleology. He talks about the emergence of autocatalytic networks as "inevitable" and he talks about humans as "we the expected," also implying inevitability. This suggests that the form of life itself, and of human life within it, is somehow pre-given.

The clearest divergence between Kauffman's approach and what we have called Transformative Teleology, however, is the importance ascribed to the struggle between individuals acting in their own selfish interest. This central feature of Adaptionist Teleology is not at all prominent in the Transformative Teleology perspective. There, movement is not driven by selfish interest but rather expresses the identity and difference of individuals and collectives at the same time. Goodwin (1994) adopts much the same view on the transformative causality of connection and relationship as Kauffman, but answers the "why" question in a different way. Where Kauffman talks about agents interacting in their own selfish interest in order to survive, Goodwin talks about the intrinsic value of creative living systems of any kind and how this intrinsic property expresses identity. For him, agents and networks of agents interact with each other in order to express their identities and in doing so, of course, delineate their differences. In saying this, he is expressing what we think of as Transformative Teleology.

What we have been describing, then, is a perspective within the theory of complex adaptive systems that implies Transformative Teleology. We argue that this represents a new paradigm, one of identity and difference. Earlier we pointed to how the 1950s saw a shift from part–whole to system–environment thinking and we are now arguing that some strands in the complexity sciences potentially point to a shift from system–environment to identity–difference thinking. It is this paradigm shift, we believe, that is radical and our interest lies in exploring what this shift might mean for making sense of life in organizations.

Review of the management complexity writers' claim

Management complexity writers claim that the natural sciences of complexity offer an alternative to the currently dominant way of thinking and talking about the management of human organizations. We argue that this amounts to a claim that the complexity sciences put forward notions of causality that differ significantly from those underlying the dominant management discourse. Put differently, the claim is that the complexity sciences provide a different answer to the central question of what causes organizations to become what they are.

In Chapter 4, we pointed to how currently dominant answers to this question are built on theories of causality imported from Newtonian physics and systems theories largely developed by engineers. In Newtonian physics, causality is of the efficient type in which there are identifiable linear links between specific causes and consequent effects, and it is these links that enable prediction. From this perspective parts add up to give wholes that move in eternally given, optimal ways. We called this view one of secular Natural Law Teleology.

In systems thinking, causality is primarily of the formative type taking a linear form in which the feedback process of the system causes its patterns of behavior, usually in a predictable way, but those patterns do not cause the system dynamics. The future forms to which such systems move are already given in their structure, including the boundary separating them from others. We called this Formative Teleology.

Chapter 3 then argued that both secular Natural Law and Formative Teleological frameworks have been imported into theorizing about human actions. Human organizations have been understood as objective phenomena rather like natural phenomena, to which the above causal principles apply. The manager or leader is implicitly equated with the scientist who observes nature in order to identify its causal structure, so enabling humans to operate upon it. The manager or leader is understood as one who observes the causal structure of an organization in order to be able to control it. There is one difference; namely, that the manager or leader is human and so are the members of the organization. This is taken to mean that the manager can choose the goals of the organization and design the systems or actions to realize those goals. We called this Rationalist Teleology. The possibility of so choosing goals and strategies relies on the predictability provided by the efficient and formative causal structure of the organization, as does the possibility of managers staying "in control" of their organization's development. According to this perspective, organizations become what they are because of the choices made by their managers. This is Rationalist Teleology, applied to a system governed by secular Natural Law and Formative Teleology.

The claim of the management complexity writers rests on whether the complexity sciences present significantly different theories of causality to these. Since the natural sciences have nothing to say about Rationalist Teleology, the question is whether the complexity sciences move from the secular Natural Law and Formative Teleologies that currently dominate the natural sciences. In reviewing what complexity scientists assume about causality in complex systems, in this and the previous chapter we suggested that the answer to this question depends upon the particular scientists one refers to, given that the complexity sciences are not a monolithic consensus. Many scientists working in the field of complexity do not make any significant move from Formative Teleology and would probably argue strenuously against doing so. A few, however, do make such a move and we think they move toward what we have called Transformative Teleology. The difference management complexity writers make to organizational thinking, therefore, will depend, in our view, upon whether they draw on scientists who work within the framework of Formative Teleology or whether they draw on work that reflects Transformative Teleology. In the former case there can be no radical rethinking of the nature of management – simply because the theory of causality continues unquestioned. The result could well be little more than another fad, that is, currently dominant views rephrased in the jargon of the complexity sciences. We hold that any useful challenge to current thinking about organizations requires drawing on those complexity scientists who make a move toward Transformative Teleology.

One example of a scientist who does not make such a move, in our view, is Gell-Mann (1994). As far as we can see, he does not depart in any significant way from the Adaptionist Teleology of neo-Darwinism. He does not ascribe any special status to the process of self-organization and emergence but argues that novelty arises in a system when it passes through bifurcations at which the particular path it follows depends entirely upon chance and its subsequent survival depends upon competitive selection. His main emphasis is on the frozen state that the system is locked into once it has passed the bifurcation. In this state, its behavior is governed by new regularities that have emerged and these provide the efficient causal links that enable prediction. This differs from notions of causality underlying the dominant management discourse in only one respect, namely the cause of emergent novelty. The idea that chance is the cause of a system changing to a novel state into which it is then locked challenges the idea that an organization becomes innovatively different because of its managers' choices. Instead, if this kind of complexity thinking applies to organizations, then they become innovatively different by chance and they subsequently find it difficult to change from that new state because of the property of "lock in." Here, the argument is exactly the same as that of organizational theorists in the Population Ecology school (Hannan and Freeman, 1989), which has had little impact on the way managers currently think. Furthermore, once in the locked-in state, dominant notions of management continue to apply in a way that is consistent with Holland's approach, characterized by Formative Teleology. The work of both Holland and Gell-Mann does not appear to us to justify the claim that the complexity sciences provide a significantly different way of understanding how organizations become what they are.

Prigogine (1997), Kauffman (1995) and Goodwin (1994) exemplify scientists who do seem to move from Adaptionist and Formative Teleology. Although very different in many respects, we think they are similar in the centrality they accord to self-organization as transformative cause. For Prigogine, self-organization refers to the spontaneous "choice" a system makes at unstable bifurcation points. The "choice" leads the system along unpredictable paths into the future. Unlike Gell-Mann, however, Prigogine does not ascribe the "choice" to accident or chance alone. He is interested in looking for the reasons why a particular fluctuation is amplified to reach a bifurcation. It is not chance but the detail of micro interactions at bifurcation point that explains how and why a system moves down one path rather than another. For him the future is under perpetual construction.

For Kauffman and Goodwin, interaction between the components of a system is the cause of the coherent pattern that inevitably, but completely unpredictably, emerges from that interaction when the system operates at the edge of chaos. The intrinsic properties of connection, interaction and relationship cause emergent coherence in the particular conditions prevailing at the edge of chaos and that emergent coherence is radically unpredictable. Efficient causality is retained as the cause of an agent's particular local response to other agents, but it is the interaction itself that operates as transformative cause of the emergent pattern of the whole system. Furthermore, that transformative causality is circular, indeed self-referential, because self-organization causes emergent patterns in itself. There is some indication of Formative Teleology in the way both Kauffman and Goodwin talk about the inevitability of a system's development. Kauffman also retains an important aspect of Adaptionist

Teleology when he argues that agents interact selfishly with each other in order to survive. Goodwin, on the other hand, suggests that agents and systems interact with each other for the sake of expressing their identity and thereby their difference from each other.

On the whole, however, we suggest that these three scientists are pointing to what we have called Transformative Teleology. We argue that this move to Transformative Teleology does challenge the notions of causality underlying the dominant management discourse on management. Perhaps it constitutes a shift from system–environment thinking to a new paradigm of identity and difference. In this new paradigm, an organization becomes what it is because of the intrinsic need human beings have, individually and collectively, to express their identities and thereby their differences. Identity and difference emerge, becoming what they are through the transformative cause of self-organization, that is, relationship. What an organization becomes emerges from the relationships of its members rather than being determined by the choices of individuals.

Conclusion: the challenge

We suggest that Transformative Teleology, illuminated by some strands in the complexity sciences, presents a challenge to the dominant management discourse because it points to:

1 *Severe limitations on predictability in the evolution of complex organizational processes*. Although short-term developments are predictable, long-term evolution emerges unpredictably. Emergent creative developments can be articulated and understood only as they emerge and cannot be predicted in advance. Creativity and uncertainty are thus inextricably linked, and if organizations are to change in novel ways then managers have no alternative but to act continually into the unknown. The invitation is for managers to reflect seriously upon how they do this. Such a perspective departs from the dominant paradigm in which the role of managers is thought to be the reduction of uncertainty rather than the capacity to live creatively in it.

2 *The centrality of self-organizing interaction as transformative cause of emergent new directions in the development of an organization*. This puts cooperative interaction, or relationship, and the conflicting constraints that relationship imposes, right at the center of the creative

process of organizational development. Since power is constraint, this perspective places power, politics and conflict at the center of the cooperative social process through which joint action is taken. Novel organizational developments are caused by the political, social and psychological nature of human relationships. This departs from the dominant discourse on management in which the role of the manager is one of removing ambiguity and conflict to secure consensus. Power is thought of as unpleasant and its importance is made undiscussable, while politics is a process that is to be minimized. Cooperation is thought to be subservient to the overriding importance of competitive advantage and competitive survival.

3   *The limits to individual choice.* If novel organizational developments emerge in power relations between people, and if they are largely unpredictable, then the notion that individuals, or small groups of them, can choose creative futures for their organization falls away. The outcomes of organizational interaction – indeed, the very dynamics of that interaction – are not within the power of any single organization to choose. Both the outcomes and dynamics producing those outcomes emerge from the interaction between organizations, with no one being able individually to choose them. The dominant management discourse is built firmly on the notion that small groups of powerful managers can and should choose the future of their organization, almost as if other organizations play no part in what happens.

4   *The sources of stability.* Stability emerges in relationships because relationships are conflicting constraints, that is, power. Individuals cannot do just what they please, precisely because they cannot survive outside of relationships and relationships constrain. Furthermore, stability is sustained by redundancy, that is, by the inefficient repetition of tasks and modes of relating. Finally, stability is sustained by the property of the edge of chaos that limits the spread of destruction through a system, namely the power law. At the edge of chaos, destruction, which is an inevitable companion of the emergent new, is controlled because extinction events are mainly small in size. In other words, organizational life is controlled because of the dynamics of relating at the edge of chaos, although no individual or group of individuals can be "in control" of the whole system. This departs from the dominant discourse in which the only alternative to an individual being "in control" is thought to be anarchy.

5   *The importance of diversity and difference.* Complex systems evolve when there is micro diversity, or fluctuations. In human terms this

means that there can be no novel organizational developments without differences between the people who comprise it. It follows that deviance, the difficult search for understanding in misunderstanding, is a prerequisite for novel change. This departs from the dominant management discourse's emphasis on harmony and consensus, now seen to be inimical to creativity.

6 *Limits to the ability to design and plan.* Complex systems have the internal capacity to change spontaneously in unpredictable ways that cannot be described as optimizing anything. Their creative development cannot be designed, planned or controlled. This departs from the dominant discourse in which designing and planning for maximal or optimal outcomes are seen as the very essence of the management role.

7 *Potential success as the paradox of stable instability.* This means that organizations have the potential to succeed in that they possess the capacity for novel change only when they combine stability and instability. This is a potential, not a guarantee, because of the destructive as well as the creative nature of evolution. This differs from the dominant discourse in which success is equated with stability alone, so ignoring the inevitability of conflict and destruction.

8 *The centrality of the expression of identity and thus difference.* This means, in relation to organizations, that the movement of stability and change in human organizations arises in the human need to express identity, both individually and collectively at the same time. Goals to do with competitive survival and profit are then seen to be subservient to this overriding need. This departs from dominant management views understanding performance as an all-important motivating force.

The conclusion, then, is that there are views within the complexity sciences, probably reflective of a minority, that do challenge the dominant discourse in important ways and so sustain the claim that the complexity sciences may offer a new way of thinking about life in organizations. However, there are also views that are probably reflective of the majority of complexity scientists, which do not form the basis of any significant challenge to currently dominant ways of thinking and talking about management. Even the most challenging, however, think in terms of systems and they try to model those systems. From our perspective, they can only provide a source domain for analogies of human action when their model or system has a life of its own. For us, human action is not a system and it is limiting to think of it as such.

Transformative Teleology represents a decisive move away from systems thinking to a paradigm of identity and difference.

The question now is just how those who write about complexity in human organizations are taking up the insights of the complexity sciences. It is to this question that the next chapter turns.

7 Differing views on complexity in organizations

The previous two chapters drew attention to three broad perspectives in the natural sciences of complexity.

First, there is a perspective that we understand as Adaptionist Teleology. From this perspective, self-organization is not regarded as a central causal principle and the causal framework is that of neo-Darwinism. Second, there is a perspective based on Formative Teleology that does elevate self-organization to the status of a central causal principle. However, it focuses on self-organizing processes of identical, or average, entities. What emerges, therefore, is forms already enfolded, as it were, in the fixed, identical interactions. The highly popular notion of simple rules producing complex order is an example of this.

When management complexity writers take these perspectives into thinking about human organizations, human choice (Rationalist Teleology) is substituted for chance mutations in the Adaptionist perspective and the simple rules are chosen by humans in the Formative perspective. The result is a causal framework that is substantially the same as that underlying the dominant management discourse, built on causal assumptions imported from physics and engineering. In this chapter we will argue that complexity writers drawing on these two perspectives continue to think that organizations become what they are because their managers choose the goals they are to achieve (Rationalist Teleology), design the feedback systems that regulate behavior required to achieve those goals (Formative Teleology) in a world characterized by regularities that can be modeled by objective rules (efficient causality), or are subjected to competitive selection (Adaptionist Teleology). These two perspectives in the thinking about complexity in the natural sciences, therefore, present no significant challenge to the understanding of causality implicit in currently dominant ways of talking about management. They are fundamentally forms of systems thinking.

The third perspective in the natural sciences of complexity does, in our view, hold out the potential for a major challenge to the dominant management discourse. This perspective, like the one of Formative Teleology, also elevates self-organization to the status of a central causal principle. However, it focuses attention on interaction between diverse, non-average entities and on how, in this interaction, the future is under perpetual construction. This leads to a very different framework for understanding causality compared to the Newtonian and engineering systems thinking underlying the dominant management discourse. Here, in becoming what they are, living systems express their identities in a self-organizing process in which identity formatively causes itself, always with the potential for transformation. These views move toward what we have called Transformative Teleology. However, they still think in terms of systems and models and so, we argue, can only provide the source domain of analogies for human action. The central proposition in Transformative Teleology is that human actions and interactions are processes, not systems, and the coherent patterning of those processes becomes what it becomes because of their intrinsic capacity, the intrinsic capacity of interaction and relationship, to form coherence. That emergent form is radically unpredictable, but it emerges in a controlled or patterned way because of the characteristics of relationship itself, to do with conflicting constraints and the self-controlled dynamics of creation and destruction in conditions at the edge of chaos. If one adopts perspectives from the complexity sciences that take something like this kind of transformative perspective, it calls for a significant rethinking of how organizations change and the role managers play in that process. They represent a move away from systems thinking.

Those writing about complexity in organizations rarely make these distinctions, instead treating the complexity sciences as if they were a monolithic consensus. Almost all of these writers claim that the complexity sciences call for thinking about management as a self-organizing system that produces emergent outcomes, as a replacement for mechanistic thinking. However, in not paying attention to the fundamental differences in notions of causality in the three perspectives, and in not attending to the limitations in systems thinking, they run the risk of simplification that subtly undermines the proclaimed challenge and merely reproduces the dominant discourse in new jargon.

In this chapter, we distinguish two different ways in which we think most management complexity writers are using notions of causality from the complexity sciences:

- First, there are writers who think about industry level dynamics in a way that moves toward Transformative Teleology to a significant extent. They model populations of organizations and draw conclusions about the nature of their evolution. Underlying what they have to say is a notion that, in becoming what they are, populations of organizations paradoxically repeat their past and potentially transform themselves at the same time. In other words, industries are characterized by simultaneous continuity and transformation of identity, the known and the unknown inextricably intertwined. Here, self-organization is interaction between diverse organizations. This perspective stresses the paradoxical, changeable nature of industries and organizations, the radical unpredictability of that change and the limited ability to control it, plus the importance of difference in the process of change. However, they do all this while continuing within systems thinking.
- Second, there is the work of those who use the language of self-organization as Formative Teleology. They focus their attention at the level of an organization and do not construct mathematical models or computer simulations, taking a loose metaphorical approach instead. This work tends to point to unpredictability but then subtly retains predictability in an implicit form which unfolds and so continues to assume that individuals can stay "in control" of organizations in important ways. This use of notions from the complexity sciences remains even more firmly within the tradition of systems thinking than the first does.

In what follows, we argue that the first way of interpreting organizational life from a complexity perspective struggles with the implications of what might be a significant challenge to current management thinking by moving toward Transformative Teleology. The drawback of this approach, however, is that by retaining the framework of systems thinking, focusing attention at the level of an industry and using models to understand it, the detail of human interaction tends to get lost. For us, the development of a perspective of Transformative Teleology for organizations needs to put detailed human interaction at the center of the explanation, simply because from this perspective it is in such micro diversity and micro interaction that the potential for transformation lies. This micro approach is what the second way referred to above seems to promise in its attention to the management of individual organizations. However, writers taking this perspective almost all continue to think within the framework of Formative Teleology, that which underlies systems thinking (see Chapter 4), and so simply re-present the dominant discourse in new jargon. We think that this qualifies as another fad, probably soon to go the way of other management fads.

How different writers focus attention and deal with causality, therefore, is extremely important because, in our view, it determines whether there is any point in managers taking an interest in the complexity sciences. If it simply leads to new jargon, they need hardly bother, but if it does challenge the basis upon which their current thinking is based, then it is surely a very important matter. Consider now these two ways of incorporating developments in the complexity sciences into thinking about organizations.

Complexity and the dynamics of industries: limits to control and the origins of novelty

This section briefly explores the work of two writers, Allen (1998a, 1998b, and in Prigogine and Allen, 1982) and Marion (1999).

The importance of deviant behavior

Allen uses the four models described in Chapter 5 to understand industrial reality.

First, he develops an equilibrium (cybernetic) model of the fishing industry and shows how it produces a policy recommendation to constrain fishing effort at, or just below, the maximum that yields a sustainable fish population. He then shows how the dynamics of fish populations and fish markets rapidly render any selected sustainable level of fishing highly inaccurate.

Second, he takes a systems dynamics model of the fishing industry and demonstrates that it generates more complex patterns of variation in fish populations and in economic conditions similar to those found in the real industry. However, because the model uses average data for all of these factors, it generates a long-term tendency toward stationary states that are not found in data on the fishing industry. In reality, there are large and continuing fluctuations in fish populations around the average, related to unpredictable factors such as movements in currents of warmer water, which the systems dynamics models do not incorporate. Furthermore, because the assumptions about average events and entities at the microscopic level are retained, the model cannot explain how the pattern of industrial activity changes.

Third is what he calls a self-organizing model of the fishing industry. He introduces "noise" into the equations to represent random fluctuations in the spatial distribution of the fish population. He also introduces the possibility of internally determined variations in factors such as responses to fish availability, levels of technology and price responsiveness. The model produces boom and bust oscillations in fishing fleet catches, reflecting patterns that can be observed in the real fishing industry, and then a spontaneously emergent small high-priced niche where fish becomes a luxury food. This model increases one's understanding of how an industry can shift spontaneously from one pattern of activity to another.

Finally, he constructs what he calls an evolutionary complex model. Here he postulates different kinds of fleet behavior. First, he distinguishes between fleets that follow rational strategies in which they are attracted to areas of highest catch and others that move more randomly in the hope of identifying new catch areas. He then adds additional fleets, each pursuing different strategies. The strategies correspond to different parameter values in the function to do with attraction to areas of catch that govern the behavior of the fleets. If a fleet pursues a failing strategy it is removed by the programmer and replaced by a fleet with new, randomly chosen parameters. Here he introduces difference in the entities comprising the model, incorporating different levels of information acquired by each fishing fleet, different attitudes to risk, different degrees of attraction to particular fishing areas, different extents to which they spy on and copy each other. By running the program, the programmer "learns" about more viable fishing strategies. The model demonstrates how effective strategies are reinforced and come to dominate the rest and how those fleets pursuing losing strategies explore and search for different ones through changing behavioral parameters. In this way, genuinely new strategies emerge and the program learns about them. Allen is able to show that being diverse is what builds a rich, sustainable system. Having and building on idiosyncrasies is the key to creating and maintaining an ecology of behaviors. If one shifts one's perspective from self-organizing to evolutionary complex thinking, therefore, one can acquire a greater understanding of the processes underlying the creative change of strategic direction pursued by different organizations in an industry and how they come to fit together in compatible clusters.

In relation to this fourth, preferred model, Allen repeatedly stresses the amplification of difference, that is, the eccentric, deviant behavior of the entities comprising the system. It is this behavior that destabilizes population identity and so leads to change. Allen also stresses radical unpredictability and the inevitability of uncertainty, arguing that even those models displaying the capacity to evolve will not necessarily do so as reality does. He thinks that evolving reality is radically unpredictable but that models may assist in thinking about the nature of the dynamic and the kind of possibilities it might imply.

Allen, we think, moves toward Transformative Teleology in his concern with how genuinely novel forms, ones that have never existed before, come into being, seeing instability, deviance and difference as essential to this process. Such a view has major implications for how one thinks about government policies for industries and what view one takes on the possibility of individual organizations within an industry choosing their strategies. The emphasis on instability and the importance of eccentricity and deviance also represents a significant challenge to the dominant management emphasis on stability and group harmony.

However, there are important limitations inherent in the activity of model building itself and in the focusing of attention at a macro level. As soon as one draws a conceptual boundary around particular human interactions and regards them as a system, even an evolving system with a life of its own, one objectifies that human interaction. The interaction is then thought of as an objective phenomenon consisting of interacting entities. It is this way of thinking about human interaction that makes it possible to formulate a model of it. The immediate consequence, however, is the rather strong possibility of proceeding as if humans were like entities in the natural sciences, assuming away the essential human quality of freedom. Rules for the interactions are then specified and the result is Formative Teleology, a way of thinking that cannot encompass novelty because it excludes freedom. Even when the models take complex evolutionary forms of the kind discussed in this section, where the models take on a life of their own, autonomous individual choice not specified by the model designer is introduced as statistical noise, probability distributions or diffusion equations. Clearly this is a proxy for, rather than an explanation of, choice and decision-making. Building macro models of human interactions, therefore, inevitably loses the quality of human freedom.

Furthermore, there is a powerful tendency to think of the model, even a model with a life of its own, as an aid to human choice in relation to the objectified phenomenon of interacting entities. Human choice is then located in the model builder, and by analogy in the managers of organizations who stand outside the system of interactions and make choices about it, as if this phenomenon did not itself consist of human choices. In other words, thinking in terms of macro models, of an industry or an organization, implicitly produces a split between the system and the human chooser, just as it does in systems thinking (see Chapter 4). The system is assumed to behave according to one kind of causal framework, usually Formative Teleology, but sometimes, as in Allen's work, something like Transformative Teleology. The model designer, or manager using the model, is implicitly assumed to be behaving according to another causal framework and this is, as far as we can see, almost always Rationalist Teleology. This is surely a problem. How can we explain human choice in terms of Rationalist Teleology, and that about which the choices are being made in terms of Formative or even Transformative Teleology, when that about which the choice is being made is itself about humans with choice? If Rationalist Teleology does explain human action, why do we not use it to explain the human action of, say, fishing? We seem to be caught in an intellectual process of regarding the human interactions we are trying to explain as equivalent to natural phenomena and then using one causal framework for the explanation of human action and another for how we might use the explanation, that use also being human action. This problem is also demonstrated in the work of Marion. He too, in the end, does not make a major shift from systems thinking.

The constraints on management choice

Marion (1999) describes the development of the microcomputer industry and uses it to illustrate his perspective on organizational complexity. Consider first a brief outline of developments in the industry.

The microcomputer industry

Mainframe computers became commercially available in 1952 and in the mid-1960s microprocessors were developed and incorporated in hand-held calculators. Small packets of technology were, therefore, emerging in a moderately coupled network of industries over the 1950s and 1960s. Then in 1975, MICS produced the first microcomputer, the Altair, which was cheaper and more accessible to a wider market than mainframes. Micros had a different architecture to mainframes and calculators, and during the initial stage of market development competition in the micro sector had more to do with architectures than anything else. There were, and still are, two architectures. One is based on the Intel chip and the other on the Motorola processor. A number of operating systems were built around these chips: CP/M; the Apple system; IBM DOS; and systems for the Commodore, Tandy, Texas Instruments (TI), NCR, NEC, Olivetti, Wang and Xerox microcomputers. The early market niche for micros was thus crowded with architectures and operating systems when, in 1981, IBM entered the micro market. The entry of IBM immediately put the fastest growing operating system, CP/M, out of business. By the mid-1980s, IBM's architecture was dominant and others adopted it in order to survive. At the same time, Apple introduced the Mac, which was not as cumbersome and difficult to learn as DOS. Later, Microsoft brought some simplicity to DOS but it is still not able to match the elegance and simplicity of the Mac. During this period, microprocessor technology was also developing: the earliest processors were 4 bits and were soon replaced by 8- and then 16-bit processors. By the mid-1990s, 32-bit technology was dominant.

Marion describes a development, then, in which there were a few people dreaming of microcomputers in 1974, a great many people wanting one by 1976, and explosive growth in the ensuing two decades. It looked as if microcomputers had suddenly appeared out of nowhere. However, the pieces were coming together long before microcomputers were ever envisioned: microcircuits, microprocessors, ROM and RAM memory chips were being used in calculators, while computer language logic was being documented in mainframes. The microcomputer was built from these pieces.

The dynamics of the microcomputer industry

Marion uses the Kauffman framework described in Chapter 6 to make sense of these developments.

You will recall that Kauffman models the emergence of autocatalytic networks of molecules, which increasingly form connections between themselves to build the chemical basis of life. Marion argues that the same phenomenon is evident in the micro industry as the bits and pieces of already existing technology come together as emergent microcomputers. He continues with Kauffman's framework to argue that the early micro niche was occupied by a large number of architectural species (high S in Kauffman's framework). These early producers were small organizations driven by a few engineering personalities. They were relatively simple organizations, lacking much internal complexity and having few internal connections (low K in Kauffman's terms). They also displayed relatively few connections with other players in the niche, since producers specialized in sub-niches – for example, Apple in the education market and Commodore at the low end of the home market. Competitive interaction was thus limited (low C in Kauffman's terms). Large numbers of species (high S), each of which is relatively simple internally (low K) and weakly connected to each other (low C), produce highly unstable, chaotic dynamics and this was evident in the rapid and unpredictable development of the microcomputer market in the early days. The industry was characterized by frequent and strong shocks, or large avalanches of extinction.

Then in the 1980s, the number of players in the architecture field diminished until IBM DOS and Mac dominated that field. In other words, the number of species declined (S declined). In addition, the entry of a highly complex organization, IBM, and the rapid growth and development of Apple, meant that internal complexity rose; that is, there was a greater number of connections between agents within the competing organizations (K rose). At the same time, the number of connections between organizations in the niche increased (C rose) because both of the main players competed with each other in all of the market niches. So S declined while both K and C rose. In Kauffman's models, this combination produces the dynamic at the edge of chaos, which combines both stability and instability. Marion argues that this intertwining of stability and instability was also characteristic of the microcomputer industry at the end of the 1980s and on into the 1990s, when changes became much smaller and more incremental, with large extinction events a rarity. IBM DOS came to dominate the architecture niche, despite the technical superiority of the Apple Mac. This is technological "lock-in", which occurs as more and more users come to rely on a particular technology so that the costs of change become too high and users stay with the technology they have, even if it is inferior.

However, there was still change as the number of micro producers increased, IBM lost its market dominance and Microsoft increased its power. The changes, of course, continue to this day.

The implications of Marion's perspective

Marion is showing how an industrial network evolves through its own internal dynamic to the edge of chaos. He emphasizes the radical unpredictability of such evolution and the continuing unpredictability when a network operates at the edge of chaos. He draws on three characteristics to reach this conclusion. The first is sensitive dependence on initial conditions (see Chapter 5), which he argues can be seen in the sensitivity of human interaction to small events. Unpredictability here is due to human inability to monitor and observe infinite detail. Second, he refers to Prigogine's work on potential energy and Poincaré resonances (see Chapter 5) to argue that intrinsic unpredictability is also a feature of complex systems. Third, he brings in self-organizing criticality and the power law (see Chapter 6) to argue that, despite its great stability and robustness, a network at the edge of chaos will be subject to many small, and a few large, extinction events and that these are impossible to predict.

He argues that all of these factors are sources of radical unpredictability in the evolution of human networks that make it impossible for an individual to be in control of such a network. In other words, no single organization in the industrial network chooses the future direction of the industry, and this means that it cannot choose its own evolution either. This suggests that managers who claim to be planning the future of their organization will not actually be doing so. Furthermore, no single organization can choose the dynamics of the industry as a whole and therefore no organization can choose its own dynamic either. In the early stages of the micro industry development, the dynamics were chaotic because of the large number of simply structured competitors, loosely connected to each other. None of them chose this. It flowed from the nature of the interaction between them. The entry of IBM was a deliberate choice, but the reduction in the number of competitors and the increase in the range of competitive interaction between the survivors was not simply IBM's choice. It depended upon what the others did too. The evolution from chaos to the dynamic at the edge of chaos was co-created through the interaction of the organizations, not chosen by one in isolation. Outcomes and dynamics continued to change in unpredictable ways, outside the power of individual organizations to choose, as the number of micro producers increased and Microsoft gained greater power over the market. Nowadays, the power of Microsoft is being challenged by lawsuits and freely available operating systems on the Internet.

Marion is making an important point here because many who take up complexity theory in relation to organizations may accept that organizations cannot choose future outcomes but then claim that they can deliberately choose the dynamic in which they operate (see the next section of this chapter). We agree this is not a conclusion that is in any way consistent with the properties of complex systems, at least from the perspective of Transformative Teleology described in Chapter 3.

The nature of control

However, Marion also repeatedly stresses that unpredictability does not lead to the conclusion that there is no control. Attractors at the edge of chaos are bounded and demonstrate a family-like similarity. Therefore it is not possible for just anything to happen. He also argues that the power law is itself a form of control because, at the edge of chaos, the numbers of extinction events, both large and small, are smaller than they are in the dynamics of stability, on the one hand, and chaos, on the other. Because of the relatively small number of large extinction events, change spreads through a network in a controlled manner. In the other dynamics, change spreads through the network in a highly destructive, continuous manner. Furthermore, the edge of chaos is characterized by coupling between agents and systems that is neither too tight nor too loose, and this – equivalent to walls separating attractors – contains the spread of change through a system when it is at the edge of chaos.

The central argument, then, is that change at the edge of chaos is controlled by the very nature of the dynamic, making it unnecessary, as well as impossible, for individuals to take control. This is an understanding of control that is very different indeed to the assumption made in the dominant management discourse where control means simply that someone is "in control" and so ensures survival. The notion that there may be a form of control that imparts stability to a whole network of networks, but no guarantee whatsoever for the survival of any individual part of the network, is a concept quite foreign to ideas of control in the dominant management discourse. Shifting the focus of attention from individuals who are in "control" to control as a characteristic of a particular system-wide dynamic implying periodic destruction of parts of the whole network, has potentially significant implications for how one thinks about the nature of organization and management.

What is the underlying framework of causality in the above analysis of the dynamics of industries? Marion is quite explicit about this.

Marion's analysis of causality in complex systems

Marion puts forward a framework that he calls Complex Natural Teleology to explain the evolution of industries (for example, microcomputers). Complex Natural Teleology is the cause of networks of interactive units forming and expressing orderly patterns of behavior and it combines autocatalytic interaction with the laws of physics, need or purpose, and natural selection. We first summarize our understanding of this framework and then comment on it in terms of the framework we have developed in Chapters 2 and 3.

The first element in Marion's causal scheme – namely, autocatalytic interaction – was discussed in Chapter 6 in relation to the work of Kauffman. It is the process of self-organization that causes the emergence of interconnections across a network and hence causes emergent patterns of behavior and change in the network. Complex systems evolve to the edge of chaos, and the properties of this dynamic, for example couplings between agents and systems that are neither too loose nor too tight, cause the combined stability and fluidity of a network's structure and behavior. Another property, the power law, is the cause of the pattern of small and large avalanches of extinction that control change. Marion draws on Prigogine's theory of dissipative structures where correlations between the behavior of agents, or resonances between them, cause the coherent order that the system displays. In the example above, Marion showed how he thinks this kind of cause applies to the development of the microcomputer industry.

The second element in Marion's causal scheme is the laws of physics. Since self-organizing interaction occurs in a physical medium for both natural and human phenomena, it is subject to the laws of physics. For example, in the micro industry, chips and processors can do what they do because of the laws of physics; that is, efficient cause.

Third, Marion argues that self-organizing interaction intrinsically seeks order (that is, coherent pattern) and is therefore characterized by teleological causality. He distinguishes between non-deliberate and deliberate teleology.

Non-deliberate, or bottom up, teleological cause is the blind need that living systems have to operate mutually on their environment in order to survive and in doing this they co-create the environment in which they live. They unintentionally affect each other's survival; indeed, they create each other's possibility of survival. For example, the organizations producing peripherals for microcomputers can only do so because microcomputers exist and microcomputers need the peripherals in order to function. The micro producers did not intend to create market niches for others but, simply by being there, they did so, and the resulting existence of the peripheral producers was essential to the operation of the micro producers. Although there is no overall purpose, intention or plan, the different kinds of organization have a mutual need to be what they are in order for any of them to survive.

Deliberate teleology arises because human agents perceive their need to survive and work deliberately to achieve that need. Humans form intentions and they set goals – for example, IBM's decision to enter the micro market.

Marion argues that both deliberate and non-deliberate types of teleological causality are operative in human systems, making it impossible for humans to control them through deliberate action alone because non-deliberate teleology and self-organizing interaction play such an important role. One human being may intentionally choose an action. However, the realization of that action will depend not simply on that choice but on the presence and action, both intentional and unintentional, of other humans. Together they co-create their environment in a way that none of them individually, or collectively, can intentionally choose, just as happened with the microcomputer industry.

The fourth element of Marion's causal framework is natural selection. The emergent structure or pattern of behavior caused by self-organization, non-deliberate and deliberate teleology, is subjected to natural selection. Marion argues that competitive selection operates on human behavioral patterns that are caused by self-organization, non-deliberate and deliberate teleology. The operation of competitive selection is obvious in the example of the microcomputer industry.

An evaluation of Marion's notion of causality

So, Marion argues that form, or pattern, in an industry is fundamentally caused by self-organizing interaction between organizational entities at a local level, constrained by the laws of physics and driven by non-deliberate, purposeless need to operate mutually on the environment in order to survive. This is essentially the same as Kauffman's argument in relation to biological evolution. Marion describes this process of self-organization in terms that are consistent with what we have been calling Transformative Teleology: the interaction between the diverse entities produces unpredictable new patterns. He then combines self-organization with non-deliberate teleology; that is, a version of the struggle for survival that is a central feature of Adaptionist Teleology.

For us, there is a major problem with what Marion does here. He focuses at a macro level and talks about a population of impersonal organizations (IBM and Apple for example) interacting with each other in a self-organizing manner, driven by an urge to survive. He is talking about this population and the organizations of which it consists as if they were no different from a population of organisms. However, what are these organizations? They are not organisms, or anything like organisms, but, rather, patterns of joint human action. Marion reifies organizations and treats them as if they were things, or organisms, apart from, or outside of humans, interacting according to principles that apply to them at a macro level, split off from the humans that constitute them. The principles governing these systems are taken to be the same as those governing non-human systems.

To this Marion adds the deliberate teleology of human beings, by which he means what we call Rationalist Teleology. The result is that humans, acting according to Rationalist Teleology, find themselves having to act within a system that is somehow independent of them, operating according to the causal principles of self-organization and non-deliberate teleology. The latter considerably restricts the scope humans have for realizing their intentions. Patterns in human action, then, emerge as the "both/and" paradigm of both human choice and a system with a life of its own.

At this point, natural selection becomes operative, with its competitive sifting between the forms presented to it. In our terms this is Adaptionist Teleology at the level of the industry.

In the terms we are using, therefore, Marion's explanation combines Adaptionist, Rationalist and something like Transformative Teleology. We regard the combination of these three causal frameworks as a completely incompatible way of explaining the evolution of human action, for reasons explained in Chapter 3. They are alternatives that logically exclude each other and we think Marion's attempt to combine them leads to a split between human individuals making choices, explained by Rationalist Teleology, and the systems they constitute. In addition to being affected by human choice these systems also have a life of their own quite independent of human choices, explained by a combination of Adaptionist and some aspects of Transformative Teleology.

Our view is that Marion's approach encounters much the same difficulty as that of Allen's. Both focus their attention at the level of a population of organizations, regard those organizations as independent entities having a life of their own, and implicitly assume some split between the macro system, to be explained according to one causal structure, and human action to be explained according to another. This is exactly what systems thinkers do (see Chapter 4). The difficulty with this is that both levels are about human action and one would, therefore, expect the same causal structure to apply to both. In seeking to develop a notion of Transformative Teleology, informed by the complexity sciences, we are interested in exploring the possibility of one causal framework applying at both macro and micro levels.

The problem with the macro approaches we have so far reviewed is that, while they reach very important and challenging conclusions about the nature of management, they leave the management process itself largely unexplored. Many other management complexity writers, however, do focus specifically on the management process and it is to these that we now turn.

Complexity and the dynamics of organizations: sustaining the illusion of control

So far, this chapter has reviewed examples of the use of the complexity sciences to make sense of organizational life that point to what Chapter 3 identified as Transformative Teleology. In doing this, they question taken-for-granted assumptions about management in important ways. However, they do so in a way that we think continues within the tradition of systems thinking to objectify organizations and so encounter difficulties in explaining the management process itself. This section turns to examples of those who use the complexity sciences primarily as a source of loose metaphor for organizations, selecting elements of thinking in the natural sciences of complexity in a way that preserves the implicit assumptions about causality underlying the dominant discourse on management. They preserve intact the framework of Formative Teleology found in the systems thinking discussed in Chapter 2. We argue that the consequence is essentially a new fad rather than a serious challenge to current ways of making sense of life in organizations.

To justify that claim, this section reviews, as examples of what we are talking about, the work of Wheatley (1992), Wheatley and Kellner-Rogers (1996), MacIntosh and MacLean (1999), Beinhocker (1999), Brown and Eisenhardt (1998), Connor (1998), Morgan (1997), Sanders (1998), Nonaka (1991), Nonaka and Takeuchi (1995), Pascale (1999), Lissack and Roos (1999), Kelly and Allison (1999), and Lewin and Regine (2000). All of these writers, implicitly or explicitly, point to the limitations of the notion of efficient causality but continue to rely on Formative Teleology in their interpretation of what the complexity sciences might mean for organizations. Running through this literature are the following three causes of emergent behavior:

- Self-organizing interaction, driven by simple rules, that reveals hidden order.
- The dynamics of far-from-equilibrium states, or the edge of chaos.
- Fitness landscapes.

Consider each of these in turn.

Simple rules and hidden order

Almost all of the writers who use the complexity sciences primarily as a source of metaphor emphasize how large numbers of agents interacting with each other according to a few simple rules can produce global, emergent patterns of coherent behavior. Chapter 6 explained why this is Formative Teleology, a causal structure that does not encompass the possibility of novelty. Consider how the concept of simple rules is used.

Wheatley (1992) makes this one of the foundations of her exposition. She holds that the "New Sciences" reveal how order is created by a few guiding principles rather than complex controls. This, she says, makes us aware of how we share our yearning for simplicity with nature and proposes that simple rules provide the basis of a simpler, more caring way of running organizations. She formulates this into an inspirational call for a return to a more natural way of managing human affairs. Wheatley talks about the need to understand the deeper reality, the hidden order, of organizational life and life in general, one that ideas from complexity can help to uncover. This resonates with somewhat "New Age" views about ancient wisdom and connection to deep levels of primal reality. This view, that there is something essential, fundamental or deep lying behind or underneath behavior and causing it, is clearly Formative Teleology. The form that emerges is already enfolded, already there, in these deep, primitive levels. This is not a transformative view in which behavior, including potentially novel behavior that is in no sense already there, emerges in the interaction of the entities and nothing more. There is no more fundamental level than these interactions.

The approach adopted by Lewin and Regine (2000) has much in common with that of Wheatley. They point to the central concern of the complexity sciences, namely interaction or relationship. They claim that human systems are complex adaptive systems and they equate interactions between abstract entities in complexity models with human relationships without any justification for doing so. Human relationships are then equated with "caring" and the notion of "soul" is imported from a completely different discourse to that of complexity, again without any justification. The simple rules idea is then brought to play to explain how human systems of caring, with soul, can be brought about. It seems that here the complexity sciences are being used as a rhetorical device to support an ideological position, rather as Wheatley does.

Brown and Eisenhardt (1998) give a more detailed account of the importance of simple rules. They talk about a few simple rules generating very complex adaptive behavior in the flocking of birds, as shown in the Boids simulation. They extend this notion to the resilience of democratic government and the successful performance of corporations, without, however, providing any justification for such an extension. In doing this, they ignore the fact that flocking is one attractor for bird behavior, one that already exists. The few simple rules that produce it will not produce spontaneous jumps to new attractors. If success for corporations over the long term requires a move to new attractors, then the metaphor of the Boids is not well chosen. However, the authors proceed, much as Wheatley does, to prescriptions to improvise while relying on a few key rules. Kelly and Allison (1999), as well as Lissack and Roos (1999) also stress this "simple rules" idea.

Morgan (1997) presents another variation on the simple rules notion. He points to the order that can emerge from interaction governed by a few simple rules and equates this with his notion of "minimum specs"; that is, avoiding a grand design and specifying a small number of critical variables to attend to. He says that minimum specs define an attractor and create the context within which a system will move to it. What he seems to ignore in this approach is, again, that if the requirement is some new form, then the rules, or the context, that will produce that form do not exist yet. If emergence depends critically on small changes then there is no way to specify what they are in advance. One could not ensure that one has detected all of them or measured them accurately enough. Morgan passes over this and recommends that managers should manage the context and allow self-organization to do the rest. He recommends surfacing the existing attractor that is locking an organization into a stable position, determining whether it should be changed and then, if it is to be changed, identifying the small changes, or leverage points, that will transform the system. Managers are called upon to identify, in advance, what the new ground rules are supposed to be.

MacIntosh and MacLean (1999) present yet another variation on this theme. They claim that dissipative structures rely on deep structure for the order they display. This deep structure is a quasi-permanent, invisible sub-structure that remains largely intact, while manifest, observable structures break down at bifurcation points. They equate this rather dubious interpretation of Prigogine's model of change with self-reference in which the self being referred to is something of a hidden essence, a hidden order already there, waiting, as it were, to be revealed. Prigogine, however, is talking about the emergence of new order that is not already there, but is truly novel. The next step, for these authors, is to equate this deep structure with a few simple rules in organizations that define business logic and operate as organizing principles. They suggest that change occurs in an organization when these hidden simple rules are surfaced, reframed and then enacted during the chaotic transformation characteristic of a bifurcation point.

The role of managers is to manage this deep structure. In this way, managers condition the emergence. The authors claim that "pure" self-organization may occur in nature but need not be accepted by people in organizations. By operating on deep structures, managers can have a limited influence on the outcomes of self-organization. They claim that self-organization in nature is spontaneous, random and unpredictable but that organizations have the capacity to change deep structure, or archetype, by creating the conditions in which successful transformation can occur. Although the outcome is dependent on sensitive conditions, managers can detect them and then amplify or damp them to bring about the change they want, more or less. Pascale's (1999) notion of designed emergence is of much the same kind as MacIntosh and MacLean's conditioned emergence, as is that of Sanders (1998). Others who take this kind of perspective on deep structure, or human essence, are Wheatley (1992) and Lewin and Regine (2000).

The causal framework

By now, it should be evident that the causal framework all of these writers are implicitly using is that of Formative Teleology (see Chapter 2) governing a system about which humans can make choices; that is, Rationalist Teleology. This is the same causal framework as that underlying the dominant discourse on management. For example, simple rules as formative cause can be chosen and their implementation guided by managers' choices. If they choose correctly then they get what they want. This amounts to a negation of self-organization and emergence. If managers are choosing what "emerges," then it is not emerging. If they have a blueprint guiding self-organization then it is not self-organization – that is, it is not agents acting purely on the basis of their own local organizing principles, but rather on the basis of simple rules chosen for them. Emergence is relegated to the level of the superficial while managers remain in control of the fundamentals. There is, for us, a contradiction between the loss of freedom this choice of simple rules and control of the fundamental implies for the many, and the call for caring relationships. The result is the dominant discourse dressed up in new jargon. Freedom here is interpreted not as freedom to choose one's own next step but to choose the state of the whole system, and as such it is confined to a powerful few and stripped from the rest, on the one hand, or equated with democracy on the other. Neither of these positions needs the complexity sciences to justify them. Furthermore, the emphasis on a few simple rules driving the behavior of all agents in an organization completely misses the fundamental importance of fluctuation and diversity.

The result is a theory that has nothing new to say about the generation of the truly novel. The way in which the concept of causality is used, therefore, has very important consequences. When causality is implicitly used as it is by those who emphasize a few simple rules, the consequence is the closing down of further thinking of the nature of control in organizations, on the one hand, and the nature of creative processes in organizations, on the other. The simple rules idea adds nothing to the dominant discourse other than new terminology, and is therefore likely to have a short life in our view.

At least as popular as the simple rules idea is that of the dynamic at the edge of chaos.

The edge of chaos

The use of this metaphor ranges from the highly simplistic to the somewhat more sophisticated. An example taken from the highly simplistic end of the spectrum is provided by the work of Brown and Eisenhardt (1998).

For Brown and Eisenhardt, the "edge of chaos" is a central concept and they interpret it in organizations as formal systems characterized by neither too little nor too much structure. Organizations at the edge of chaos are those that are only partially structured in formal terms. This interpretation of the "edge" metaphor immediately loses the paradoxical quality of the edge of chaos. Partial structure is not a state of contradictory forces that can never be resolved but, rather, a simple balance: too much structure produces stability and too little produces chaos, while a balance between the two produces the dynamics of the edge of chaos. When an organization is at the edge, its managers allow a semi-coherent strategy to emerge; that is, one that is neither too fixed nor too fluid.

This approach completely loses the sophisticated concept of self-organizing criticality in which a system evolves to the edge of chaos through its own internal dynamic, where self-organization produces potentially novel strategies, again through the system's own internal dynamic. Instead, in Brown and Eisenhardt's version, managers are "allowing" strategies to emerge.

The edge of chaos is a dynamic that occurs when certain parameters fall within a critical range – for example, critical rates of information flow, degrees of connectivity and diversity between agents. When Brown and Eisenhardt take the edge of chaos as a metaphor for organizations, they immediately collapse these parameters into one of formal organizational structure, which then becomes a choice for managers to make. Managers can choose to install just enough structure to move their organization to the edge of chaos, where it can experience relentless change. Brown and Eisenhardt provide a questionnaire that managers can use to identify whether they are at the edge of chaos or trapped in one of the other dynamics. They then give prescriptions for moving to the edge, if they are not already there. Managers should foster frequent change in the context of a few strict rules. They should keep activity loosely structured and also rely on targets and deadlines. They should create channels for real-time, fact-based communication within and across groups. Self-organization as local interaction amongst agents producing emergent outcomes is lost. Complexity may mean that managers cannot choose detailed outcomes, but according to this simplistic view of the dynamics at the edge of chaos, they certainly can choose the dynamic of their system. This is pure Rationalist Teleology.

The power law

This move completely ignores a key feature of the edge of chaos; namely, the power law. The small numbers of large extinction events and the large numbers of small extinctions that occur periodically mean that there is no guarantee of survival at the edge of chaos, only the possibility of new forms emerging that might survive. Managers cannot choose these extinction events, nor can they avoid them since they are a property of the internal dynamic of a complex system. Nowhere do the authors mention this power law. Instead, they make a simplistic equation between being at the edge of chaos and success. Because they implicitly think within a framework of Formative and Rationalist Teleology, they miss the constraints in self-organization. As Marion convincingly argues, managers in a single organization cannot choose the dynamic for their industry or their organization because the dynamic emerges from the interaction within the whole population of organizations in an industry. Also conspicuously absent in the Brown and Eisenhardt argument is the importance of fluctuations and diversity so often emphasized by Allen.

Morgan (1997) also ignores the power law. He uses chaos and complexity theory as the basis of one of his metaphors for organizations, namely the organization as flux and transformation. He says that some kind of ordering is always likely to be a feature of complex systems. However, this is not necessarily so. A complex system can self-organize into disintegration just as it can into a rigid, repetitive pattern. Furthermore, even when it operates at the edge of chaos there is the potential for the emergence of a new form, which no one can know the shape of in advance, and it may well not be one that leads to survival because of the power law and competitive selection. For Morgan, the manager is also one who identifies the minimum specs and then creates the context for them to produce self-organization capable of novelty. He also talks about managers "allowing it to happen." Here too, the essential generator of novelty – diversity – receives little attention.

Wheatley (1992) claims that living systems do not seek equilibrium but, rather, maintain themselves in a state of off-balance so that they can change and grow. She finds this a natural and therefore comforting notion, one that returns us to ideas more in keeping with an affinity to the primitive forces of nature to be found in ancient wisdom. For Wheatley, then, organizational functioning in states of non-equilibrium is natural and non-threatening to people, at least once its nature is understood, because there is always recognizable pattern in the change.

The edge of chaos as crisis

However, others describe that state in much more threatening terms. For example, Connor (1998) talks about the need to promote change relentlessly, as do Sanders (1998) and Brown and Eisenhardt (1998). For them, the comfortable notion of equilibrium yields to a view of organizational life that is hectic and pressured. Nonaka and Takeuchi (1995), Pascale (1999), and many other writers, equate the edge of chaos with crisis and a state in which managers are stretched and stressed. They then recommend that managers should create crisis and stretch/stress conditions in order to push their system to the edge where it can be creative. Although MacIntosh and MacLean (1999) draw a distinction between far-from-equilibrium conditions and the edge of chaos, a distinction that they never explain, they use the former in much the same way as the other authors already referred to. Having identified the new archetype, or deep structure, that they want, managers are then supposed to move their organization to a far-from-equilibrium state to create the space for the new archetype to take hold. They talk about this occurring through a bifurcation, which sounds very much like the crisis and stretch that the other authors refer to. They also incorrectly draw a distinction between far-from-equilibrium states and the edge of chaos, arguing that the former has to do with major discontinuous change while the latter only explains continuous change. This is incorrect because, once again, it takes no account of power law dynamics at the edge of chaos, which are essentially about both small continuous and large discontinuous change. For us, this perspective loses the paradox of stability and instability altogether by moving from the stability pole to its opposite – endless instability. Systems are *either* stable and so cannot change, *or* they are unstable and so can change.

Yet others retain the notion of equilibrium to some extent by describing system change in terms of a cycle. For example, Beinhocker (1999) understands the evolution of a complex system in terms of punctuated equilibrium, in which stable states are interrupted by significant discontinuous change before moving to other stable states. This view of the relationship between stability and instability is also to be found in MacIntosh and MacLean. They use Prigogine's phases of development far-from-equilibrium to posit a cycle of change in organizations that moves from stability, or normal equilibrium, through a bifurcation that is described in terms of crisis and chaos and a period of experimentation, out of which emerges a new order. Hurst (1995) also proposes a cyclical view of movement from conservation, through creative destruction (crisis and confusion requiring charismatic leadership), to renewal (creative networking), then exploitation (choice and entrepreneurial action) and back to conservation through strategic management. When the dynamics of change are described in these terms, the paradox of stability and instability is also lost, this time by proposing a sequential process incorporating *both* stability *and* instability that follow each other *sequentially*.

It seems to be very difficult to hold the paradox of both stability and instability simultaneously in order to grapple with what it might mean for making sense of life in organizations.

The edge of chaos and the very similar concept of far-from-equilibrium conditions are formative causes. In other words, the behavior of a complex system is formed, or caused, by the dynamical qualities of the edge of chaos or far-from-equilibrium state. The entities comprising the system are not the causes of the pattern in a direct sense. It is not the individual entities but their dynamic interaction in "edge" conditions that cause the emergent pattern of behavior. The dynamic conditions at the edge are not chosen by any entity in the system, but evolution to the edge is itself a property of, and is caused by, the internal dynamic of the system; that is, the interactions between entities. Marion's (1999) example of the microcomputer industry illustrates how this happens in industries. The internal dynamic of a system cannot be chosen by a system on its own because it is in interaction with other systems that the internal dynamic of each is formed as a property of the network of networks.

The question then becomes whether this is a useful metaphor for understanding organizations. It is evident from the above review that the writers referred to are claiming to use the "edge" as a metaphor, but in ignoring the importance of the internal dynamic as formative cause they are in fact not using it at all. Their metaphors may be useful but it is misleading to claim that they are derived from concepts of the edge of chaos or far-from-equilibrium conditions. The metaphorical uses surveyed in this section all fall within the causal frameworks of combined Formative and Rationalist Teleology.

The concept of fitness landscapes is less frequently used, but when it is it tends to be done with much the same implicit notions of causality as those underlying simple rules and the edge of chaos.

Fitness landscapes

An example of how the concept of fitness landscapes is used is provided in a paper by Beinhocker (1999). He suggests that an organization's strategies can be thought of as a population searching a fitness landscape, where fitness is defined in terms of profit. He directly transfers to human organizations the notion of genetic networks in biology searching a landscape where fitness is defined in terms of survival (see Chapters 3 and 6).

A random mutation in a gene is thought of as a move across the landscape, climbing toward a peak if the mutation increases fitness and descending toward a valley if fitness is reduced. Mostly the moves are incremental (that is, to a nearby state), but sometimes the genetic network jumps across the landscape in a discontinuous change. The shape of the landscape is determined by the internal connectivity of agents within a system and the external connectivity with other systems, the latter causing the landscapes of each system to heave about. The shape of the landscape operates as formative cause in the following sense. If the landscape is too rugged and heaves about too much because connectivity is too high, then moves will not often increase fitness. The whole system will be racked with frequent large extinction events. If the landscape is too smooth, systems can easily get trapped on sub-optimal peaks and the whole network of networks will be too easily affected by system moves so that frequent avalanches of large extinction events will also be likely. When landscapes are rugged, but not too rugged, both small moves and large jumps are more likely to increase fitness and thus survival.

Beinhocker conceives of a population of strategies in the same way. Some strategies represent incremental moves up profit peaks or down profit valleys, and other strategies amount to discontinuous jumps to other parts of the profit landscape. He says, following Kauffman, that the rules for success are the same for strategies as they are for genes; namely, a small number of jumps combined with a large number of incremental moves. He then ignores how the shape of the landscape is determined by the internal dynamic of the network of networks, the connectivity, or interaction between systems, and proposes that managers should manage a population of multiple strategies rather than have a single focus. In effect, he assumes that the profit landscape for a particular organization is given. This is Formative Teleology again. This is supposed to make it possible for managers to "harness" the forces of evolution through a population of strategies that is more robust and adaptive than a single focus. He claims that this adaptive population *will* produce positive results under a wide range of conditions, even though the results may not be optimal. Again, the power law is ignored. The prescriptions are for managers to keep moving, which means creating a culture of restlessness and discomfort with the status quo, simultaneously employing multiple strategies and mixing incremental and discontinuous changes. He provides a questionnaire for managers to determine whether their population of strategies is robust and adaptive enough. He offers his approach as an alternative to political processes of decision-making. He admits that his conclusions are not new but claims that complexity shows them to be essential. Once again, complexity is taken to mean hectic action, stress and discomfort.

Kauffman (see Chapter 5) uses fitness landscapes as a metaphor for a dynamic temporal process internal to a system, but since it is a spatial metaphor the temporal nature of what it points to can easily be lost. When that happens, the fitness landscape is no longer thought of as depicting the system's own internal dynamic but as some condition or context within which the system is moving. The result is the kind of description given above of a population of "strategies" wandering across a space, with some more or less "fit" than others. The connections between them and how the dynamics of those connections create the landscape is lost. The same thing happens when bits of knowledge are thought of as moving across a landscape (Roos and Oliver, 1999).

Again, those using the notion of a fitness landscape as a metaphor for organizations do so within the framework of Formative Teleology and management choice as Rationalist Teleology. This has implications for predictability.

Predictability

Almost everybody who uses insights from the nonlinear sciences refers to the problem of predictability, but usually with enormous ambivalence. For example, Connor (1998) states that it makes no sense to maintain a sense of balance by foreseeing distinct events in an unstable environment. However, he is adamant that this should not stop managers trying to guess what will happen because they might just be right. He claims that success becomes a matter of guesswork and taking bets with long odds. In other passages, however, he talks about how important predictability and personal sense of control are. He talks about a continuum from predictability to instability, viewing the latter as a temporary and rather unfortunate phenomenon to be dealt with by reliance on responsive processes. In this way, the "nimble" organization secures a sense of control. Beinhocker (1999) also points to the limits to predictability and concludes that reliance on a single strategy is inappropriate. Instead, managers should develop a population of strategies so that at least some of them will turn out to be successful.

Those who do recognize radical forms of unpredictability, and therefore the limitations of strategic planning, nevertheless emphasize the need for vision. They usually explain that by this they do not mean a picture of a future state, or a destination, but clarity about purpose and direction. Wheatley (1992), for example, sees vision as an invisible field that permeates an organization and shapes desired behaviors. For Hurst (1995), vision is the formulation by an individual of a transcendent, over the horizon, goal for an organization. In both cases the underlying causality is, once more, that of Formative Teleology. However, the problem of what is desired behavior and what are appropriate goals in a system whose future is radically unpredictable is not normally addressed. If the future is radically unpredictable this means that one cannot rely on the desired outcome of an action. How then does it help to formulate such a desire for the whole system?

Yet others make even more unsuccessful attempts to deal with the recognized problem of unpredictability in nonlinear systems. For example, Sanders (1998) claims that pictures of strange attractors allow one to see the order hidden in disorder. However, strange attractors are not "real" pictures. They are abstract mathematical concepts. She says that it is possible to identify a system's initial conditions because it is deterministic, but that it is difficult to predict its future state because it is nonlinear. Of course, this statement is wrong because it is impossible to forecast the long-term state of a nonlinear deterministic system precisely because it is not possible to identify the initial conditions to the infinite exactness required. Determinism is a theory of causality and implies nothing whatsoever about the ability to measure initial conditions.

However, Sanders proceeds to argue that despite an inability to make predictions of long-term states it is possible to provide qualitative descriptions of whole system behavior over time. This may be true, but only for the attractor that the system is currently drawn to. It would not be possible to describe any new attractor that some system was capable of spontaneously jumping to, until the jump occurred. Sanders tries to get around this by saying that it is possible to identify what she calls "perking" information. These are the new initial conditions to which a system may be sensitive, that is, changes or developments that are already taking shape just below the surface. It takes peripheral vision, or well-developed foresight skills, to recognize a system's initial conditions as they are emerging. This enables one to see change coming and so influence it to one's advantage. Recognizing these conditions before they emerge is the new leverage point. This attempt runs into the same problem as before. It is not possible to identify all of the initial conditions and measure all of them with infinite accuracy. So how can you have foresight if you cannot predict? What is peripheral vision? Unpredictability is mentioned and then, in effect, ignored.

Brown and Eisenhardt (1998) take a similar tack. They talk about strategy as an unpredictable, uncontrollable, relentless struggle for competitive advantage. They then immediately state that managing change means reacting to the unexpected as a defensive tactic and anticipation, that is, gaining insight into what is likely to occur and then positioning to meet it. It could also mean foreseeing the emergence of new customer segments. For them, the highest level of managing change is leading change by dominating markets, setting the rhythm and pace for the others. So, on the same page they talk about a strategy that is unpredictable and uncontrollable and then prescribe foresight and the domination of markets. They imply that this is a choice that it is possible for managers to make all on their own. Having said that the future is unpredictable, they immediately call for anticipation and foreseeing the emergence.

The ambivalence about the unpredictable nature of complex systems is, of course, tightly coupled with the concern about control. If one holds the paradox of predictability and unpredictability, it requires a continuing exploration of what control means in such situations. What it is unlikely to mean, of course, is that powerful individuals can be "in control" of their organization. This is at least unpalatable to many and anxiety-raising to most, both leaders and led. The result is talking about unpredictability in a manner that never leaves the dominant discourse because it stays within the split between a system governed by Formative Teleology and a chooser governed by Rationalist Teleology.

Conclusion

This chapter has explored the implicit and explicit assumptions that are being made about the nature of causality when notions of complexity in the natural sciences are used to explain the functioning of human organizations and the roles of their managers and leaders. Many of those now writing about complexity in organizations select one or more of three insights from the complexity sciences for application to human activity, and the way these are then used depends upon the implicit or explicit assumptions that are made about causality.

The most popular of these insights is the demonstrated possibility that coherent behavioral patterns of great complexity can emerge when large numbers of agents interact with each other in a self-organizing way according to simple relational rules. This immediately places them within the causal framework of Formative Teleology. The next implicit move is to assume that the manager can choose the simple rules that will yield a desired pattern of outcomes. This immediately places them in the framework of Rationalist Teleology. The result is a causal framework that is exactly the same as that to be found in the dominant management discourse. It is hardly surprising, then, that the conclusions drawn about what complexity means for management have to do with being in control. Self-organization becomes another term for empowerment, which is really a more idealistic word for delegation. This immediate drive to reduce complexity to simplicity, with its focus on "rules," leads to no new insight into how organizations function. This matters, because the call for new ways of thinking about management arises, it seems to us, from the repeated, frustrating experience of managers who find that they cannot do what they are supposed to do, namely to stay in control. Simply reproducing the dominant discourse does not help to make sense of that frustration; that is to say, it does not help us in talking about how people are really "getting things done."

When one succumbs to the powerful drive to reduce complexity to simplicity one loses sight of what is so striking about the possibility of self-organizing interaction producing emergent coherence. This is a striking proposition because it suggests that the internal dynamic of a network of relationships is itself the cause of the coherent patterns of behavior displayed by the network and the cause of transformations in those coherent patterns. This points to Transformative Teleology.

There is another aspect to this powerful desire to reduce complexity to simplicity. It rapidly leads to the notion of an already existing hidden order waiting, as it were, to be revealed or unleashed. This is then reflected in the notion of deep structures underlying coherent behavior and a Romantic call for a return to more "natural," more primeval, more harmonious ways of behaving – one that humans can choose. This sidesteps the essential role, in the emergence of novelty, of diversity and the conflicting constraints that relationships impose. It sidelines the fundamental transformative cause of power relations and politics in relation to human action. The drive to simplicity slides over the fundamentally paradoxical nature of the transformative processes producing novelty. Novelty means coherent pattern that has never existed before, not some hidden form that already exists but has not yet been revealed. Diversity and conflicting constraints (that is, power relations) are all essential to the emergence of true novelty. This is one of the central insights coming from the complexity sciences that is simply missed when one thinks in terms of hidden order and deep structures. Creativity is intimately intertwined with destruction and this insight is concealed when harmony and sharing are placed at the center.

The move from thinking about what emerges as hidden order to what emerges as novelty also has important implications for how one thinks about causality. The latter is not the reproduction of a pre-given form, the realization of a hidden, real identity. It is, rather, both the repetition and potential transformation, the perpetual construction, of its identity. As we see it, a central problem running through the work we have reviewed is this. When one thinks of the organization as an objectified system, it is easy to take principles used to explain a system in nature and apply them directly or metaphorically to "the organization" as if it were like a natural system. The easiest and most familiar way to do this is within the framework of Formative Teleology. Then the human manager, like the natural scientist, enters the picture and operates within a Rationalist Teleology in order to manipulate "the organization," rather like the applied scientists manipulates nature. Then Adaptionist Teleology, incorporating competitive selection might be applied. These ways of thinking are deeply rooted in Western thought and are very difficult to get out of.

The real difficulty is that "the organization" is people and "the manager" and "the leader" are amongst them. Applying one causal framework to the organizations and another to management choice continues in the tradition of systems thinking and is, therefore, a very approximate and rather dubious move. Our interest in exploring the implications of Transformative Teleology for life in organizations could not, therefore be accomplished simply by substituting Transformative Teleology for the Formative one. A further extension is required, that of dropping Rationalist Teleology and thinking about life in organizations, about choice, intention and action all within the same causal framework, that of Transformative Teleology.

8 Complexity and human action

Understanding human action from the perspective of Rationalist Teleology (see Chapter 2) focuses attention in a particular way. First, the human individual is taken as primary and that individual is understood as autonomous. This means that it is the individual who autonomously chooses goals and actions. The motivation for such choice arises in the individual and the choice comes before action, which is directed toward other humans and the non-human world. Second, this autonomous individual chooses goals, and the actions to achieve them, in a rational manner. In other words, individuals think about what they should, or want to, achieve in a given situation and then use reason to work out how to achieve the goal in that situation. The reasoning individual need not be, and usually is not, fully aware of the process of choice, especially when the action is highly skilled. Then individuals may choose on the basis of implicit or tacit knowledge.

Rationalist Teleology, therefore, places the individual at the center of any understanding of human action and regards groups as collectives formed by individuals, collectives that might constitute the main features of the situation in which the individual acts. The group situation might enable, or might constrain, what the individual seeks to do, or both. This Rationalist Teleology underlies mainstream thinking in functionalist sociology, as well as in cognitivist and humanistic psychology. Psychoanalytic theories also understand human action in these terms, with one important difference. The process of choosing goals and actions is not purely, or even mainly, rational but, rather, unconscious and irrational.

This chapter first describes how the dominant discourse on management is built on Rationalist Teleology. It then argues that when management complexity writers employ concepts from the complexity sciences, they make the translation to human action primarily using the framework of Rationalist Teleology, just as systems thinkers do. This move, we believe, makes it very difficult to hold onto the challenge that concepts from the complexity sciences could present to current management thinking. Finally, the chapter describes thinking in sociology and psychology about human action that seems to us to reflect Transformative Teleology. We believe that it is this kind of thinking, potentially illuminated by concepts from the complexity sciences, that holds out the potential for challenging the dominant discourse on management. For us, it represents a decisive move away from systems thinking.

Human action in the dominant management discourse: focusing on the individual

Chapter 4 pointed to the development of management science in the early years of the twentieth century by the engineers Taylor and Fayol. Taylor (1911) held that individuals were more efficient than groups, believing that individuals were pulled down to rabble-like behavior when they were "herded" into groups. His aim was to remove emotion and other forms of irrationality from organizational processes, and Fayol ([1916] 1948) took the same view. Both made the same assumption, namely that human action is essentially individual action and that managers are objective observers who stand outside the processes of the organization and design them according to rational criteria to do with goal achievement. This was meant to remove emotion so that the organization could operate most efficiently in realizing its goals, all quite consistent with the behaviorist psychology of the time. Chapter 4 also pointed to the views of social psychologists in the Human Relations School who thought that individuals formed groups; that groups were the sum of the individuals in them; and that groups were only effective when individual members were motivated, loyal and shared the same beliefs and goals. Managers should, therefore, choose conditions and motivators that lead to group harmony. This whole way of thinking about human action clearly reflects the causal framework of Rationalist Teleology.

These ideas continue to underlie the dominant management discourse's assumptions about the relationship between the individual and the group and the importance of conformity, but they have been added to in significant ways by the development of cognitivist psychology. It is cognitivist psychology that forms the foundation of Rationalist Teleology in today's dominant discourse on management.

Computers, cognitivism and the importance of conformity

Chapter 4 referred to the overlap between the development of systems theories, computers and cognitivist psychology. The cognitivist claim, which rapidly replaced behaviorism, is that human brains and minds are cybernetic systems, or deductive machines that function according to logical processing principles like computers (Gardner, 1985). Just as computers process digital symbols, so the human brain processes symbols taking the form of electro-chemical activity in the brain to form representations of external reality into internal templates that are more or less accurate pictures of that external world. According to this view, the brain acts as a passive mirror of reality and the mirror images of the world are said to be stored in specific parts of the brain in the sense that a stimulus, say a particular light wave, always triggers the same sequence of firing neurons. The brain is said to directly register already existing real properties of the world external to it, and the templates so formed are the basis upon which humans know and act. Repeated exposure to the same stimulus supposedly strengthens connections along a specific neuronal pathway, so making a perception an increasingly accurate representation of reality. The template so formed is said to be stored in the memory and then compared with other stimuli and categorized, forming the basis of the responses of the body. Representing and storing are essentially cybernetic processes in that there is a fixed point of reference (external reality), and negative feedback of the gap between the internal picture and external reality. There is a self-regulating process that closes this gap. Knowing, knowledge creation and learning are essentially adaptive feedback processes, according to this theory.

Furthermore, cognitivism holds that there is a separate entity that does this representing and storing. This is a "centered" theory in the sense that the biological individual is at the center of the whole process of knowing and acting, and also in the internal sense of processes centered in particular parts of the brain. Since all normal individuals have much the same biologically determined brain structures, and all their brains are processing symbolic representations of the same pre-given reality, there is no fundamental problem in individuals sharing the same perceptions as far as cognitivism is concerned. The transmission of messages from one brain to another, and the sharing of information between them, is simply not thought to pose significant questions.

It is this view of human behavior, entirely consistent with systems thinking, that forms the fundamental assumptions about human action underlying the dominant discourse on management. It is quite evident in the Argyris (1990) construct of mental models and similar notions of schemas, cognitive maps and rules of behavior. These notions amount to the proposition that as people act, they build up mental models and maps of the world in which they are acting and of the way in which they respond to this world. Such thinking may also take a more constructivist form (von Glasersfeld, 1991); that is, one that recognizes limited human cognitive capability, requiring people to select parts of reality for attention, so excluding other parts. The result is a framework of major importance to the theory of the learning organization and is increasingly becoming part of the vocabulary of practicing managers.

Argyris and Schön (1978) developed the notion of mental models into a theory of learning that underlies discussion about the learning organization. They distinguished between single and double loop learning. In single loop learning people hold their mental models constant and act according to them. This works while the environment in which they built the model remains the same. However, it gives rise to skilled incompetence if the environment changes and the person carries on behaving according to the same mental model. Double loop learning is then required to change the mental model to a more appropriate one, a change that humans can supposedly choose to make on an individual basis.

Mental models are said to be largely below the level of awareness, but it is held that people are able to surface the unquestioned assumptions they are making about the world and change them. Argyris (1990) pointed to how difficult people find this and how, as a consequence, they employ many defensive routines to avoid having to do so. For example, they make matters undiscussable. The notion that most knowledge is below the level of awareness has come to feature prominently in the theory of knowledge creation in organizations (Nonaka and Takeuchi, 1995). It is often expressed in terms of the difference between the explicit knowledge of which people are aware and the tacit knowledge, below the level of awareness, which is the basis of skilled behavior (Polanyi and Prosch, 1975). It is then thought that knowledge creation in an organization requires managers to share mental models and to make implicit knowledge explicit so that it can be codified and so retained by the organization. The problems of what it is that they share and how they come to share it are usually dealt with by suggesting that people mimic each other.

This is what Rationalist Teleology means in current organizational theorizing. The theory focuses on the autonomous individual, and relating to other humans is an action that might affect the individual's mind but plays no fundamental role in constructing it. Notice what happens in the cognitivist argument about the nature of an individual mind. It is understood as a system, or model, which the individual having the mind can observe and choose to change. The individual becomes the objective observer of his own mind, understood like other objectively observed systems to be governed by a causal framework other than Rationalist Teleology, which governs only the choice about changing the mind. In cognitivism the observed mind is assumed to be a system governed by Formative Teleology in that it is a model of the world, already containing assumed features of the world. Double loop learning is then the choice of someone (Rationalist Teleology) standing outside this system, which is governed by another causal framework (Formative Teleology). This point was made in Chapter 4 in relation to systems thinking.

This focus on the autonomous individual and the split it entails between the individual mind as a system subject to one kind of causality and a chooser subject to another, is also central to the use of humanistic psychology in organizational theory.

Humanistic psychology

While the cognitive psychologists focused on the cognitive capacities of individuals, a number of other psychologists in the humanistic psychology tradition focused on relationships and human motivation. McGregor (1960), Hertzberg (1966) and Maslow (1954) were the principal developers of this perspective.

In scientific management and systems-based management theories, individuals were thought to be motivated to perform tasks by financial rewards. Those writing in the Human Relations tradition argued that people were more efficient when motivated to operate in teams. McGregor (1960), however, was more interested in relationships, distinguishing between autocratic and participative styles of management. He argued that autocratic styles were based on the view that people disliked work and avoided it if they could. They needed to be coerced into working, being punished if they did not and rewarded if they did. This is the "stick and the carrot" that is still so prevalent in management speak. The participative style, however, was based on the view that people were naturally creative and motivated by achievement and would direct and control themselves. McGregor argued that the participative style led to greater efficiency. The last two decades have witnessed the resurrection of this idea in the call for empowerment of individuals in an organization.

Hertzberg (1966) distinguished between hygiene factors to do with pay and working conditions and motivational factors to do with achievement, advancement, growth, recognition and responsibility. If the hygiene factors were not perceived to be adequate then people became dissatisfied with their work, but these factors were not sufficient to motivate people to work well. In addition, the motivating factors had to be present. Maslow (1954) presented a similar argument, drawing attention to a hierarchy of human needs. People could not be motivated to do much if basic needs for food, shelter and safety were not met. However, once these were met, people were motivated by factors relating to growth, such as love and belonging, the esteem of others, and self-esteem. Again, once met, they no longer had much effect as motivators and self-actualization became the highest level of motivation. Maslow described self-actualization in terms such as individuality, wholeness, uniqueness, goodness, aliveness, beauty and truth. In other words, he argued that people were motivated to become more themselves, to realize their true selves. Maslow thus argued that people would work effectively when their work enabled them, as individuals, to realize their full potential as human beings. The call for a sense of mission, inspiring visions and organizational designs that enable people to realize their individual potentials, is today's resurrection of Maslow's ideas.

These notions had, and continue to have, a substantial effect on personnel and human resource policies and on the training of managers in appropriate leadership styles. Notice, however, that although importance is ascribed to human relationships, that concern is expressed in terms of the motivating effect of "good" relationships on the individual in which it is not the relationships but the individual that is prior and primary. This view also implies the kind of split referred to in relation to cognitivism. First there is an essential, true self, already there. This is Formative Teleology. Then, within the framework of Rationalist Teleology, the individual chooses actions, or those in authority choose conditions and motivators, that realize the essential or true self.

Consider now how interaction in complex systems, the abstract analogy of relationship in human systems, is taken up in the complexity sciences.

Human action in complexity: retaining the individual focus

Most natural scientists working in the complexity sciences talk about the shift from a focus on individual entities to the interaction between entities comprising a complex system. However, many of them do so in a way that retains the notion of autonomous individual agents.

For example, Langton (1989) talks about the inability to provide a global rule, or algorithm, for changes in a complex system's global state, making it necessary to concentrate on the interactions occurring at a local level between agents in the system. He says that it is the logical structure of the interactions, rather than the properties of the agents themselves, which is important, thus potentially elevating interaction to primacy. However, he retains the view that agents are individual information processors, thus continuing a strong link with cybernetics and, therefore, when translated into human terms, a link with cognitivist psychology. Holland (1998) is quite explicitly cognitivist when he talks about individual agents having strategies, that is, prescriptions telling them what to do as the game unfolds. Gell-Mann (1994) also makes cognitivist assumptions when he talks about adaptive agents constructing schemata to describe and predict one another's behavior. Kauffman (1995) also talks about agents interacting locally in their own self-interest.

For most scientists working in the complexity sciences, then, individual agents are schemas or algorithms representing the world they act into. The agents manipulate and process information according to their schemas as the basis of their interaction. Algorithms drive the behavior of the agents, although no algorithm can be identified for behavior at the global level. Despite talking about the importance of interaction the primacy of the autonomous individual is preserved in the sense of agents as systems that individually represent a world, and then act autonomously and selfishly on the basis of those representations. In human terms, this amounts to a cognitivist, cybernetic theory of action.

There are some, however, who take a different view, most prominently Prigogine (1997) and Goodwin (1994). Prigogine casts his theories in terms of entities resonating with each other and evolving as collective ensembles. Goodwin emphasizes the intrinsically creative nature of relationships between entities in the evolution of a system.

Consider now how management complexity writers take from the complexity sciences those notions of relationship and individual agency that preserve individual autonomy, rather than those that place relationship at the center. This is the easy route to follow, of course, because it is so consistent with the individual-centered psychological assumptions underlying the dominant management discourse.

What the management complexity writers have to say about relationship

Almost everyone using the complexity sciences in relation to organizations stresses the importance of interaction and relationships, just as almost all natural scientists working in the field of complexity sciences do. However, just as with most natural scientists, management complexity writers emphasize individual agency. Individual agents form the relationships rather than the relationships forming the individual agents. Consider first those writers who turn to the complexity sciences as a source of metaphor and then those that use a more analogical approach.

Complexity metaphors and human relationships

Wheatley (1992) is quite explicit about the importance of relationship when she says that individuals cannot exist independently of relationships. However, she then says that self-organization succeeds when an organization supports the independent activities of individuals by giving them a frame of reference, usually the vision of an individual leader. She talks about freedom to evolve to greater independence. Cleary it is the individuals who are primary and the goal of their evolution is freedom and independence. Relationships require leaders to empower and include. In this way, self-organization is equated with empowerment and often with democracy (Purser and Cabana, 1998). Wheatley says that creative individuals can have an enormous impact on their system when that system is far-from-equilibrium. In the same conditions, individuals can gain access to the deep structures guiding their behavior (MacIntosh and MacLean, 1999). All the other writers that we have come across who use complexity science as a metaphor retain the importance of the individual in this way (see, for example, Lissack and Roos, 1999; Kelly and Allison, 1999). They all talk about leaders having a vision that guides their organization. For Roos and Oliver (1999), as well as Nonaka and Takeuchi (1995), knowledge is stored in the heads of individuals. Indeed Roos and Oliver regard individuals as autopoietic systems in that information may come from outside an individual but the knowledge that is constructed from it depends entirely on the individual, that is, the history-based structure of the individual mind.

Running through this writing is a view of human relationship that is individual centered and, furthermore, one that stresses harmony and sharing. This view presents an idealized view of human relating that completely abstracts from power relations and conflict, ignoring the transformative causal importance of conflicting constraints in complex systems. They talk about "good" relationships in which behavior, purpose and values are all aligned with each other. Individual differences are smoothed over by calling for "inclusive diversity," and the destructive processes of human relating – as well as their connection with human creativity – are ignored in a focus on caring relationships (Lewin and Regine, 2000). The general call is for freedom for individuals, for providing them with a context to find their "true selves," for coalescing around inspiring visions, for harmony and "good" relationships. The complexity sciences are here being used as rhetorical devices to justify a particular view of human behavior that clearly reflects cognitivist and humanistic psychological underpinnings and has only loose connections with the sciences of complexity themselves.

There are at least four important points to be made here. First, the easy equation of self-organization with individual empowerment and democracy has the effect of covering up the issue of power. Self-organization, as it is used in the complexity sciences, refers to the process of interaction in which entities interact with others according to their own principles of interaction. Interaction is local and organized by principles at the level of that local interaction. There is nothing in this process that necessarily implies equality or any other particular distribution of power. The essence of self-organizing dynamics is the conflicting constraints, or power relations, that agents impose on each other. Power relations between agents are thus one of the phenomena to be understood, not simply dismissed by a call for equality and caring.

Second, when notions from the complexity sciences are used as metaphors for organizations it is quite clear that they are translated from the one domain to the other on the basis of implicit cognitivist assumptions about human behavior. There are two important elements to this view. First is the assumption that the individual is prior and primary, that mind is a property of an individual brain. Second is the assumption that this individual brain processes information about a pre-given environment to form a map, schema or model as the basis of action. Most writers import both of these assumptions without acknowledging them. Some, such as Roos and Oliver (1999), reject the second proposition to do with representation but quite explicitly retain the first. They move from a purely cognitivist to a constructivist psychology. The latter focuses on the constraints on individual cognitive capacity arising from both biology and personal history. However, the central focus on the individual as prior and primary is retained. When Roos and Oliver claim that individuals are autopoietic systems, they enhance the primacy and priority given to the individual.

Third, no substantial importance is attached to differences between people, or to the destructive aspects of human relating. This is the straightforward importation of humanistic psychology.

Fourth, the split continues between the individual mind or social relationships, on the one hand, and choices made by leaders about them, on the other. The former is implicitly understood as Formative Teleology and the latter as Rationalist Teleology.

In Chapter 7 we argued that writers turning to the complexity sciences as a source of metaphor simply retain notions of causality found in systems thinking. Here we are arguing that they also retain, without examination, the psychological assumptions made in systems thinking, the most important being the fundamental importance accorded to individual agency. It is for both these reasons that this writing does not depart from the dominant discourse in conceptual terms, only in terms of vocabulary.

Consider now the position on individuals and groups taken by those writers who draw more careful analogies between complex systems in the natural sciences and human organizations.

Analogies for human relationship in the complexity sciences

Marion (1999) uses his concept of Complex Natural Teleology (discussed in Chapter 7) to explain human action. First, he relates the formative causality of autocatalysis in natural systems to human behavior. He asks what catalyses social behavior and concludes that it is the selfish need of the individual. Selfishness is local and personal, an individual trait that does not depend upon any external force. Humans are said to cooperate because that is the best way of achieving individual goals. In addition, individual human action is catalyzed by symbols: ideas, concepts, opinions, beliefs, emotions and projections. Humans assign meaning to symbols and mental constructs that catalyze human action to create complex social structures. This clearly places the individual as fundamental and thought before action. Before there can be the social there have to be individual humans with their selfish interests, and before they act, they think and make selfish choices.

Later, however, Marion argues that an individual's personality is the product of complex interactions and complex histories. He says that personality is not easily changed and cannot be changed by efforts that ignore social context. Change is a group rather than an individual process, so it is wrong to think that by changing an individual one can change a group. Change in one individual will not change the pattern of inter-actions. Here, he appears to be making the group fundamental. He seems to be saying that individuals form groups, which then affect how those individuals evolve. This is similar to psychoanalytic theory in which the individual mind is structured by the clash between the inherited selfish need to discharge drives for pleasure, on the one hand, and social constraint, on the other. It retains the idea that individuals are primary.

The social

The split that Marion makes between an individual and a social level becomes clearer when one considers his argument about social forces. He takes from Dawkins (1976) the concept of the meme, the social equivalent of the gene. Kelly and Allison (1999) also make use of the notion of memes. From a neo-Darwinian perspective, the genes of an organism are a blueprint that determines the biological structure of that organism. Marion argues that memes – that is, ideas, concepts, beliefs, scientific theories, ideologies, fads and fashions – provide the blueprint for social and organizational structure. These memes produce the content of culture; that is, the shared understanding of how things should be. Just as there are mechanisms that translate genes into biological structure, so there are mechanisms that translate memes into social, cultural and organizational structure. These mechanisms are processes of mimicry, interaction, correlation, teaching and learning through which societies and organizations imprint people with the memes of the parent culture (for example, the beliefs of an organization's founder).

For Marion, memes are the agents, or species, that interact cooperatively and competitively in a complex adaptive system to evolve in potentially novel ways through cross-fertilization between species of memes. Cross-fertilization is made possible because people, imprinted by memes, belong to more than one group. While genes are efficient causes of biological structure, that biological structure never causes the genes. With memes, he argues, it is different because although memes cause social structure, individuals in that structure can deliberately affect the memes. This makes it possible for cultural evolution to proceed much faster than biological evolution: major novel changes in memes can appear fully blown and be transferred to the young within a single generation. Competitive selection means that less-fit memes perish while fitter ones survive, modifying cultural and organizational structures so that they fit the environment.

Memes, then, are portrayed as somehow existing above the level of the individual as a kind of group mind or transpersonal process. They are described as the agents of a complex adaptive system with a life of their own, reproducing and potentially changing. They form a cultural blueprint, quite apart from the individuals upon whom they act. Memes are said to be translated into social structures as they imprint individuals who reproduce them through processes of mimicry and learning. Memes produce and choose behavior. However, in turn, individuals can deliberately choose to influence memes but the memes will choose which of these efforts is to succeed. Marion's main argument splits individuals and groups into two distinct but interactive levels. There are both individual and group processes and they affect each other but in a sequential rather than a simultaneous manner. Marion says that individuals join groups, motivated by symbols that are implicitly outside them, and when they do so they create more than the sum of their individualities. Each individual is like an attractor and when individuals come together to form a group, they resonate with each other, producing through their communication the social attractor. The split comes at this point because social attractors are now said to reproduce themselves and in the process they may change. He says that under the surface of the social, individual resonances harmonize in the sense that people develop a shared view. One operates within one kind of causal framework, this time something approaching Transformative Teleology; the other operates according to another, again Rationalist Teleology. In this argument, therefore, Marion stays within the dominant paradigm. However, another part of his argument indicates a significant difference.

Throughout, Marion stresses the robustness and stability of organizations and cultures and the difficulties that this creates when it comes to change, particularly deliberate, intentional change. He does couple this, however, with frequent references to the potential for the emergence of novelty in organizational and cultural evolution, and claims that this lies in human irrationality.

The importance of the irrational

Marion points to how complexity theorists in the natural sciences describe interactions between agents in complex systems in terms of simple stimulus and response; that is, according to rational rules. He draws on a number of sources in organizational theory – for example, Weick (1979) on enactment and Cohen *et al.* (1972) on garbage can decision-making – to argue that this is too simplistic when it comes to human decision-making and action. The basic argument here is that when humans must make decisions in situations in which causality is poorly understood, where there is considerable uncertainty, where people hold different beliefs, where they have personal biases, where they do not understand each other and where they lack all the required technical expertise, then decisions are made and actions taken on an irrational basis. People even make decisions before there is a problem, the problem arriving to find a solution. Problems do not arise in an inert environment but in the relationship between organizations and environment in which they create each other, and this makes a purely rational, logical, algorithmic approach impossible. Marion argues that order emerges because of interaction and it does not matter whether the interaction can be described as rational and logical or as irrational.

He goes further to argue that the very nature of the irrational and the random is essential to the emergence of novel structures. He ties creativity and the emergence of novelty firmly to the unpredictable aspect of the dynamic at the edge of chaos. He argues that without irrationality there would be stagnation. He sees irrationality as the social equivalent of the Poincaré resonances that Prigogine regards as essential to the emergence of new structures in nature (see Chapter 5). The diverse and surprising order in the world arises because life takes unexpected directions. Marion thinks about human learning as a process of tinkering, often without much thinking. People tinker, and as they do so they sense patterns. These patterns organize their perception and understanding, and as they tinker further those perceptions and understandings restructure, which in turn affects what people observe. He claims that learning occurs because humans are irrational. Perfectly rational decision-makers have nothing to discover and hence nothing to learn. Heroic leaders do less than we think they do, but they do act as symbols of a cause and they do rally unified behavior.

Having taken a radical position on causality, predictability, equilibrium, limits on human ability to change social processes through deliberate action alone, and so in many ways decentering the individual, Marion ends up with a view of human psychology and social relating that is not all that radical, apart from the way he stresses the irrational and the need for deviant behavior. He stays within the dominant paradigm to the extent that he sees human behavior resulting from a mimetic blueprint that humans have limited capacity to change of their own choice, with any choice having, in a sense, to be ratified by the memetic blueprint. He implicitly ends up with rather mysterious notions of a social mind or transpersonal processes. What has happened to the non-mysterious, fundamentally self-organizing nature of human action that Marion refers to, action that produces emergent patterns of behavior in the absence of a blueprint? What has happened to the importance of relationship? What he ends up with is a split between human action explained according to one causal framework and human choice explained according to another, just as systems thinking does. Since both are human, this is hardly tenable.

We now turn to approaches to understanding human behavior that put relationship at the center and do not split action and choice into different levels governed by two different causal frameworks, and in so doing we make a decisive shift away from systems thinking.

Transformation and human action: focusing on relationship and participation

In the 1920s and 1930s, during the period in which behaviorism dominated psychology and individual-centered psychoanalysis was coming to have a major impact, three social psychologists took a different view of the relationship between the individual and the social and of the causal framework within which human action might be thought about.

Mcad (1934) in thc Unitcd Statcs, and Vygotsky (1962) and Bhaktin (1986) in the Soviet Union developed, apparently independently of each other, a similar perspective on human action. There are differences in their approaches, of course, but the concern here is with the similarities between them.

For all of these writers, human beings are distinguished from other animals by their sophisticated processes of cooperating with each other and their use of tools to "make a living." In other words, the distinctive feature of human animals is their social behavior and it is distinctive in that human social processes are conducted in the medium of symbols. Humans cooperate with each other in the medium of symbols, and their primary tool to accomplish that social cooperation is language. As they cooperatively interact, humans interact with their environment using tools, their very cooperation in this regard being made possible because they talk to each other.

Mind as social process

Chapter 3 referred to Mead's (1934) argument that all social animals communicate with each other through a conversation of gestures: movement, touch, sound, visual display and odor. Each gesture by one animal calls forth a response from another, and together gesture and response constitute a social act; that is, an act that is meaningful to those gesturing and responding. This is what the social, in general terms, means to him: a responsive process in which animals signal meaningfully to each other in a continuous cycle of cooperative interaction. However, although there is meaning in such a process, there may be no mind or consciousness. Mind is a process in which a gesture can call forth the same response in the one making it as in the one to whom it is made. It is only through the capacity that the one making a gesture has to call forth in him/herself the same attitude being called forth in the other that the maker of a gesture can be aware of what it means. For example, this capacity enables one to be aware that the gesture of shouting at someone may arouse fear or anger in that someone. That awareness is possible because the gesture of shouting arouses the potential of fear or anger in oneself. Such a gesture is what Mead calls a significant symbol. It is significant because it means the same thing to the maker of the gesture and to the recipient.

The elaboration of vocal gestures into language enables a more elaborate development of mind. Language enables the maker of a gesture to be aware, in advance, of the likely response of the recipient and it enables the maker of the gesture to signal to the recipient how the act is likely to unfold. The maker of the gesture is, thus, conscious and can think, that is, hypothesize likely responses to a gesture in a kind of role-play. To have a mind means to be aware of the possible consequences of actions, as those actions unfold, by means of silently conducted conversations in the pauses between gestures and responses. Mind is silent, private role-playing of gesture–response conducted during the vocal, public interaction of gesture–response that is social cooperation. This is not a view of the autonomous individual first thinking and then choosing an action, but of individuals in relationship continuously evoking and provoking responses in each other, responses that each paradoxically also selects and chooses. The private, silent conversation of a body with itself is the same process as public, vocal conversation between bodies; in this sense mind is always a social phenomenon even though it is an individual conducting the private silent conversation. This theory of mind is firmly linked to the body because mind as a silent conversation of gestures requires a body. The conversation involves more than words; it is always interwoven with feelings and direct communication between bodies in the medium of feelings.

The individual mind is then logically the same process as social relating, in that both are cooperative interaction. The only difference is that one is silent and private while the other is vocal and public. It is impossible to have a mind in advance of vocal, public interaction, just as it is impossible to have that vocal, public interaction, that sophisticated social cooperation typical of humans, in the absence of minds. Neither form of conversation is primary nor prior to the other. They must both arise together, simultaneously. This immediately renders problematic the labeling of one as more or less fundamental and suggests that the individual and the social are at one level of analysis, not two. Meaning is not something that is going on in a mind as thought before action but, rather, arises, and continually re-arises, in the conversation of gestures, in the action and interaction, through social relationships conducted in significant symbols. It is no longer necessary to postulate that something separate, called an idea, for example, has to be expressed in language so that it can pass from one mind to another. An idea is already in language, otherwise it is not an idea, and instead of passing it between them their gestures are calling forth similar responses in themselves as they do in others. There is no need to postulate a separate social level programmed by memes, or any kind of transpersonal processes, or any notion of a group mind.

Mead takes the argument a step further with his concept of the generalized other. By this he means that one does not simply call forth in oneself the attitude to one's gesture of a particular other but comes to call forth in oneself the collective attitude toward one's gesture. In other words, in the private role-play of silent conversation the attitude of one's group toward one's actions finds a voice. This is a social form of control, arising simultaneously in the group and the individual.

Mead then goes further to suggest what it means to be self-conscious. One is self-conscious when, as a subject, one becomes an object to oneself. To be an object to him/herself, an individual must experience him/herself from the standpoint of others; he or she must talk to him/herself as others talk to him or her. This happens as an individual learns to take up the roles of others to him/herself, as a unique identity, in a form of role-play with him/herself. The silent conversation then involves a "me" (that is, an identity), which is the attitude of one's group toward oneself. The individual's response to this "me," is the "I"; that is, the action that an individual takes in response to the perceived community view of him/herself. The "I" response is potentially novel and hence unpredictable. The "I" response has the potential to change others, opening up the way for simultaneous individual/group evolution.

In this process, an individual takes the attitude of the whole community toward him/herself, as well as the attitude of individual others toward him/herself and the attitude of others toward each other. It is through this process that individual and community display controlled cooperative behavior. This sophisticated human social process is possible only in language. It follows that the self is a social construction emerging in relationships with others and only animals that possess language can possess a self that they are aware of. This does not mean that an individual cannot have the solitary experience of a self, only that one can never start life as a hermit. Mind and self do not emerge out of a clash between something that is already there in the individual and social constraint. Mind and self emerge in social relationships and they are "internalizations" of those social relationships. Individuals are forming and being formed by the group at the same time. Mind and self arise between people rather than being located in an individual.

We have already said in Chapter 3 that Mead's explanation of mind, self and society is an expression of Transformative Teleology. In this explanation, it is in the detailed interaction between people, their ongoing choices and actions in their relating to each other, that their minds and selves arise. They arise in patterns that display both continuity and potential transformation. At the same time, the social, the cooperative interaction of humans, is also formed as continuity and transformation. The movement here is paradoxical in that it is both continuity and transformation at the same time, the known and the unknown at the same time, the individual and the social at the same time, all arising in the micro detail of interaction. In this explanation there is no split between mind and social governed by one kind of causal framework, and human choice by another. All aspects of human choice and action, individual and social are explained in the same causal framework. Choice and action are not either rational or irrational, either logical reasoning or unconscious fantasy, but both at the same time, constituting forms of human relating. Mead was not alone in thinking in this way.

Dialogue and novelty

For Bhaktin (1986), all social phenomena are constructed in the ongoing dialogical relationships between people. He stressed the multiplicity of discourses, symbolizing practices and speech genres that are to be found in any culture. He talked about language as simultaneously structuring and being structured by people so that individuals are not simply the effects of social relations, nor are social relations simply the sum of individuals. He stressed the unpredictable and unfinished nature of dialogue and its capacity to produce the novel. Utterances never simply expressed something given and final outside the individual but always created something new and unrepeatable. He also stressed the dialogic tension between centripetal forces seeking expression in unity, merging, agreement and monologue, on the one hand, and centrifugal forces seeking expression in multiplicity, separation, disagreement and dialogue, on the other. This tension accounts for the emergence of official ideologies: centripetal forces push toward unity and order, giving voice to particular beliefs, while the centrifugal forces of multiplicity and diversity come to be denied expression. Power relations determine which words can be used officially and which can only be used unofficially.

Vygotsky also thought of mind as "inner speech" that has the same back and forth character as "outer speech" in which people continually negotiate their actions with each other. Thoughts come into existence through words and originate in the vague, unordered sense of the situation a person is in with others. Thoughts do not arise in an organized form at some center of an individual's being to be expressed to the other but, rather, thoughts are organized in the very back-and-forth negotiation between people in dialogue with each other.

Symbols, power and ideology

Elias (1989) defined the human mind in terms of the capacity to utilize symbols to explore potential reactions to an action before undertaking that action. He particularly stressed the use of language and symbols of all kinds in the elaboration of private fantasies. He saw people interacting with each other through symbols to form competitive and cooperative relationships that imposed enabling constraints on each other, so creating figurations of power relations. He located power in relationships rather than in an individual imposing his will on another, maintaining that power relations were co-created. Particular ways of talking are used to signal and enhance power, binding people together through the medium of symbols. Individual minds are formed by power relationships at the same time they are forming those power relationships. He defined individuals as interdependent people in the singular and society as interdependent people in the plural, so emphasizing the point that he sees individual and society as two aspects of the same phenomenon.

For him, language is not a tool used to express a thought because a thought is already in language. Thinking is born of concrete activity that takes place between people. It is because people are interdependent that they must communicate if they are to express their identities, and the means of communication is language. Language, therefore, expresses the power relations of the social figuration. Language orients one in the world – that is, it is knowledge – and its themes organize experience.

Elias equates mind with silent conversation, just as Mead did before him, and mind, therefore, emerges in social relationships. In fact mind is the "internalization" of social relationships and is, therefore, just as much structured by power relationships as social figurations are.

Elias, therefore, introduces a fundamental aspect of social relationships, namely the constraints they impose on members of a group and, therefore, the power differentials they create. He points to a basic social impulse – to maintain power differentials – and links this to the role of ideology, which categorizes groups into binary opposites, making power-preserving behavior feel natural. He identifies how gossip plays a central role in constantly reinforcing the ideology and so preserving power differences (Elias and Scotson, 1994). Foulkes (1948) combined psychoanalysis with the work of Elias and an understanding of human interaction in network terms to develop a group analytic practice of psychotherapy. He points to the connection between mental health and patterns of conversation, associating health with richly connected, free flowing conversation. People become ill, always in the context of some group, when they are caught in repetitive patterns of conversing and thinking.

Bhaktin, Vygotsky, Elias, and to some extent Foulkes, then, all present ways of understanding human action that reflect what we are calling Transformative Teleology and there are other developments that do so as well.

The construction of social reality

Another line of development that illustrates what we mean by Transformative Teleology is that of social constructionism (Gergen, 1999; Shotter, 1993). From this perspective, people create and are created by their social reality. Mind emerges in relationship and the notion of a mind inside someone disappears. An individual's mind arises between that individual and the others with whom he or she is in relationship. It is between them, not in one of them. Mental phenomena, including the sharing of meaning with others, all arise in social or group relationships, although they may be experienced as phenomena pertaining to the individual.

Shotter (1993) emphasizes communication and language as the medium of relationship in which mind arises. He distinguishes between representational–referential and rhetorical–responsive modes of communication. In the first, individuals form representations of the world they are acting in and then refer to those representations in order to act. This is of course cognitivism. Shotter does not deny that sometimes humans think and talk in this way, but he argues that the latter form is of far more importance and it is completely ignored in cognitivism. Rhetoric is the art of persuasion and in the ordinary everyday conversations that make up the bulk of human life, people are responding to each other as persuasively as possible. In ordinary, everyday life people have to justify themselves to others. They have to give an account of themselves and explain what it is they are doing and why. When they do this, they are practicing the art of rhetoric, persuading others to let them do what they want and even cooperate with them, just as they are responsively being persuaded to accommodate others. This is the sophisticated social act of cooperation in the medium of symbols that Mead spoke about. People together shape what they perceive and hence the context in which they jointly act. They do so by pointing to this and inviting people to look at that. They are together constructing their social reality.

Developmental psychology

The social constructionist way of thinking about how mind and social relationships emerge simultaneously in interaction is supported by detailed studies of infant development (Stern, 1985, 1995). Stern, for example, uses experimental evidence to explain how an infant's self emerges in the mutual relationships with family members in a conversation of gestures. Parents hold, look at and direct sounds to an infant and these gestures evoke responses from the child, who cries, stops crying, makes noises and returns the parental gaze. In this manner infant and parents, as well as other people, communicate with each other in ever more elaborate ways, which eventually include language. This communication is the infant's experience just as it is the experience of those relating to the infant. Initially, the communication takes place in the medium of varying body states or feelings. As they interact with each other, the feeling state of one body affects the feeling states of other bodies as they resonate with each other. For example, a crying infant immediately evokes feeling states in the bodies of caregivers. The same thing happens, of course, between adult bodies. Stern sees an infant in a family whose members are continuously responding to each other and suggests that each member relates to other members in accordance with schemas that organize their experience of being with each other. As an infant's experience of relating to others continues, more and more organizing principles emerge and some of them become tied together by a common theme or feature. For example, they may cluster around the themes of feeding, playing, or separation.

Intersubjectivity

A similar view of human action has been developed by a number of psychoanalysts (Stolorow *et al.*, 1994) who have moved away from Freud's individual-centered psychology.

Putting it rather simplistically, the focus of attention in the classical Freudian theory is the individual drives and how they are constrained by social prohibition to form the mind. Object relations theory shifts the focus to the structuring impact of an individual's inner fantasy of his or her nurturing and prohibiting relationships with significant others. Self-psychology extends this to incorporate representation of self and others as object to, or of, the self in inner-fantasy life. Throughout these developments, as relationship is increasingly emphasized, the individual remains prior and primary. These theoretical perspectives look for universal developmental phases and universal mechanisms of development, without regard to historical cultural or any other context. The radical nature of intersubjectivity arises from its challenge to all of these central assumptions.

First, meaning is not located in the inner world of an individual, according to an intersubjective perspective. Informed by the detailed research into infant development already mentioned, this theory posits relationship itself as the structuring process for mind and personality. As infant and caregiver interact with each other empathically, resonating and attuned emotionally to each other to varying degrees, the infant mind is structured into principles that organize the experience of that infant. The organizing principles arise in the experience between the mother and infant and are not, therefore, simply located in either. This process is elaborated when language develops as the medium of relating, and each party to the relating elaborates experience according to the principles of their own subjective world, much of the elaboration occurring imaginatively, or as fantasy. Such organizing principles are largely unconscious. Here, then, there is no longer a reified idea of "the unconscious" consisting of repressed wishes concerned with drive expression, or sexual and aggressive fantasies, but principles organizing experience of relating that those relating are largely unaware of, many of those principles themselves being elaborated in a "fantasy" manner.

This mode of psychological structuring does not place the individual prior to and primary *vis-à-vis* the social world of relationship. Infants are born with the urge, indeed the necessity, to relate to others, and the development of their subjective worlds arises in the pattern of relating. The energy and motivation for behavior comes from the need to modulate affect in relationship and from the need to maintain the organization of experience, that is, identity. Relating itself is the intersection of different subjective worlds.

The emphasis on relationship in a particular context, and the impact of history on current patterns of relating, means that the social process is self-referential. In other words, patterns of relating now refer back to patterns of relating.

A word on memes and mimicry

Earlier on, this chapter referred to the use by some complexity writers of the concept of memes by analogy with genes. To recapitulate, genes are said to be the fundamental biological units, providing a blueprint translated by chemical mechanisms into biological structures. Memes (that is, ideas, concepts, theories and the like) are taken as the fundamental units of human culture and are said to be translated into social structure and behavior through the mechanism of the individual mind's capacity for mimicry. This seems to be a popular concept for some complexity writers (for example, Marion, 1999) because it provides an immediate candidate for the agents in complex adaptive systems. The move is then away from the notion of memes as blueprints to the notion of memes as agents in a complex adaptive system. Memes can then be thought of as interacting with each other in a self-organizing manner to produce emergent new memes. These new memes, it is assumed, can be transmitted to other individual minds through the process of mimicry, and once enough people come to share them they can be said to be part of the culture. Culture then imprints yet other individual minds with these memes through the process of mimicry. This implies that there is a complex adaptive system called "culture," in which the agents are memes, and a complex adaptive system called "an individual mind," in which the agents are also memes. Memes in the culture system then interact to yield cultural evolution that impacts on individual human minds through imprinting; that is, mimicry. Similarly, memes in the individual human mind interact to yield individual mental evolution. Emergent memes in the individual mind may then enter into the complex adaptive system called "culture," again through mimicry. The whole idea depends upon the transmission of memes from one mind to the cultural system and back again into other minds through the process of mimicry.

For us, there are a number of problems with this idea. First, it splits the individual and the social into two levels of description: the macro social and the micro individual. The approach we have been outlining in this section suggests that the private role-play of individual mind and the public communication of the social are the same phenomenon. Even if one argued that memes can be thought of as interacting only in individual minds and then passed from one to another without postulating a higher level of culture, there is the second problem.

Second, the concept of the meme implies that an idea or concept lies behind, beneath or below its articulation. It implies that there is an idea that is put into words. The approach we have been outlining in this section argues that ideas are already words and actions. There is nothing lying behind, below or above them. What else could an idea be but the words in which it is expressed?

Our third objection is that the concept of the meme requires a process by means of which "something" called an idea is transmitted from one individual mind to another. The "idea" itself has to move out of one mind and into another, and the process proposed for this transmission is that of mimicry. Other processes identified are learning and teaching, but these are understood as forms of mimicry. One person copies what is in the mind of another into his own mind. However, just what is it that is being transmitted and copied? How could we ever know that what is in our minds is the same as that which has been received into the mind of another? The notion that people communicate by copying each other's mental contents makes it difficult to explain how anything new could arise between them. Interaction between diverse memes in the complex adaptive system "individual mind" or in the system "culture" could produce a new meme, but to get further than this the meme has to be copied by others. The evolution of a relationship would have to depend upon the emergence of a new idea in the mind of one of them transmitted into that of another by a process of copying. Or, it would have to depend upon the emergence of a new idea in an abstract system called "culture," quite split off from humans. This surely is an impoverished idea of relating, leaving no scope for relationship itself to play a part in what emerges between people.

The approach outlined in this section places interaction (that is, relationship) at the center of self-organization. In doing so, it avoids the difficulties identified above by focusing on relational communication as the bodily gestures of one person and the bodily response they call forth in her/himself and in others at the same time. Here nothing is passing between their minds at all. What is happening between them is continuous bodily action of gesture and response calling forth meaning in each at the same time. This meaning does not have to be the same for both. Here bodily communications may well have different impacts on the two communicating bodies.

Conclusion

This chapter has argued that the dominant management discourse, including systems thinking, is built, explicitly or implicitly, on Rationalist Teleology as an explanation of choice and Formative Teleology as an explanation of how the choosing mind, or the web of social relations, works. This is expressed in psychological theories that accord priority and primacy to the choosing individual over the social. It is a view of minds as information processing devices that make representations of a pre-given world, formed into maps and models that are the basis of subsequent action. Alternatively, individuals may be thought of as having deep, true identities and they are motivated, ultimately, by contexts that allow them to express their true natures. The social – that is, the cooperative and competitive relating between people – is important as an enabling context for the expression of true, enfolded identities. From this perspective the complexity sciences are taken as supporting essentially cooperative processes in organizations. Or they are understood as a split between individual and social, where each is at a different level. The social then comes to be thought of as impersonal social forces, memetic programs, transpersonal processes or group minds.

We then pointed to a cogent and persuasive alternative to individual-centered psychology coming from early social psychologists, some strands in group analytic theory, more recent psychoanalytic theories, research in developmental psychology and social constructionism, together amounting to what we are calling relationship psychology. These ways of thinking provide a cogent view of individual and collective identities emerging in interaction of a primarily conversational nature configuring power relations and their sustaining ideologies. Relationship, and its inherent power relations, is the transformative cause of such emergent identities. The result is a view of self-organizing processes of conversational interaction that simultaneously constitute identity and difference. Relationship is continuously recreating identities with the potential for transforming them. The causal framework here is Transformative Teleology applicable to all levels of human action. This view of conversational relating between people resonates strongly, we argue, with an interpretation of the complexity sciences as Transformative Teleology and it represents a decisive move away from systems thinking. It is this perspective on human action, one that locates agency in relationship, in the simultaneous emergence of individual and group identity, that we are interested in using to interpret the complexity sciences in human terms.

9 Getting things done in organizations: from systems to complex responsive processes

It seems to us that the past few decades have witnessed the vigorous revival of age-old questions. Are we to understand change in our world only as the unfolding, or revelation, of forms that are there in some way? Or, are we also to understand change as a process that brings into being new forms that have never existed before? Put slightly differently, the question becomes whether our future is knowable or whether it is in the process of perpetual construction and, therefore, unknowable. The question is whether there is no true novelty in experience or whether there is.

Questions of this kind exercised the minds of pre-Socratic philosophers such as Parmenides and Heraclitus nearly 3,000 years ago. They were taken up by Plato and then Aristotle and continued to be debated in ensuing centuries. Chapter 2 took up the discussion at the time of Kant, who provided a unique proposal in the history of Western thought for splitting our understanding of the natural world and the world of human action. That chapter described how he thought of causality in nature in terms of what we are calling Formative Teleology, a causal framework that answers the age-old question referred to above in a particular way. Formative Teleology applied to nature means understanding our non-human world as the unfolding or revelation of form that is enfolded in movement forward to a future that is knowable. In this explanation, there is no novelty in nature. Chapter 2 also described how Kant applied Rationalist Teleology to human action in order to take account of human freedom. This means understanding ourselves as changeful and productive of the new through rational choices as expressions of universal ethical principles. This ingenious answer did not satisfy Hegel, who argued that we cannot understand our world in this "both/and" way. Instead, he argued that both the natural and the human aspects of the world could be understood in a causal framework that we are calling Transformative Teleology. The answer to the age-old question is, then, that change is process that brings forth the new in both nature and human action in the same way. That way lies in the continual, detailed interaction between entities, which paradoxically brings forth both continuity and potential transformation at the same time. It is this micro interaction that perpetually reconstructs the future.

As far as the natural sciences are concerned, there can be no question that Kant's thought has now taken a dominant position. Although Marxist interpretations of Hegel lived on in the social sciences, Kant tended to predominate there too, although not as he would have intended. Although he argued that what we are calling Formative Teleology could never be applied to human action, that is just what mainstream social sciences do. They regard systems of human action in the same way that natural scientists regard systems in nature and apply Formative Teleology to those human systems. Like nature, human systems are assumed to change in ways that unfold or reveal what is already there, and their futures are therefore knowable. However, it is also assumed that, like nature, these human systems can be operated upon by humans standing outside them and choosing, in accordance with Rationalist Teleology, what future they should unfold. By this move, both Formative and Rationalist Teleology are applied to human action in a way that splits the chooser, governed by Rationalist Teleology, from the chosen, governed by Formative Teleology. The answer to the age-old question as far as human action is concerned then becomes rather confusing. It seems that for those humans who have the freedom, or power, to choose and design there is the possibility of choosing new forms that have never existed before. They can choose to construct the future in a truly novel way and design the system of human interaction required to produce that future by making rational choices. Once they have made the choices, it is as a given that the human system of interaction unfolds. The problem with this way of thinking is that the humans who choose the novel future are also humans who interact with others in the system they design. They must therefore step outside the system, become very special kinds of choosing humans, and then make a choice for the whole system's future. In that moment they exercise human freedom while no one else does. But this freedom only lasts for a moment because they too are then subject to the system they have designed, unless of course they decide to design another. The freedom to choose is therefore confined to special people and special moments. This, it seems to us, is the foundation upon which contemporary systems thinking about human organizations is built.

The option that freedom is a daily ongoing characteristic of all human action and interaction is then completely lost. In fact the whole scheme can only work if freedom is lost in this way because if human members of the designed system do exercise freedom on a daily basis then the system will take on a life of its own, quite likely to depart from the design and thus the future chosen for it. This immediately undermines the possibility of someone stepping outside the system and choosing its future and designing it to achieve that future.

This split way of thinking leads to the confusing experience of a presumed loss of freedom while still being required to exercise it if the system is to work. It leads to the experienced inability to choose and design in the way that one is supposed to. This is the experience we described at the beginning of Chapter 1. The whole way of thinking focuses attention, for most, on the designed system, but it never proves sufficient, and they have to "get things done anyway," almost despite the system. What they are not encouraged to do, by this very way of thinking itself, is to pay attention to the detailed interactions between them, through which they "get things done." Combining Rationalist and Formative Teleology to thinking about life in organizations, as systems thinking does, is a thoroughly stressful daily experience for people.

It is this experience, we think, that gives such importance to the relatively recent revival of the age-old questions about change. In the previous chapter we referred to how developments in the social sciences revive these questions in the form of social constructionism, developmental psychology, intersubjectivity theory in psychoanalysis, and group analytic theory. These developments point to answers to the questions from the perspective of Transformative Teleology. They describe the detailed human interactions that bring forth novel patterns of behavior that are not pre-given. They explore how true novelty arises in the detail of interaction between people who differ from each other as they perpetually and unpredictably construct their future.

The sciences of complexity interest us because they are also raising again the age-old questions about change. In Chapters 5 and 6 we described how we see some complexity scientists pointing toward Transformative

Teleology, while others continue within the causal framework of Formative Teleology. The work of the former resonates, for us, with some strands in the social sciences that also take the perspective of Transformative Teleology. In our view, most management complexity writers are taking concepts from the natural complexity sciences and applying them to organizations within the framework of combined Formative and Rationalist Teleology, just as systems thinking does. What they do, therefore, runs into the same fundamental problems as the existing dominant discourse. It follows that they can have little new to say about change in organizations. Even those who make a move toward Transformative Teleology do so within a framework that preserves the split between human chooser and human system to which the choice is applied.

Key elements of our project

Our project, the project that this series of books is intended to take up, is different. We are interested in exploring how the perspective we are calling Transformative Teleology might offer ways of thinking about life in organizations that takes account of novelty and the ordinary daily freedom of human interaction, hopefully leading to less frustration.

Complex responsive processes of relating

First, we want to move away from the notion that human action and interaction is a system or can usefully be thought of as a system, when it comes to understanding change of a transformational kind.

The difficulties we see in thinking about human interaction as if it were a system were spelled out in Chapter 4 and have been referred to in subsequent chapters. This is not to say that systems thinking has no use at all. It clearly does when one is trying to understand and, even more, trying to design interactions of a repetitive kind to achieve kinds of performance that are known in advance, that are already given. Even then, however, systems thinking is not enough because people in organizations hardly ever accomplish their joint action on an ordinary day-to-day basis in a way that is entirely determined by the designed systems they operate within. No system can encompass every eventuality and, therefore, ordinary daily human freedom is exercised to weave actions into and around the system, the known, in order to cope, at the same time, with the daily unknown. This acting, in an ordinary day-by-day way into the known–unknown, requires an explanation that systems thinking on its own cannot provide because this thinking always entails some human chooser standing outside the system and acting upon it (see Chapter 4). Even more difficult for systems thinking is the less-frequently experienced major discontinuities that represent novel change. Although systems thinking is extremely useful when it comes to understanding the unintended and unexpected consequences of human action, its theory of causality does not allow for the emergence of true novelty.

What we are getting at is the need to understand human intentions, choices and actions as essential to, as operating within, the dynamic of daily interactions between people. We are arguing for a move away from understanding "the organization" as a system subject to one kind of causality (whether that be Formative or Transformative), and "the manager" or "the leader" as the maker of human choices operating according to another causality (Rationalist Teleology). We are interested in understanding the process of organizing as the ongoing joint action of communication. We are arguing that organizing is human experience as the living present, that is, continual interaction between humans who are all forming intentions, choosing and acting in relation to each other as they go about their daily work together. This is not the kind of interaction between "entities" forming a system about which some humans make choices, on which they act as if the system, or the organization, were a tool they use to do what they need to do. Instead, there is a process of interaction, or relating, which is itself a process of intending, choosing and acting. No one steps outside it to arrange it, operate on it or use it, for there is no simply objectified "it." There is only the responsive process of relating itself. Instead of understanding "the organization" as a tool humans design and use, we seek to understand organizing, that is, experience as the living present. Instead of understanding human action as Rationalist Teleology split off from a tool structured by Formative, or even Transformative, Teleology, we want to explore how the detail of human choice and action itself operates as the process of organizing understood in terms of Transformative Teleology.

Humans accomplish sophisticated cooperative, joint action through their capacity for communicating with each other in the medium of symbols, particularly those that constitute language. For us, "the organization" is not the tool of joint action. It is joint action, that is, a pattern of cooperative interaction continually recreated and potentially transformed at the same time. Our project, then, focuses on communication in all its forms in organizations and we seek to understand how people accomplish the joint action of organization in this communication. Of particular interest for this purpose are the ordinary everyday conversational forms of communication. When people communicate with each other, conversationally or otherwise, to accomplish the joint action of living and acting together, they are, of course, continuously relating to each other in a responsive manner.

The move we want to make, therefore, is away from thinking about an organization as a system, to thinking about organizing as highly complex, ongoing processes of people relating to each other. We refer to this as Complex Responsive Processes of relating in order to differentiate what we are talking about from any notion of a system. In this process, people will design and use information and control systems of a procedural nature as part of their ongoing communication with each other, but these are particular kinds of communicational tools devised to speed up communication of a standardized, repetitive nature. Systems here are tools used to facilitate communication, most importantly by establishing what is legitimate and what must be subjected to negotiated choice. "The organization" is not a system or a tool; rather, systems are some of the tools of communication employed by people in their relational processes of organizing joint action. In our view it is quite unrealistic to think of information and control systems as simply equivalent to engineering systems. Information and control systems
in organizations do not function separately from humans. They do not regulate themselves or have any kind of life of their own, because at every step humans use them, negotiating with each other what is legitimate, how to get around the systems, how to deal with exceptions to them, and so on. One only has to think of the practical activity of operating within a financial budget to see how ordinary choices are made all day long about how to categorize an item of expenditure or revenue. Systems are simply tools of communication, ways of talking, similar to any other in an organization, with the important difference that they are formalized and provide legitimation for talk and other action.

We seek to understand Complex Responsive Processes of relating within the causal framework of Transformative Teleology. This means, for us, that the relational processes of communication, within which people accomplish joint action, are actively constructing the future as the living present and that future is unknowable in advance. Throughout, the process is characterized by the paradox of the known–unknown and in it emerges the aims people formulate, the goals they set, the intentions they form and the choices they make. What is being expressed here is individual and collective identity at the same time.

How does novelty arise in these ordinary, daily processes of complex responsive relating between people? Those who think in terms of what we are calling Adaptionist Teleology, or aspects of it, answer this question in terms of chance. For them, it is chance variations at the individual level that generate variety. In their models, they incorporate this as a random factor, a probability distribution, statistical "noise," and the like. This amounts to saying that the source of novelty is variety, something that just happens without any cause, a deviation from the regular, an aberration. In the Transformative Teleology we are interested in exploring in relation to human action, we want to avoid an appeal to chance, an appeal that would split the regular and chance aberrations from it. For us, the notion of fluctuations, or irregularities, as inextricably interwoven with regularity is more consistent with what we mean by Transformative Teleology. We are talking about regularly irregular patterns that cannot be separated out into regular and irregular components. We are saying that complex responsive processes of relating between people are movements in time that are simultaneously regular and irregular. Here instabilities are intrinsic and thinking in this way focuses attention on bifurcations in the process of relating. In other words, it focuses attention on the essential diversity in the real-life process of relating itself. The diversity arises in the scope for different interpretations open to people communicating with each other. Instead of thinking in terms of chance, error or misunderstanding as the generators of variety in communication, we want to think of the ever-present, ordinary detailed differences of interpretation in communication between people as the generators of variety and, hence, the source of novelty. It is in these ongoing differences of interpretation that individual and collective identities are continually recreated and potentially transformed.

The individual and the social

This perspective of Complex Responsive Processes accords priority and primacy neither to the individual nor to the social. It regards both as the same phenomenon, forming and being formed by each other at the same time. The individual, following Elias (1989), is the singular of the phenomenon of human relating, with the social being the plural of that phenomenon. This means that there is no distinction between micro and macro levels in human interaction. Individual and collective identities are continuously formed and transformed in the process of relating. The key features of these processes are as follows:

- *They are processes of action and interaction through which people in organizations act jointly, transforming their environment and their identities.*
- *They are the action of relating.* This places relationship at the center of understanding life in organizations. However, by this we do not mean an idealization of human interaction. We do not take this emphasis on relationship to mean the elevation of humans caring for each other or treating each other well in some way. Of course, it includes this, but relationship, as we all know only to well, also includes dark and dreadful ways of treating each other. We are interested in understanding relationship in organizations in a way that encompasses the caring and the harming, the creative and the destructive.
- *These actions of relating are bodily actions of communicating, both directly in the medium of feelings and in the form of language.* We are interested in how people accomplish joint action in organizations through their conversational life.
- *They are therefore processes of power-relating, that is, processes that both enable and constrain action.* We are interested in understanding how the action of communication between people in organizations gives rise to power relations. It is particular ways of talking that establish the power dynamic enacting who is included and who is excluded.
- *They are actions of communication and power reflective of human freedom.* Here we are not talking about freedom as a noble, idealized human aspiration. We are referring instead to the ordinary, daily freedom of communicating, forming intention and making choices in myriad small ways. We are interested in how people interact freely and spontaneously with each other in transformative ways and how they get caught in repetitive forms of interaction that curtail or even destroy that ordinary freedom.
- *They are actions of communication and power-relating open to the detail of varying interpretations.* It is the difference of interpretation that generates variety in human action and thus constitutes the source of novelty and creativity.
- *They are actions of communication taking the form of bodily gestures and responses, including the vocal ones of language, which call forth responses in others.* Communication here does not involve the

transmission of anything from one mind into another and therefore does not have to rely on the notion of mimicry to explain how such transmission occurs.

Insights from the natural sciences of complexity

We think that the natural complexity sciences are relevant in a number of ways to the features of our project outlined above. First, as Chapter 4 pointed out, the dominant management discourse, from which we differentiate our approach, is directly built on notions imported from the natural sciences. If some of these keys notions are being questioned within the natural sciences themselves, it becomes very important to examine the implications for thinking about organizations. If the foundations of their ways of thinking are being undermined in the area from which they were imported it seems inconceivable for management thinkers to ignore this. Second, we have already mentioned how natural scientists working in the complexity sciences are, in effect, reviving age-old questions about the nature of change. The way they are doing this, we think, is illuminating for those whose interest is in these questions in the social sciences. Third, and most important, we think that the natural scientists are developing concepts about complexity and ways of talking about it that are potentially of great use to management thinkers.

For us, the complexity sciences are a source domain of abstract relationships from which we believe it is possible to derive insights about human interaction by way of analogy. Appendix 2 sets out what we mean by this. Briefly, we are not proposing to use the complexity sciences as a source of loose metaphor because we think that route easily leads to yet another management fad. Nor are we interested in constructing models of organization using the techniques of the complexity scientists. This is because models inevitably treat human interaction as if it were a system and we have argued against this perspective. This does not mean that we think such models have no use. They may well develop important insights. It is simply that our interest lies in directly understanding real human interactions in organizations, and mathematical models and computer simulations cannot, in our view, represent human interaction.

For our project, therefore, we look to the complexity sciences as a domain of abstract relationships, as demonstrations of possibility, potentially providing a source of insight and a way of talking about human action in organizations. The principal insights relevant to our project are as follows:

- *The demonstration that it is possible for the same set of abstract relationships to display distinctively different kinds of dynamic in different conditions.* One dynamic has the characteristic of Formative Teleology in that it repetitively reveals an already given pattern. Another dynamic has some of the features of Transformative Teleology in which novelty emerges. In yet another dynamic the same set of relationships produce disintegration. Our interest is in understanding these dynamics in human terms as patterns of repetitive interaction in which people get "stuck" and as patterns of spontaneous, creative relationship in which the possibility of transformation arises.
- *The demonstration of the properties of abstract relationships, which seem to have the intrinsic capacity for self-organization to produce emergent patterns of coherence in themselves.* This suggests that there is a way of understanding how coherence, or order, arises in organizational life that does not rely exclusively on global intention and design.
- *The demonstration that abstract relationships are capable of emergent novelty only when the relationships are between diverse entities in the presence of fluctuations.* This can be interpreted to mean that the source of novelty lies not simply in chance but in the very diversity and irregularity in the pattern of relationship. This insight, if it applies to human relating, obviously has very interesting implications for how we think about transformative change.
- *The demonstration that abstract relationships produce emergent change that is paradoxical in that it is both predictable and unpredictable, known and unknown, stable and unstable, all at the same time.*
- *The demonstration that abstract relationships can produce emergent change, which is radically unpredictable, and that this is what novelty means.* This insight directs attention to how people go on acting as they come to know what they are doing.

None of these insights can simply be transferred from the source domain of abstract relationships to human action. They must be interpreted in terms of some understanding of what it means to be human. In our project, we make this interpretation in terms of what we are calling relationship psychology, as briefly indicated in the previous chapter.

A participative approach

A move away from thinking of organizations as systems, and a belief that formal models cannot capture the human interaction we wish to understand, has implications for methodology. It means trying to understand human action in organizations from within that action, as a participant in it. Our interest is to move from the position that equates the researcher, the consultant, the manager or the leader in an organization with the objective observer, to one that sees them all as participative inquirers. We are interested in what it means to understand Complex Responsive Processes of relating through our own participation in organizational life, indeed, to understand ourselves in this way. This does not mean that we cannot talk and write in a rigorous and abstract way about complex responsive processes or that we have to rely only on narratives and stories. This whole book is theoretical, parts of it providing an abstract description of complex responsive relating. The point we are making about participation is that the abstract descriptions and explanations must be about processes that are essentially participative. It means that our descriptions and explanations of the processes cannot be taken as models to be applied or as sources of universal, context-free prescriptions.

The books in this series

At the start of Chapter 1 we described how managers repeatedly report long lists of things that went wrong with their plans, systems and procedures, and then ignore how they "got things done, anyway." They move instead to prescriptions for yet more systems, procedures and plans. We suggest that they do this because they are thinking within a framework imported by engineers from the natural sciences in earlier decades. The same point applies to complaints about inaccessible information and the call for information systems to replace the knowledge arising in personal contacts, never considering whether the gaining of knowledge through personal contacts might be the most appropriate way in situations of rapid change. These complaints reflect systems thinking. This currently dominant frame of reference structures the conversations of people in this way through placing individual choice about whole systems as the central cause of how an organization comes to be what it is. It is the dominant discourse that makes it feel quite natural to think about the manager as one who steps outside the organizational processes in order to design systems and stay "in control."

We are suggesting that members of organizations explore a shift in their way of thinking to a way that places relationships between them as the transformative cause of organizational identity. This focuses attention on conversation as the central activity of organizing, especially that spontaneous and fluid conversation characterized by ongoing differences of interpretation. This means that people jointly create the meaning of what they are doing when they act into the unknown, co-creating their future in interaction with others. From this perspective, they are all participants in the joint inquiry into what they are doing together. This way of thinking is a decisive shift from systems thinking.

The series of books, of which this is the first volume, is intended to provide a vehicle for the exploration of this kind of challenge to the dominant discourse on management, particularly systems thinking. The second volume will consider how knowledge creation and management might be thought about from the perspective of Complex Responsive Processes of relating. The third will explore the nature of organizational change as Complex Responsive Processes of relating. The fourth volume will take up the important matter of leadership and ethics in Complex Responsive Processes. The fifth will consider innovation in organizations, and the sixth will take a detailed look at the nature of managerial control.

Appendix 1: The origins of Western notions of causality

Some 3,000 years ago, thinkers referred to as the "pre-Socratic" philosophers speculated, over a number of centuries, about the nature of reality. Their thought traces out the transition from understanding change in a purely mythological sense to the "logos" which became the core of Greek philosophy. Two of these thinkers, Parmenides (*c.* 450 BC) and Heraclitus (*c.* 500 BC) still symbolize today what seem to be mutually exclusive perspectives on change. Parmenides held that reality was stable without change, that is, being. Heraclitus argued that reality was all flux and change, that is, becoming. The tension between these two positions has echoed through the ages, and much of the discussion about stability and change in the complexity sciences harks back to it.

Plato tended toward the Parmenidian position and argued that reality is eternal forms, given from the beginning and continuing without change. What humans perceive as change is an illusion, the fallible perceptions of the shadows of the eternal forms. This notion still finds its way into how mathematical models are sometimes used as pure forms describing the reality that lies behind what humans perceive. The consequence of Plato's thought is that humans cannot trust their experience. Aristotle, however, argued that change is not an illusion but that humans actually experience nature as change. Reality is not some eternal given but an experience one perceives. Humans can trust their experience; indeed, this is the only way they have of making any sense of reality. To back this position up, Aristotle introduced a theory of causality, for the first time in human thought, which brought together elements of various other thinkers of his time. Aristotle had studied for decades at Plato's Academy and his theory of causality represented the core of his movement away from Plato, taking up the polarities stated by Parmenides and Heraclitus and reaffirming "becoming," which he argued had been lost in Plato's thought.

Aristotle first introduced this theory of causality as a way of understanding the human experience of physical nature (*Physics*, Book II). For him there was one overarching source of change, or becoming, and three others that he distinguished as subordinate to it. The overarching source of change was what he called teleological (from the Greek work "telos," meaning the goal or end for the sake of which an act is understood) or final cause (from the Latin work "finis," meaning the end). He was arguing that humans experience nature in the way that they do because nature acts toward final ends. The fundamental source of becoming is that everything tends toward some end, or form. For example, an animal moves from the form of fertilized egg, to infant, to young adult, to mature adult. An acorn moves from this form to a sapling, to a fully grown tree. This is the beginning of evolutionary theory, that is, a theory of movement or change. Within this movement toward a final form or end, Aristotle distinguished other sources of becoming that are subordinate to the overarching teleological movement:

- One of these sources is what has come to be known as "formal cause." This is the human experience of the form of the phenomenon as it moves toward its final form. In other words, this is the human experience of pattern, of the given sequence of changes in the form. So, while the teleological is concerned with the final form, the formal source of change is the changes in form that lead up to it. In the above examples, these are the infant and the young adult, or the acorn and the sapling. This is what is meant by the formal source of becoming.
- Next, Aristotle distinguished a source of becoming which has come to be known as "efficient causality." Here humans experience change in terms of what went before the present state. For example, a tree is now experienced as being on fire because in the preceding state it was hit by lightning. This link between the lightning strike and the subsequent fire is what developed into the if-then sequence of efficient causality.
- Lastly, Aristotle talked about what has come to be known as "material cause." Here humans experience change as they do because one source of becoming is the material of which a thing is made. For example, a tree is experienced as a tree because it is made of wood.

The translation from Aristotle's sources of becoming to what we understand today as causality is rather difficult because causality has become so identified with efficient causality of the if-then kind. Furthermore, Aristotle was talking about the source of human experience of change in physical nature whereas today one thinks of causality as pertaining to that physical nature itself rather than the human experience of it.

Human organizations can, however, be understood in terms of all of today's modern descendants of Aristotle's four causes. For example, a pharmaceutical company is as it is because of material cause in the sense that it depends upon the nature of the chemicals it produces. Change and stability in the organization depend in this way on change and stability in chemical matter. An organization can also be understood in terms of efficient cause when, for example, reward systems are used to motivate people. If sales incentives are increased, then sales people sell more products. Formative cause would identity the source of change and stability in the functioning of a system – for example, an information and control system. Then, the processes of, say, the accounting system would be formatively causing the organization to become what it becomes. Teleological cause would be the objectives that the organization was seeking to achieve – for example, the profit objectives. This kind of definition of the four causes seems to us to be typical of the dominant discourse on management. It is a definition that takes for granted the source of change.

However, this way of thinking about the descendants of Aristotle's four causes does not capture the manner in which goals and values, the motivators of human action, continually emerge in the self-organizing complex responsive processes we discuss in this volume. Instead, the motivational process (that is, the source of goals and values) is hidden within the categories of efficient and formative cause. In this sense teleology is subordinated to the other causes, rather than embracing them as in Aristotle's thinking. In the above examples, what motivates people is reduced to a cause (sales incentive) and effect (change in sales) link, or is simply stated as a profit goal without taking account of how such a goal arises in the self-organizing complex responsive processes we are pointing to. In using the term Transformative Teleology we are trying to draw attention to the self-organizing complex responsive processes of emerging values, goals, strategies, and so on. This restores teleology to its overarching position in a theory of causality.

It is in his *Nicomachean Ethics* and *Politics* that Aristotle again takes up teleological causality as his core argument in understanding change:

> If, then, there is some end of the things we do, which we desire for its own sake . . . and we do not choose everything for the sake of something else . . . clearly this must be the good and the chief

good . . . and we see even the most highly esteemed of capacities to fall under this, e.g. strategy, economics, rhetoric; now since politics uses the rest of the sciences, and since, again, it legislates what we are to do and what we are to abstain from, the end of this science must include those of the others, so that this end must be the good for man.

(*Nicomachean Ethics*, Book I)

It is in this sense that we are arguing that neither the social sciences (including management theory) nor the natural sciences can ignore the question of teleological causality.

Appendix 2: Complexity sciences as sources of analogy

The purpose of this appendix is to set out the ways in which the complexity sciences are drawn upon to think about life in organizations. It considers two questions: Are the natural complexity sciences valid sources for management thinkers to turn to? If so, how might it be valid to use them in order to understand human action? Some make direct applications of the ideas in the complexity sciences to organizations. Others use the science in a loose metaphorical way. Yet others regard the sciences as source domains for analogies. This appendix sets out our position.

The validity of the complexity sciences

Many (for example, Rosenhead, 1998) argue that there are a considerable number of findings in the complexity sciences that have passed the test of scientific validity – for example those relating to the weather (chaos theory) and fluid dynamics and chemical clocks (the theory of dissipative structures). The test is that real world events should fit the predictions of the theory, as shown by repeatable observations. On these grounds most of the insights derived from computer simulations fail the test because they are not firmly grounded in empirical findings. Many natural scientists using those computer simulations pose the same question to themselves and point to the tentative nature of their "findings." This certainly calls for careful examination of the concepts management writers draw from the complexity sciences, but we do not accept the positivist test of repeatable observations as the only test of valid knowledge.

A positivist approach to science involves moving from the domain of theory and models to the domain of the phenomenon they seek to explain in order to test theory and model together by examining whether their predictions match the behavior of the phenomenon in some relevant way. McKelvey (1999), however, follows Suppe (1989) and others to present a semantic, rather than a positivist, conception of the scientific method. While the positivist method tests both theory and model together in one step, the semantic method adopts two steps:

- First, theoretical propositions are used to make predictions of behavior in a model and then the progression of the model is used to test the propositions of the theory. The justification for this test is as follows. A theory is an abstract description of selected aspects of some phenomenon in terms of parameters and relationships, and a model is some representation of that abstract description, consisting of idealized structures or processes postulated by the theory. Neither the theory nor the model predicts the progression of the phenomenon itself because both theory and model are abstractions of certain selected aspects of that phenomenon. Instead, the theory predicts the progression of the model. The adequacy of the theory is established by how well it predicts the empirical behavior of the model. The model may be expressed in the abstract form of mathematics, or in the always artificial form of some prototype or laboratory experiment, or, more contentiously, in the abstract form of a computer simulation. When one is dealing with phenomena that are too complex to be formulated in mathematical models and that cannot be captured in laboratory experiments without losing their very nature, then the appropriate model is a computer simulation. Taking this view, computer simulations are a perfectly acceptable way of performing the first scientific step; that is, testing fit between theory and model. They are demonstrations of possibility.
- Second, the model is compared with the phenomenon, exploring whether salient features of the model are present in the phenomenon. This second step is a comparison in that features that are well understood in the model are used to describe similar features that are less well understood in the phenomenon. In other words, it is a procedure of translation. The natural sciences rely on a transfer from an abstract symbolic source domain, such as mathematics or computer simulations, or from the domain of idealized physical situations as in a laboratory, to a target domain such as chemical or biological phenomena located in nature. What is important, then, is not whether making a transfer is valid or not, for humans have no other way to proceed, but rather what can be said about the nature of the transfer

(Tsoukas, 1993). Consider two different ways in which knowledge might be transferred from one domain to another.

The first kind of transfer is the use of metaphor, which can take two forms. The first is literal similarity where the attributes of an object and the relationships between those attributes are transferred from a source domain to a target domain. For example, when one says that wine is like water one is referring to attributes such as wetness and to the chemical structure. When management complexity writers say that an organization is, or is like, a complex adaptive system, they transfer, from the science to organizations, attributes of the scientific models (such as large numbers of agents) and the relationships between them (such as simple rules of interaction).

The second type of metaphor is the mere matching of appearance in which there is a transfer of only the attributes of an object in the source domain to an object in the target domain – for example, describing water as being as clear as glass. When management complexity writers talk about fitness landscapes of strategies or knowledge, they are mostly transferring an attribute of complex adaptive system models without the connections or relationships between the agents. This device of metaphorical transfer is used in literature, but natural scientists also use it when they employ intuitive insights in model construction. However, having done this the scientist leaves the original metaphor behind and constructs abstract models informed by the metaphor.

Analogy is often used as a synonym for metaphor, but Tsoukas (1993) distinguishes between the two. An analogy transfers a relationship, but not the attributes, in the source domain to a similar relationship in the target domain and in so doing operationalizes a metaphor. For example, parts of a machine functioning together to produce integrated motion could be an analogy for departments in an organization functioning together to produce collective action. What is being transferred here is an explanatory structure. Management complexity writers do this when they transfer notions of self-organization as formative cause from the complexity sciences to the human domain. This differs from the metaphor in that it is the relationships without the attributes that are transferred. The analogical transfer, therefore, requires an act of interpreting the attributes of the objects in the relationship. This non-transfer of attributes, and the consequent need for careful translation, is what distinguishes the analogical from the metaphorical transfer.

In the case of a source domain that is an abstract relational structure containing only abstract principles and generalized entities, as in mathematical and computer models, what is transferred from the source to the target domain is this abstract set of relational principles without any attributes of the objects. This is done, for example, when notions of causality are transferred from scientific models to the phenomenal target domain. The careful interpretation required to bring in the attributes of the objects in the target domain is done when the mathematical equations, computer simulations and laboratory experiments of the complexity sciences are translated in terms of the features of physical, chemical and biological phenomena in their natural locations. There is no reason why social scientists should not adopt a similar approach, provided that a careful interpretation is made to incorporate the distinctive attributes of human beings.

It is important to distinguish between transfer from complexity models to organizational theory by analogy and transfer by metaphor. Writers such as Morgan (1997) suggest that metaphors liberate the imagination and draw attention to alternative realities. The more metaphors used, the more sophisticated the understanding. The implication is that one metaphor is about as useful as another, and if one does not illuminate then another should be tried. However, from the perspective of analogical transfer, it might be argued that complexity sciences provide more useful abstractions and analogies than other approaches and that they do not provide simply yet another loose metaphor amongst many. The procedure we intend to follow is one in which the relationships in the theories and the models are taken from the complexity sciences and then compared with the phenomena of human organizing and managing. In other words, the approach is to make a translation in terms of human sociology and psychology with the purpose of seeing whether this procedure illuminates the experience of life in organizations. The theories and models of the complexity sciences are then used as an analogy for human activity. They also motivate particular ways of examining organizational phenomena.

The use of analogy has two requirements. First, a concept being transferred analogically from one domain to another must be better understood in the source domain than in the one it is being transferred to. Even though the complexity sciences are in their infancy, the phenomenon of complexity is *better* understood in its application in the natural sciences than it is in current management theory. Second, concepts in the sciences must be put in one-to-one relation with concepts in management, and causal connections in the first must be preserved in the second. For example, when self-organization as formative cause in the complexity models of the natural sciences is transferred to the social domain by analogy, then those social phenomena must be understood to be emerging from the self-organization itself, not from some choice imposed from outside.

Validated evidence in relation to organizations

Rosenhead (1998) also argues that there is no validated evidence that complexity based prescriptions produce the results claimed for them. There are two points to note here; namely, the focus on prescriptions and the requirement for valid evidence.

Take the matter of evidence first. Instead of evidence, management complexity theorists are said to rely on anecdotes, making it impossible for others to judge their representativeness. Again, this criticism rests on an implicit assumption that the only valid form of knowledge is that of empirically supported general propositions, that is, a positivist epistemology. That assumption relies for its authority on the widespread acceptance of *the scientific method*. However, this is not the only valid form of knowledge, especially when it comes to very complex human dynamics. It is then that narrative knowledge comes into its own. Narrative knowledge is embedded in anecdotes and stories, as well as the evaluation of those stories. The point is not whether they can be empirically validated or not, but whether they resonate with the experience of others and assist them to make sense of that experience. Furthermore, implicit in Rosenhead's criticism, there is the implication that a validated body of management theories already exists and that the methods that have been used to validate them are themselves valid.

But is this so? First, as we have argued in this book, dominant management theories are also based on frameworks imported from the natural sciences. The whole notion of empirical validation and the methods for that validation have been imported along with the theoretical frameworks. In applying the imported notions of empirical validation, management researchers test their propositions with data gathered from surveys, questionnaires and interviews, often utilizing various statistical analyses. However, just how valid is this? It is likely that people in organizations will respond to questionnaires and interviews in terms of the legitimate dominant discourse, rather than in terms of the more marginal shadow discourses. This raises major question marks over the reliability of so-called empirical validation. This is because statistical analyses make particular assumptions about the distribution of variables around means. In other words, they make assumptions about the dynamics of the system being modeled. If those dynamics are incorrectly identified then the statistical analysis will say more about the time period chosen than the system (Stewart, 1989). Furthermore, Allen's (1998a, 1998b) work indicates that the assumptions made about distributions around means in statistical analyses are a way of avoiding the complexity of micro dynamics and so ignoring a system's internal capacity to change. The easy equation of such empirical findings with "validity" becomes highly questionable.

Now take the way Rosenhead (1998) selects the *prescriptions* made by writers on complexity theory in organizations. He justifies his focus on *actionable proposals* deduced from complexity theory with the argument that it is the proposals for action that provide managers with a reality test and that it is only through specific actions that management practice will change. This kind of justification makes an implicit distinction between thinking/talking and acting. It assumes that people first think and talk about what they are going to do and then do it. It assumes that people can only judge the usefulness of a framework for thinking by its immediate action implications. In other words, people first develop a mental model and then test its action implications; that is, they behave like scientists. This is elevating the positivist scientific method to a form of general behavior that applies to any sensible person. It is a typically cognitivist interpretation of human action. However, complexity frameworks provide ways of thinking that resonate with experience. In other words, the conceptual framework itself may assist to make sense of that experience, quite apart from actionable proposals. This is the subjective reality test for any reader. The question is whether the concepts resonate with lived experience. If they do, then as thinking shifts so does behavior because the two are so intertwined. The question, then, is not whether a proposal for action is plausibly beneficial. Indeed, this cannot be the question in circumstances where the long-term outcomes of actions are radically unpredictable. We think that management practice does not change through specific actionable proposals but through the evolving ways of thinking and talking of groupings of managers that produce emergent action.

The objective observer

There is one feature of computer simulations in the natural sciences for which there is no analogue in human interaction. The computer simulations are always designed by programmers and those programmers take the position of objective observer, drawing insight from running the program. In human interaction, there is no objective observer who prepares a minimal design and then watches the program running. Even the most powerful human is a participant in human interaction. This means that people can only come to know about human systems through their own conversational and empathic participation in them. There is a large literature on appreciative or participative inquiry (for example, Reason, 1988) as a method of research, and a rapidly growing literature on the analysis of conversation and discourse as action in organizations (for example, Grant *et al.*, 1998).

Despite any differences between them, complexity management writers seem so far to have adopted a common methodological position. They explicitly or implicitly assume the stance of the objective observer standing outside the organization as a system and formulating the principles of its functioning. This is demonstrated quite clearly when statements are made about applications and implications of the theoretical developments proposed. For example, Pascale (1999) talks about managers designing emergence and unleashing the potential of self-organization. MacIntosh and MacLean (1999) talk about managers surfacing the deep structured, designing changes to it and conditioning the emergence. Managers are exhorted to "allow" self-organization to take place. Wheatley (1992) talks about managers giving opportunities to self-organizing systems. Brown and Eisenhardt (1998) talk about managers identifying whether they are at the edge of chaos and then designing the conditions required to move their organization to the edge if it is not already there. Nonaka and Takeuchi (1995) advise managers to create crises to move their organization to the edge. Another strand emphasizes the need for managers to understand the whole system. For example, Wheatley talks about taking the whole-system view. Purser and Cabana (1998) prescribe future search conferences and other techniques for getting the whole system into the room.

This approach to methodology and application sidesteps a number of points. If human organizations are similar to self-organizing systems in anything other than the purely superficial, then they must always have evolved through self-organizing processes producing emergent outcomes.

To talk of installing or designing self-organizing systems or processes is to ignore this. To talk of unleashing and allowing self-organizing processes is to ignore the point that they must already be there. When managers are advised to change the dynamic of their organization to the edge, the insight is lost that the system's own internal dynamic and its connections with other systems determines the dynamic. If the metaphor makes any sense then it will be beyond the capacity of managers to determine the dynamic. The whole notion that managers can observe their whole system ignores the central feature of self-organization, namely that patterns emerge though local interactions in the absence of any one agent understanding the whole. If organizations are metaphorically or analogically like complex adaptive systems then managers are agents in those systems and are themselves such systems interacting at their own local level. They are participants unable to step outside, make objective observations, then design and choose the dynamics. The dynamics and the emergent behavior arise through their participation not their acts of design.

Appendix 3: The movement of our thought

In co-authoring this volume, the three of us have recognized how the thought of each of us has moved in our conversations together both before and during our work on this book. In this appendix, we each say something about that movement. We are sure that this book is not the end product because the nature of thought is movement.

Ralph D. Stacey

This book seeks to locate the work of management complexity writers in the history of Western thought and it argues that much of their work misses the opportunity of radical challenge to the currently dominant discourse on management. The reason suggested for this is that they remain within the framework of systems thinking and compatible assumptions about human action drawn from cognitivist psychology. I feel the need to say that similar points apply to much of what I have written over the past decade. My purpose here is to indicate how I have moved away from systems thinking and cognitivist psychology.

I started my working life as a lecturer in applied economics, having just completed a doctorate at the London School of Economics. The research for that doctorate was based on econometrics and amounted to developing and testing a particular model of macro patterns of economic development in underdeveloped countries. One of my first academic papers was a test of the success of forecasts made by an economics bureau in South Africa. The forecasts were clearly not all that successful and I argued that a sophisticated econometric model of the economy would yield better results. My first consultancy assignment was to develop such a model for a bank in South Africa. I completed the model, but it was never used because the manager who commissioned it was removed after losing a political battle. I then took up a position as an economist at British Steel where I was concerned with building models to forecast steel demand. Later I moved to a construction company where part of my role was to forecast the demand for construction services. A few years later, I became the corporate planning manager of this company so that my work expanded to include investment appraisals and all the other tasks of corporate planning. Years later, I moved to a financial investment house where I was supposed to give advice on the movement of capital markets. Once again this involved trying to understand the financial markets as systems in order to predict their evolution.

Then I returned to academic life, combining it with work as a strategy consultant to top management teams. Clearly my way of thinking was systemic and one of my interests was building models of systems. However, I became increasingly dissatisfied with the contribution this model building and systems thinking actually made to my work. In 1990 I published a book based on my experience of the previous fifteen years and concluded that organizations hardly ever move into the future in accordance with their long-term plans. Recalling my past experience as a manager in organizations and the then current experience as a consultant to managers, I suggested that the plans and many other procedures simply covered up what we were actually doing, namely a process of interaction and politics that led to what we did together. Influenced by my work with the Tavistock Institute I also concluded that these strategic plans were mainly defenses against the anxiety aroused by not quite knowing what we were doing. However, I felt dissatisfied with what I had written because I could not explain why we found ourselves in the situation of not being able to predict the future to a useful enough extent and just how we might understand what we did behind the cover of plans and the like.

It was then that I chanced on Gleick's (1988) book on the new science of chaos. I immediately thought that this must have something to do with the questions that were exercising me most. After reading Gleick I wrote *The Chaos Frontier* (1991). In this book I claimed that organizations were literally chaotic systems and that was why we could not forecast their futures. I used the work of Prigogine and Stengers (1984) as an analogy to claim that what happened to organizations resulted from a political process of agenda building. I talked about the need to understand what managers were doing when they did not know what they were doing. I emphasized the paradoxical nature of the management process. Next I wrote a book called *Managing the Unknowable* (1992) in which I succumbed to pressure to present some kind of prescription for actions flowing from thinking that organizations were chaotic systems. I had great difficulty with this and produced a set of prescriptions that amounted to the current discourse presented in new jargon. I tried to move away from this in *Strategic Management and Organisational Dynamics* (1993), where I drew a distinction between the legitimate system of an organization, which could be understood in the terms of the dominant discourse, and the shadow system, where I brought in some ideas from psychoanalysis. I stressed that people in organizations operated in both of these systems at the same time, but whenever I talked about it I noticed how people immediately thought about moving from one system to another, sometimes in one and sometimes in another. I found it very difficult to explain my disquiet at this move.

Then I found out about complexity theory and quickly realized that this was much more relevant to thinking about organizations than chaos theory because it was about systems that could learn, whereas chaos theory was about systems that were deterministic. So in *Complexity and Creativity in Organizations* (1996) I claimed that organizations were literally complex adaptive systems. I picked this up in the second edition of *Strategic Management and Organisational Dynamics* (1996) and further developed the distinction between legitimate and shadow systems. In all of the work I had done so far, I had attempted to translate the complexity sciences into human terms using a combination of cognitivist psychology and psychoanalysis. My early interest in models and my systemic way of thinking clearly persisted to this point. Whenever I tried to say anything prescriptive, it came out in the terms of the dominant discourse expressed in a different vocabulary.

When I began to take an interest in the complexity sciences I concluded that if organizations did not move according to plans then they presumably moved in ways that arose from the way people interacted in groups. I felt I knew so little about groups that in 1992 I embarked on a lengthy training as a group psychotherapist. I also started to run a doctoral group focusing on complexity and organizations, and the members of this group brought the areas of social constructionism and philosophy to our work. These experiences led to an increasing dissatisfaction with what I had written before. I moved away from cognitivist and early psychoanalytic assumptions about human action when I wrote the third edition of *Strategic Management and Organisational Dynamics* (2000), appealing instead to what I called relationship psychology drawn from social constructionism, intersubjectivity in psychoanalysis and group analytic theory. I also moved away from thinking that organizations were complex adaptive systems, seeing the sciences of complexity as a source of analogy instead. As my co-authors and I worked on this volume we reached the conclusions we present here that there is a fundamental problem with thinking about organizations entirely in terms of systems. Hence our interest in moving away from systems thinking and pursuing what it might mean to think of organizations as Complex Responsive Processes of relating, drawing on the complexity sciences as a source domain for analogies.

Douglas Griffin

Looking back, I can now see that an important strand of my thought has evolved very much around understanding knowing as a process. This has often fixed on key phrases that kept coming back to mind because I had a very strong sense of both understanding and not understanding them. During graduate studies in Theology I was awakened by a statement at the core of the work of the Thomist philosopher Bernard Lonergan: "Man is the unrestricted desire to know." At the same time Lonergan refers to this as a long and painstaking process. A central theme formed, knowledge and time, which has continued to evolve up to the present. I linked Lonergan's idea to Piaget's work on the cognitive development of children and wrote a thesis investigating the question of the judging or discerning powers necessary for the sacrament of confirmation. During my last semester of Theology I discovered in Edmund Husserl's phenomenology the concepts of inner time consciousness and intersubjectivity. This proved to be my first real move away from a taken-for-granted focus on the individual.

The interest in Husserl's thought generated further graduate studies in Germany. In the lectures of one of Husserl's last assistants, who was just about to go into retirement, I first heard of St Augustine of Hippo's concept of time and memory. This concept of "memoria" is at the core of Hegel's understanding of his dialectic as the movement of thought and is best summed up in a phrase often used by one of the professors who was looking at Husserl's thought from a Hegelian perspective: "Meaning is only meaning as meaning." Today I would translate this roughly as: the phenomenon, the object of meaning, is meaning for us as subjects in the unique lived present in which it is the movement of experience.

I also encountered systems thinking for the first time in the sociology of
Niklas Luhmann, who in his early writing tried to use Husserl's thought
as a way of thinking about the individual. Luhmann had studied under
Talcott Parsons in the USA and was attempting to further develop the
grounding of the social sciences in systems theory. Leaving the university
and going to work in organizations, in what was then called human
resource development, I encountered in the early 1980s the rise of
systems theory to its present dominance of management theory – for
example, culture, the learning organization, leadership. In working with
each new fad over the past two decades, it became increasingly clear that
the new jargon of each fad was only a thin veneer over a repetitive and
temporally flat notion of the process of knowing as a function or role.
The unique history and striving of the persons in such systems are
excluded in order to describe the system. The "three-dimensional"
snapshot of interaction, as for example in Senge's beer game, is a better
one than that of one-dimensional behaviorist models, but still temporally
flat. The "time" he so emphatically includes is not that of human sense-
making.

Encountering complexity theory in the mid-1990s I immediately sensed a
way of challenging systems thinking, but I first thought that this would be
from within systems thinking. After initially understanding cultures
literally as complex adaptive systems, I found in the work of G. H. Mead
a way to understand social interaction that resonated strongly with what
I believed to be the consequences of complexity theory for the social
sciences. In a doctoral thesis in 1998 I attempted to demonstrate that
Mead's theory of the emergence of mind, self and society builds directly
on Hegel's concept of time and that this has far-reaching consequences
for our understanding of communication and participation in
organizations. At present I am interested in examining the process of
knowing in terms of ethics and leadership.

Patricia Shaw

The movement of my thinking has been closely allied to periods in my
life as an organizational development practitioner when I lost conviction
in my existing ways of speaking about my practice. At such times a
painful gap would open between ways of accounting for my experience
as a consultant, which were common currency in my profession, and a
scarcely articulated sense of what I was actually engaged in with my

clients and colleagues. One recurrent concern for me has therefore been the nature of the relation between theory and practice.

My earliest experience of this dilemma was as a Physics graduate with what was then a large public utility. My job as an Operations Research Analyst was to create optimizing models of various aspects of the business that senior managers could use to guide them in making key decisions about resource allocation and working practices. During this time I became interested in the nature of modeling and the kind of models being used, inside a taken-for-granted acceptance of systems thinking. The fact that such models were simplifications of complex interactions was a trivial observation not worth discussing. It was in the nature of models to simplify in order to make messy situations more tractable and allow managers to exercise appropriate control. My world was split. Sometimes I spent days in conversations with people all over the organization making sense of their practice worlds. At other times I spent days back in the Operations Research group where we strove to create simulations of these activities that would help managers grasp intellectually the most effective way to organize and then implement this. Already then I had a dim sense that the sense-making work in conversation had immediate consequences that were different in kind to my later conversations with "client" managers teaching them to use the dynamic models I had devised to help them look at and operate on the business world.

This question about what was going on in the conversational world of human sense-making led me to undertake five years of study and intensive experiential training in Gestalt approaches to change in groups and organizations. At the same time I moved to work as a tutor at a management institute, specializing in the human aspects of organizing business. The theorizing in my Gestalt training drew on an eclectic mix of holism, Freudian and Jungian ideas, humanistic psychology, Lewin's field theory, existential philosophy and the phenomenology of Husserl and Merleau-Ponty. Gestalt maintained a focus on individuals and groups as systems with clear boundaries and intervention was spoken of in terms of boundary disturbances to "contact." What proved most significant for me in this training was the experiential emphasis on process, relationship and the paradoxical nature of change in groups. It was this combination of systems thinking and the skills of spontaneous engagement creating unpredictable shifts of meaning in experience that I took with me into my work as an independent OD consultant.

The theory–practice dilemma arose again, as I became involved in "change program" in a number of large multinational organizations. Despite my systems thinking becoming more sophisticated and including a second-order, reflexive perspective, I felt a queasy unease growing in the conversations I had with colleagues and clients whenever we tried to account for our designs and intentions for enabling "systemic" change. I identified with Torbert's description of mature practitioners in joint living inquiry who have developed a certain consciousness in the midst of their activity. This is a consciousness in which action and reflection interpenetrate as a heightened awareness of the possibilities of the "living moment," in which the experience of time has a different quality. He notes that this quality of attention is both somatic and intellectual simultaneously. My frustration was growing in that I could not speak about my practice with the same coherence with which I engaged in it, and I felt this was a serious matter that undermined my sense of integrity.

It was in this period that I became interested in understanding self-organizing processes and the emergence of both familiar and new patterns of activity in networks of agents. I asked myself whether it was possible to "facilitate" emergence in patterns of communicative action and this led to a doctoral thesis which began to reshape the nature of Organization Development practice as a quality of participation in the conversational life of an organization.

Bibliography

Ackoff, R. L. (1981) *Creating the Corporate Future*, New York: Wiley.

—— (1994) *The Democratic Organization*, New York: Oxford University Press.

Allen, P. M. (1998a) "Evolving complexity in social science," in Altman, G. and Koch, W. A. (eds) *Systems: New Paradigms for the Human Sciences*, New York: Walter de Gruyter.

—— (1998b) "Modeling complex economic evolution," in Schweitzer, F. and Silverberg, G. (eds) *Selbstorganization*, Berlin: Dunker & Humbolt.

Argyris, C. (1993) *Knowledge for Action*, San Francisco: Jossey-Bass.

—— (1990) *Overcoming Organizational Defenses: Facilitating Organizational Learning*, Needham Heights, Mass.: Allyn & Bacon.

Argyris, C. and Schön, D. (1978) *Organizational Learning: A Theory of Action Perspective*, Reading, Mass.: Addison-Wesley.

Ashby, W. R. (1945) "The effects of control on stability," *Natura* 155: 242–243.

—— (1952) *Design for a Brain*, New York: Wiley.

—— (1956) *Introduction to Cybernetics*, New York: Wiley.

Bak, P. and Chen, K. (1991) "Self-organized criticality," *Scientific American*, Jan.: 46–54.

Bateson, G. (1973) *Steps to an Ecology of Mind*, St Albans: Paladin.

Bateson, G. and Bateson, M. C. (1987) *Angels Fear: Toward an Epistemology of the Sacred*, New York: Macmillan.

Bateson, W. ([1894] 1970) *Materials for the Study of Variation, Treated with Special Regard to Discontinuity in the Origin of Species*, New York: Robert Schalkenbach Foundation.

Beer, S. (1966) *Decision and Control: The Meanings of Operational Research and Management Cybernetics*, London: Wiley.

—— (1979) *The Heart of the Enterprise*, Chichester: Wiley.

—— (1981) *The Brain of the Firm*, Chichester: Wiley.

—— (1994) *Beyond Dispute: The Invention of Team Syntegrity*, New York: Wiley.

Beinhocker, E. D. (1999) "Robust adaptive strategies," *Sloan Management Review*, Spring: 95–106.

Bhaktin, M. M. (1986) *Speech Genres and Other Late Essays*, Austin, Tex.: University of Texas Press.

Bortoft, H. (1985) "Counterfeit and authentic wholes: Finding a means for dwelling in nature," in Seamon, D. and Mugerauer, R. (eds) *Dwelling, Place and Environment*, Dordrecht: Martinus Nijhoff Publishers.

—— (1996) *The Wholeness of Nature: Goethe's Way of Science*, Edinburgh: Floris Books.

Boulding, K. E. (1956) "General systems theory: The skeleton of science," *Management Science* 2: 197–208.

Brown, S. L. and Eisenhardt, K. (1998) *Competing on the Edge: Strategy as Structured Chaos*, Boston, Mass.: Harvard Business School Press.

Checkland, P. B. (1981) *Systems Thinking, Systems Practice*, Chichester: Wiley.

Checkland, P. B. and Schles, J. (1990) *Soft Systems Methodology in Action*, Chichester: Wiley.

Churchman, C. West (1968) *The Systems Approach*, New York: Delacorte Press.

—— (1970) *The Systems Approach and its Enemies*, New York: Basic Books.

Cohen, M. D., March, J. G. and Olsen, J. P. (1972) "A garbage can model of organizational choice," *Administrative Science Quarterly* 17: 1–25.

Connor, D. R. (1998) *Leading at the Edge of Chaos: How to Create the Nimble Organization*, New York: John Wiley & Sons.

Darwin, C. (1859) *The Origin of Species by Means of Natural Selection or, The Preservation of Favoured Races in the Struggle for Life*, London: John Murray.

—— (1871) *The Descent of Man*, London: John Murray.

Dawkins, R. (1976) *The Selfish Gene*, New York: Oxford University Press.

Eldridge, N. and Gould, J. (1972) "Punctuated equilibria: An alternative to phyletic gradualism," in Schopf, T. J. M. (ed.) *Models in Paleobiology*, San Francisco: Freeman, Cooper & Co.

Elias, N. (1989) *The Symbol Theory*, London: Sage Publications.

Elias, N. and Scotson, J. (1994) *The Established and the Outsiders*, London: Sage.

Fayol, H. ([1916] 1948) *Industrial and General Administration*, London: Pitman.

Fisher, R. A. (1930) *The Genetic Theory of Natural Selection*, Oxford: Oxford University Press.

Flood, R. L. (1990) "Liberating systems theory: Towards critical systems thinking," *Human Relations* 43: 49–75.

—— (1999) *Rethinking the Fifth Discipline: Learning Within the Unknowable*, London: Routledge.

Forrester, J. (1958) "Industrial dynamics: A major breakthrough for decision-making," *Harvard Business Review* 36, 4: 37–66.

—— (1961) *Industrial Dynamics*, Cambridge, Mass.: MIT Press.

—— (1969) *The Principles of Systems*, Cambridge, Mass.: Wright-Allen Press.

Foulkes, S. H. (1948) *Introduction to Group Analytic Psychotherapy*, London: William Heinemann Medical Books Limited.

Gardner, H. (1985) *The Mind's New Science: A History of the Cognitive Revolution*, New York: Basic Books.

Gell-Mann, M. (1994) *The Quark and the Jaguar*, New York: Freeman & Co.

Gergen, K. J. (1999) *An Invitation to Social Construction*, Thousand Oaks, Calif.: Sage.

Gleick, J. (1988) *Chaos: The Making of a New Science*, London: William Heinemann Limited.

Goldberger, A. L. (1997) "Fractal variability versus pathological periodicity: Complexity loss and stereotypy in disease," *Perspectives in Biology and Medicine* 40, 4: 553–561.

Goodwin, B. (1994) *How the Leopard Changed its Spots*, London: Weidenfeld & Nicolson.

Goodwin, R. M. (1951) "Econometrics in business-style analysis," in Hansen, A. H. (ed.) *Business Cycles and National Income*, New York: W. W. Norton.

Grant, D., Keenoy, T. and Oswick, C. (eds) (1998) *Discourse and Organisation*, London: Sage.

Griffin, D., Shaw, P. and Stacey, R. (1998) "Speaking of complexity in management theory and practice," *Organization* 5, 3: 315–340.

—— (1999) "Knowing and acting in conditions of uncertainty: A complexity perspective," *Systemic Practice and Action Research* 12, 3: 295–310.

Griffin, J. D. (1998) "Dealing with the paradox of culture in management theory," unpublished Ph.D. thesis, University of Hertfordshire.

Haldane, J. B. S. (1932) *The Causes of Evolution*, New York: Harper Brothers.

Hannan, M. T. and Freeman, J. (1989) *Organizational Ecology*, Cambridge, Mass.: Harvard University Press.

Hegel, G. W. F. (1807) *Phänomenologie des Geistes*, Bamberg: Joseph Anton Goebhardt.

—— (1830) *Enzyklopädie der philosophischen Wissenschaften*, Hamburg: Felix Meiner.

Hertzberg, F. (1966) *Work and the Nature of Man*, Cleveland, O.: World.

Holland, J. (1998) *Emergence from Chaos to Order*, New York: Oxford University Press.

Hurst, D. K. (1995) *Crisis and Renewal*, Boston, Mass.: Harvard Business School Press.

Huxley, T. (1863) *Man's Place in Nature*, New York: D. Appleton.

Kant, I. ([1790] 1987) *Critique of Judgement*, trans. W. S. Pluhar, Indianapolis, Ind.: Hackett.

Kauffman, S. A. (1993) *Origins of Order: Self Organization and Selection in Evolution*, Oxford: Oxford University Press.

—— (1995) *At Home in the Universe*, New York: Oxford University Press.

Kelly, S. and Allison, M. A. (1999) *The Complexity Advantage: How the Science of Complexity can Help your Business Achieve Peak Performance*, New York: McGraw-Hill.

Langton, C. (1989) "Artificial life," in Nadel, L. and Stein, D. (eds) (1991) *Lectures in Complex Systems*, Reading, Mass.: Addison-Wesley.

—— (1993) "Artificial life," in Boden, M. A. (ed.) (1996) *The Philosophy of Artificial Life*, Oxford: Oxford University Press.

Levy, S. (1992) *Artificial Life*, New York: First Vintage Books.

Lewin, R. (1993) *Complexity: Life at the Edge of Chaos*, London: J. M. Dent.

Lewin, R. and Regine, B. (2000) *The Soul at Work*, London: Orion Business Books.

Lewontin, R. C. (1974) *The Genetic Basis of Evolutionary Change*, New York: Columbia University Press.

Likert, R. (1961) *New Patterns of Management*, New York: McGraw-Hill.

Lissack, M. and Roos, J. (1999) *The Next Common Sense: Mastering Corporate Complexity Through Coherence*, London: Nicholas Brealey Publishing.

Locke, J. (1962) *Second Treatise of Civil Government*, in Barker, E. (ed.) *Social Contract: Essays by Locke, Hume and Rousseau*, London: Oxford University Press.

McCulloch, W. S. and Pitts, W. (1943) "A logical calculus of ideas imminent in nervous activity," *Bulletin of Mathematical Biophysics*, vol. 5.

McGregor, D. (1960) *The Human Side of Management*, New York: McGraw-Hill.

MacIntosh, R. and MacLean, D. (1999) "Conditioned emergence: A dissipative structures approach to transformation," *Strategic Management Journal* 20, 4: 297–316.

McKelvey, B. (1999) "Complexity theory in organization science: Seizing the promise or becoming a fad?," *Emergence: A Journal of Complexity Issues in Organization and Management* 1, 1: 5–31.

Marion, R. (1999) *The Edge of Organization: Chaos and Complexity Theories of Formal Social Systems*, Thousand Oaks, Calif.: Sage Publications.

Maslow, A. (1954) *Motivation and Personality*, New York: Harper Brothers.

Maynard Smith, J. (1976) "Evolution and the theory of games," *American Scientist* 664, 1.

Mayo, E. (1949) *The Social Problems of Industrial Civilization*, London: Routledge & Kegan Paul.

Mead, G. H. (1934) *Mind, Self and Society*, Chicago: Chicago University Press.

—— (1936) *Movements of Thought in the Nineteenth Century*, Chicago: Chicago University Press.

—— (1938) *The Philosophy of the Present*, Chicago: Chicago University Press.

Miller, E. J. and Rice, A. K. (1967) *Systems of Organization: The Control of Task and Sentient Boundaries*, London: Tavistock Publications.

Morgan, G. (1997) *Images of Organization*, London: Sage.

Nicolis, G. and Prigogine, I. (1989) *Exploring Complexity: An Introduction*, New York: W. H. Freeman & Company.

Nonaka, I. (1991) "The knowledge-creating company," *Harvard Business Review*, Nov.–Dec.: 96–104.

Nonaka, I. and Takeuchi, H. (1995) *The Knowledge Creating Company: How Japanese Companies Create the Dynamics of Innovation*, New York: Oxford University Press.

O'Donohue, J. (1993) *Person als Vermittlung: Die Dialektik von Individualität und Allgemeinheit in Hegel's "Phänomenologie des Geistes,"* Mainz: Matthias Grünewald.

Pascale, R. T. (1990) *Managing on the Edge: How Successful Companies Use Conflict to Stay Ahead*, London: Viking Penguin.

—— (1999) "Surfing the edge of chaos," *Sloan Management Review* 40, 3: 83–95.

Phelan, S. (1999) "A note on the correspondence between complexity and systems theory," *Systemic Practice and Action Research* 12, 3: 237–246.

Philips, A. W. (1950) "Mechanical models in economic dynamics," *Econometrica* 17: 283–305.

Pluhar, W. S. (1987) "Introduction to the Critique of Judgement," in Kant, I. (1790) *Critique of Judgement*, trans. W. S. Pluhar, Indianapolis, Ind.: Hackett.

Polanyi, M. and Prosch, H. (1975) *Meaning*, Chicago: University of Chicago Press.

Prigogine, I. and Stengers, I. (1984) *Order Out of Chaos: Man's New Dialogue with Nature*, New York: Bantam Books.

Prigogine, I. (1997) *The End of Certainty: Time, Chaos and the New Laws of Nature*, New York: The Free Press.

Prigogine, I. and Allen, P. M. (1982) "The challenge of complexity," in Schieve, W. C. and Allen, P. M. (eds) *Self-Organization and Dissipative Structures: Applications in the Physical and Social Sciences*, Austin, Tex.: University of Texas Press.

Purser, R. E. and Cabana, S. (1998) *The Self Managing Organization: How Leading Companies are Transforming the Work of Teams for Real Impact*, New York: The Free Press.

Ray, T. S. (1992) "An approach to the synthesis of life," in Langton, G. C., Taylor, C., Doyne-Farmer, J. and Rasmussen, S. (eds) *Artificial life II, Santa Fe Institute, Studies in the Sciences of Complexity, Volume 10*, Reading, Mass.: Addison-Wesley.

Reason, P. (ed.) (1988) *Human Inquiry in Action*, London: Sage.

Reynolds, C. W. (1987) "Flocks, herds and schools: A distributed behavior model," *Proceedings of SIGGRAPH "87," Computer Graphics* 21, 4: 25–34.

Roos, J. and Oliver, D. (1999) "From fitness landscapes to knowledge landscapes," *Systemic Practice and Action Research* 12: 279–294.

Rosenhead, J. (1998) "Complexity theory and management practice," London School of Economics, Working Paper Series.

Sanders, T. I. (1998) *Strategic Thinking and the New Science: Planning in the Midst of Chaos, Complexity and Change*, New York: The Free Press.

Senge, P. (1990) *The Fifth Discipline: The Art and Practice of the Learning Organization*, New York: Doubleday.

Shaw, P. (1997) "Intervening in the shadow systems of organizations: Consulting from a complexity perspective," *Journal of Organizational Change Management* 10, 3: 235–250.

——— (1998) "An exploration of the role of organisation development intervention in fostering emergence and self-organisation," unpublished Ph.D. thesis, University of Hertfordshire.

Shotter, J. (1993) *Conversational Realities: Constructing Life Through Language*, Thousand Oaks, Calif.: Sage Publications.

Stacey, R. (1991) *The Chaos Frontier: Creative Strategic Control for Business*, Oxford: Butterworth-Heinemann.

——— (1992) *Managing the Unknowable*, San Francisco: Jossey-Bass.

——— (1993) *Strategic Management and Organisational Dynamics*, London: Pitman (2nd edn, 1996).

——— (1996) *Complexity and Creativity in Organizations*, San Francisco: Berrett-Koehler.

——— (2000) *Strategic Management and Organisational Dynamics: The Challenge of Complexity*, London: Pearson Education.

Steier, F. (1991) *Research and Reflexivity*, Thousand Oaks, Calif.: Sage Publications.

Stern, D. N. (1985) *The Interpersonal World of the Infant*, New York: Basic Books.

——— (1995) *The Motherhood Constellation: A Unified View of Parent–Infant Psychotherapy*, New York: Basic Books.

Stewart, I. (1989) *Does God Play Dice?*, Oxford: Blackwell.

Stolorow, R., Atwood, G. and Brandschaft, B. (1994) *The Intersubjective Perspective*, Northvale, N.J.: Jason Aaronson.

Suppe, F. (1989) *The Semantic Conception of Theories and Scientific Realism*, Urbana-Champaign, Ill.: University of Illinois Press.

Taylor, F. (1911) *Scientific Management*, New York: Harper Brothers.

Trist, E. L. and Bamforth, K. W. (1951) "Some social and psychological consequences of the long wall method of coal getting," *Human Relations* 5: 6–24.

Tsoukas, H. (1993) "Analogical reasoning and knowledge generation in organization theory," *Organization Studies* 14, 3: 323–346.

Tustin, A. (1953) *The Mechanism of Economic Systems*, Cambridge, Mass.: Harvard University Press.

von Bertalanffy, L. (1968) *General Systems Theory: Foundations, Development, Applications*, New York: George Braziller.

von Foerster, H. (1984) "On constructing reality," in von Foerster, H. (ed.) *Observing Systems*, Seaside, Calif.: Intersystems.

von Glasersfeld, E. (1991) "Knowing without metaphysics: Aspects of the radical constructivist position," in Steier, F. (ed.) *Research and Reflexivity*, Thousand Oaks, Calif.: Sage Publications.

Vygotsky, L. S. (1962) *Thought and Language*, Cambridge, Mass.: MIT Press.

Waldorp, M. M. (1992) *Complexity: The New Science at the Edge of Order and Chaos*, London: Viking.

Webster, G. and Goodwin, B. (1996) *Form and Transformation: Generative and Relational Principles in Biology*, Cambridge: Cambridge University Press.

Weick, K. (1979) *The Social Psychology of Organizing*, Reading, Mass.: Addison-Wesley.

Wheatley, M. J. (1992) *Leadership and the New Science: Learning about Organization from an Orderly Universe*, San Francisco: Berrett-Koehler.

Wheatley, M. J. and Kellner-Rogers, M. (1996) *A Simpler Way*, San Francisco: Berrett-Koehler.

Wiener, N. (1948) *Cybernetics: Or Control and Communication in the Animal and the Machine*, Cambridge, Mass.: MIT Press.

Wright, S. (1931) "Evolution in Mendelian populations," *Genetics* 16: 97–159.

—— (1940) "Breeding structures of populations in relation to speciation," *American Naturalist* 74: 232–248.

Index

and interactions/relationships 164–6; and
the irrational 169–70; and the social
167–9, 189–91
industry dynamics: and constraints on
management choice 133–7; and deviant
behavior 130–3; and nature of control
137–8; and unpredictability 136–8
intersubjectivity 178–9

Kant, I. 19–29, 41, 62, 67
Kauffman, S.A. 21, 25, 45, 110–12,
113–19, 122–3, 135, 138, 151, 163
Kelly, S. and Allison, M.A. 142, 143, 167

Langton, C. 163
language 174–6
Lewin, R. 1; and Regine, B. 142, 145, 165
life-time development 47–8
Lissack, M. and Roos, J. 142, 143
Locke, J. 24
Luhmann, N. 211

McGregor, D. 161, 162
MacIntosh, R. and MacLean, D. 142, 144,
148, 149, 165, 205
McKelvey, B. 200
management: constraints on choice 133–7;
definition 61
Marion, R. 21, 130, 133–41, 147, 150,
167–70, 179
Maslow, A. 161, 162
Maynard Smith, J. 45
Mayo, E. 63
Mead, G.H. 33–4, 35, 36–7, 49, 171–4, 211
mechanistic thinking 17–19
memes 167–9, 179–81
mental models 160–1
micro diversity 99–102
microcomputer industry; described 134;
dynamics of 134–6
mind: as inner speech 175; as social
process 171–4; and symbols, power,
ideology 175–6
Morgan, G. 142, 144, 147–8, 202

Nash equilibrium 45
Natural Law Teleology 25, 26, 27, 28, 120;
comparison with other teleologies 52–4;

and complexity 167; and scientific
management 67–8; and systems thinking
57, 58, 62, 82; and unknowable future
31, 34, 38, 48–9
neo-Darwinians 44–7, 109, 167–8
Nicolis, G. and Prigogine, I. 92
Nonaka, I. 142; and Takeuchi, H. 142, 148,
160, 165, 205
novelty 40–1, 174–5; emergence of 106–26

objective observer 69–71, 205–6
O'Donohue, J. 35
organizational dynamics 141–2; and edge
of chaos 146–50; and fitness landscapes
150–2; and predictability 152–4; simple
rules/hidden order 142–6
organizations: activities 61; alternative to
systems thinking in 9–11; cause/effect
approach 22–5, 29; change in 63–4;
ignoring interaction in 61–4;
mechanistic/systemic split 58–61;
paradoxical situation of 3–6; part/whole
thinking 17–19; Rationalist/Formative
split 57–8; self-organization/emergence
19–21; splitting choice/interaction in
646; stability/change in 12; ways of
thinking in 6–9

Parmenides 195
Pascale, R.T. 105, 142, 145, 148
Phelan, S. 75, 76
Philips, A.W. 64, 65
Plato 195
Pluhar, W.S. 21
Polanyi, M. and Prosch, H. 161
predictability 88–9, 123, 152–4
Prigogine, I. 92, 93, 94, 96–8, 107, 138,
144, 149, 164; and Allen, P.M. 99, 130;
and Stengers, I. 92, 101–2, 208
Purser, R.E. and Cabana, S. 165, 205

Rationalist Teleology 24–5, 26, 27–8, 120,
137, 140–1, 181; and boundaries 72–4;
comparison with other teleologies 52–4;
and human action 158–9; and scientific
management 68; and systems thinking
57–8, 62, 82–4; and unknowable future
35, 36, 38, 39, 50